CALIFORNIA AND THE AMERICAN TAX REVOLT

Proposition 13 Five Years Later

Terry Schwadron, Editor

Paul Richter, Principal Writer

Introduction by Jack Citrin

University of California Press
Berkeley   Los Angeles   London

Staff Writers contributing to the book:

John Balzar
Patrick Boyle
Bill Boyarsky
Frank Clifford
Lee Dye
Tom Greeley
Ray Hebert
Michael A. Hiltzik
Robert A. Jones
Paul Jacobs
Kristina Lindgren
Carol McGraw
Penelope McMillan
Harry Nelson
Jeffrey A. Perlman
Anne Roark
David G. Savage
Lynn Smith
Ronald L. Soble
William Trombley
Daniel M. Weintraub
Leo Wolinsky

University of California Press
Berkeley and Los Angeles, California

University of California Press, Ltd.
London, England

Printed in the United States of America
1 2 3 4 5 6 7 8 9

Library of Congress Cataloging in Publication Data
will be found on the last page of this book.

Contents

Preface

California's tax revolt was born of emotion and frustration. It was a movement that was to have a profound impact on changing the structure of local government in California, on cutting back government services, on forcing local government to devise new ways to raise money. It was a movement that would quickly influence other states and other populist efforts to cap tax spending.

Still, some five years after passing Proposition 13 and adopting other tax-cutting measures, California voters really did not know the full effects. Despite some discouraging projections from government officials, Deputy Managing Editor Noel Greenwood believed that The Times indeed could set out to try to document the effects of the tax revolt in cities, counties, school districts and special districts across the state. Seldom, it was felt, has a single initiative had such a broad impact, and it was the newspaper's responsibility to try to chart the changes. The result was a nine-part series published in June, 1983, in conjunction with the fifth anniversary of the Proposition 13 vote.

Eventually, the Times effort included Terry Schwadron, Metro executive news editor as project editor, financial writer Paul Richter as the principal writer, researcher Susanna Shuster, and 18 reporters in Los Angeles and Sacramento in an effort that took up to six months for some of those involved. Other reporters filed additional stories for editions of The Times distributed in Orange and San Diego counties.

The Times set out to measure a broad range of topics—the effects on public employment, the impact on public services, the changes in philosophy of government and the political impact, among others. The newspaper wanted a sense of how changes were felt statewide, and, at the same time, how they affected the taxpayer, the consumer, in getting the public services for which he believed he was paying.

Adoption of tax-cutting measures has meant new fees to drive through a city park in Los Angeles, new fees to attend museum exhibitions in San Diego, longer waits for a new book to hit the public library bookshelves in Oakland. It has meant much lower property tax bills for some, and higher ones for the new neighbors buying an identical house. It has changed the way local school districts arrange for their money. Still, while the trends may have become clear, no one knows comprehensively the full, statewide effects of cutting property taxes, of permanently indexing state income-taxes, of repealing state gift and inheritance taxes.

When The Times set out to measure these impacts, the most apparent problem was that the state itself lacked detailed, comprehensive information on spending and taxing by some 5,000 units of local governance in California. It was necessary for the newspaper to devise and conduct its own survey to cover a few key areas of government spending, a survey described fully in the Appendix. To help devise, test and supervise the survey, The Times hired Kevin M. Bacon of the Sacramento consulting staff of Price Waterhouse. Bacon, an economist, was formerly a consultant with the California Assembly Office of Research, where he wrote a 1981 study of local government finances in the aftermath of Proposition 13. Assistance in the design and execution of the survey came from I.A. "Bud" Lewis, director of the Times Poll, Susan H. Pinkus, Times Poll field supervisor, and Mary Klette, Times Poll assistant director.

Deciding California's tax system at the ballot box has meant relying on insufficient and sometimes misleading information. It turns out, for example, that repeal of inheritance taxes has mainly aided the wealthy, rather than middle-class survivors, as had been argued during the campaign. In campaigns for hotly contested initiatives, such as Proposition 13, both sides spend large amounts of money for slick drives that barrage voters with slogans and catchy ads; as a result, voters must decide sweeping initiatives by balancing emotional appeals, rather than comparing detailed data about the state's finances. Voters know that property-tax bills would be cut, but had no way to decide how the changes would affect government spending or the search for substitute revenues.

In the past, there arguably has been less demand for statewide, centralized spending data. But with the adoption or Proposition 13 in 1978 and Proposition 4 in 1979, which limited governmental appropriations, taxing power and revenue allocation have been concentrated at the state level, and there is a new need for comparative data. Working against such a centralized source of financial information are many factors. Among them:

■ Cities and special districts lack uniform accounting systems, which effectively blocks analysus of government spending patterns. Counties have more uniform accounting systems, but reporting procedures vary. What one agency reports as police spending might including operating costs along; what another agency shows as police funds might also include pension payments. Because of such discrepancies, it is impossible to know for certain what some argue is try—law-enforcement officials, for instance, claim that probation departments have suffered th most extensive cuts as a result of Proposition 13. But hard data is lacking.

■ While the state controller does collect spending reports by cities, counties and special districts, the office does little analysis of the figures. It is nearly impossible to determine how much all of California's local jurisdictions spend on such things as recreation, garbage collection, parks and libraries, and differences in what is reported from one year to the next make comparisons risky.

■ State spending reports are out of date. The latest available records from the state controller that show spending and revenue by cities and counties are almost two years old. And the state recently changed its method of keeping such reports, making analysis difficult. Trying to determine how cities and counties have adjusted to the end of state bailout funds, for example, The Times was told by the state Department of Education that computerized records covering two years worth of spending could not be located.

■ Agencies have difficulty producing comparable information to such quantitative questions as police response times. Some agencies determine average time only for response to emergency calls, others to all calls. Obviously, guaging uniform effects to such qualitative things as the condition of roads and changes in library book purchases is more subjective.

■ Many social service programs, including health and welfare programs, defy efforts to analyze local financial impact. Federal and state runds and rules have so mixed with local funds that it is hard to know whether it was change in federal, state or local attitudes which has caused longer waits at public health clinics or fewer home visits by social workers.

The Times received completed surveys from more than 700 government agencies and school districts, for an overall response rate of about 55%. Responses came from 105 police agencies, whose jurisdictions included 55% of the state's population; 157 streets and roads agencies, representing 60% of the population; 188 parks departments, representing 58% of the population, and 91 school districts, representing about 30% of California public school students.

Preparation of this book in conjunction with the University of California Press came about with the assistance of Jack Miles, executive editor of the UC Press, Bozena Syska, a Times graphic designer, Managing Editor George Cotliar, Deputy Managing Editors Greenwood and John Foley, and Bart Everett, a Times news editor.

Following publication, there were many developments in Sacramento and elsewhere. The change in the national economy boosted state revenues, and Governor Deukmejian and the Legislature did begin to restore some of the cutbacks, particularly those for the community college system, although the lawmakers did initiate student fees.

For the newspaper, the unusual effort in reporting and publishing the tax revolt series has had two major effects: It has heightened interest in pursuing the effects of other initiatives; and it has challenged reporters to learn how to read, understand and translate the statistical information of financial reports into its impact on government services and on people.

—*Terry Schwadron*

Introduction:
The Legacy
of Proposition 13

By Jack Citrin

Nothing is forever. The passage of Proposition 13 in June 1978 ended an era of fiscal feast in California. The next five years were painful for those in government. Politicians used to doing good by doing more had to learn to say no, as they squirmed in a budgetary straitjacket which a suspicious electorate refused to loosen. Administrators gave up planning new programs for social betterment in order to master the intricacies of cash-flow management. With revenues scarce, costs rather than benefits dominated official thinking; and by 1983 it appeared that government spending, which had moved inexorably upward for so long, actually could come down.

Yet this slowdown too may not last. Economic recovery has relieved California's fiscal predicament, and a long line of claimants for additional funds has already formed. The prospect of burgeoning state revenues has encouraged Governor Deukmejian, a conservative whose 1983-84 budget *cut* state spending by 2 percent from the previous year's level, to propose a 1984-85 budget that would *increase* expenditures by 13 percent, without raising taxes *(1)*. This new shift in the turbulent budgetary climate makes it especially timely to assess the impact of the taxpayers' revolt on California politics and to ask what its legacy will be.

This volume undertakes such an assessment by publishing in book form the Los Angeles Times' in-depth report on the condition of state and local government in California on the fifth anniversary of Proposition 13. The Times articles summarize trends in taxes, services and intergovernmental relations on the basis of extensive new information, which is buttressed here by Kevin Bacon's statistical report on a survey of how local governments have fared. This introductory essay broadens the investigation by comparing California's adjustment to a new fiscal order with the experience of other states, most notably Massachusetts, that have also come under the taxpayers' gun.

My analysis has these main purposes. It charts the course of the tax revolt nationwide in order to assess public support for efforts to limit the taxing or spending powers of government and to identify the conditions under which such efforts have succeeded. It describes how public officials have responded to voter-imposed fiscal restrictions, in order to measure the fit between budgetary outcomes and popular preferences and to determine whether the coping strategies of politicians in diverse contexts are similar. Finally, this essay examines the current state of public opinion on taxing and spending issues to speculate about the future of the tax revolt in California and elsewhere.

To preview the conclusions of the account which follows, the adoption of limits on state and local government taxes and spending has led neither to the millennium promised by the proponents of these restrictions nor to the Armageddon predicted by their detractors. Yet there has been change—in the size and distribution of the tax burden, in the pace of public expenditures, and in the pattern of relationships among state government, local officials, and citizens. How much change in the size of the public sector occurred was determined largely by how well the private economy performed. As should be obvious but is often overlooked, when budgets must be balanced economic growth is the solvent that allows government to expand without exacting a price in private consumption.

The pattern of adjustment to fiscal adversity was quite consistent across the various states. There are rules for "decremental" budgeting (2) and these rules are highly political, emerging as officials search for a safe path through the minefield between the voters' generalized desire for lower taxes on one side and intense organized pressure for maintaining services and public employment on the other. Walking this road while at the mercy of the business cycle is hazardous indeed, and explosions are to be expected. So notwithstanding several recent defeats for the tax revolt, it seems premature to conclude that this movement "sleeps with the fishes" *(3)*. Yogi Berra's caution is more apropos: "It ain't over till it's over."

CONTOURS OF THE TAX REVOLT: 1978-83

Resistance to high taxes, of course, is an ancient and widespread phenomenon, so the term "tax revolt" is used here to refer specifically to the popular movement that erupted in many American states in the late 1970s. Impatient with the ordinary processes of legislation, angry citizens took matters into their own hands to propose far-reaching and enduring restrictions on the authority of elected officials to tax and spend. Like bands of guerrilla army in the process of formation, state and local units of tax rebels sprung up independently and operated with relatively little coordination. Indeed, the tax revolt never has developed a central command structure, and even now relationships among the various organizations dedicated to reducing the size of government tend to be informal and spasmodic. Led by political outsiders and recruited mainly from groups on the fringe of the dominant institutions in American society, the tax rebels, particularly at the beginning of their campaign, found themselves arrayed against a coalition of establishment forces comprising most elected officials, public employees, the trade unions, and the large corporations *(4)*.

Proposition 13 was not the first successful action in the grass-roots uprising, but as the most dramatic and best publicized it came to symbolize the public's disgruntlement and its desire for cheaper and humbler government. After the passage of Proposition 13, the tax revolt proceeded on two fronts. The insurgents still employed their favorite weapon—the ballot initiative—to cut taxes and limit public spending. But increasingly they found allies in high places. In California and elsewhere, politicians had heard the message. Some enthusiastically embraced the religion of public austerity; others simply swallowed hard and adopted a policy of self-restraint. A combination of conviction and prudence thus added legislated tax relief to the reductions mandated by the voters. And once the recession further eroded revenues and the federal government failed to come to the rescue, the result was a substantial and rapid retrenchment at the state and local levels. As Table 1 on the following page shows, state and local government taxes, expenditures and employment all declined between 1978 and 1982, after rising steadily for decades *(5)*.

The election of Ronald Reagan to the presidency in 1980 marks the apogee of the tax revolt. With this, the proclaimed goals of Howard Jarvis, the sponsor of Proposition 13 who until 1978 had been a neglected, though shrill, voice in the California political wilderness, became enshrined as national policy. People were to pay less and government to do less. And these objectives were substantially realized. The 1981 Economic Recovery Tax Act included an across-the-board reduction of 25 percent in federal income tax rates, spread over three years. Large reductions in non-defense spending also were enacted, leading to a sharp decline in federal aid for state and local budgets. In 1978 federal outlays to state and local governments were $231 per capita; by 1982 this had fallen to $174, in inflation-adjusted terms *(6)*.

Targets of the Tax Revolt.

Local government in America has always relied heavily on the property tax as its principal instrument for generating revenue, so it was natural for the tax rebels to single out this highly visible and much-hated levy for attack. Assault tactics ranged from sniper-fire—circuit-breaker programs to shield poor and elderly citizens—to heavy artillery along the lines of Proposition 13— permanent reductions on the maximum property tax rate and ceilings on increases in assessment or the total amount of jurisdiction could raise in property taxes.

The effort to lower property taxes was effective, at least in the short run. The passage of Proposition 13 triggered an unprecedented rush of property tax reductions, as state officials has-

TABLE 1

Changes in the Size of State and Local Government

TAXES

Total State and Local Taxes per $1000 Personal Income (1)

	1972-73	1977-78	1982-83
All States	$128	$126	$110
California	**$146**	**$156**	**$108**

SPENDING

Total State and Local Expenditures per $1000 Personal Income (2)

	1966-67	1977-78	1981-82
All States	$15.57	$19.43	$18.72
California	**$18.41**	**$21.29**	**$19.15**

Average Annual Increase in Real per Capita State and Local Spending

	1957-58	1978-81
All States	4.4 %	0.54%
California	**4.11%**	**-0.73%**

EMPLOYMENT

Full-Time Equivalent: State and Local Employees per 10,000 Population (3)

	1966-67	1977-78	1981-82
All States	377	492	476
California	**408**	**489**	**458**

Average Annual Increase in State and Local Employment
per 1000 Population

	1957-58	1978-81
All States	2.7%	1.8%
California	**1.8%**	**-2.2%**

(1) Source: Legislative Analyst, State of California
(2) Source: Advisory Commission on Intergovernmental Relations (ACIR)
(3) Source: ACIR

tened to use accumulated reserves to expand programs of property tax relief for local governments. Between 1978 and 1980, then, fully forty-three states adopted new limitations on local property taxes or new property tax relief plans, either on official initiative or as a result of the electorate's decision *(7)*. In 1977-78, property tax revenues provided 80.6 percent of the revenues collected by local governments; by 1982 this had declined to 76.6 percent *(8)*.

The tax rebels also took aim at state taxes. Prior to the late 1970s, voters tolerated legislated increases in taxes to pay for expanded services, and governments also benefited both from inflation, which automatically boosted income and sales tax revenues, and from a heavy flow of federal aid. As a result, many states and localities acquired substantial budgetary surpluses, of which California's became the most notorious. After 1978, however, plebiscites and legislation reduced or repealed a number of specific taxes. Between 1978 and 1982, fifteen states reduced their general income tax rates and ten indexed their personal income tax systems, thereby giving up the bonus resulting from inflation. During the same period, seven states eliminated their gift taxes and six repealed their inheritance taxes *(9)*. The cumulative effect of these actions was to lower state and local revenues as a percentage of personal income from a high of 15.0 in 1977 to 13.7 in 1980; the tax revolt had succeeded in cutting taxes *(10)*.

On the expenditure side, constitutional or statutory ceilings on spending now confront a number of state and local governments. To be sure, these measures, which usually were adopted with official acquiescence, if not enthusiasm, vary in how tightly they draw the fiscal noose. Most exempt certain categories of spending from the limit, allow for adjustments to take account of population growth or inflation, and provide for emergency escape routes. Yet most state and local politicians are reluctant to use the statutory loopholes or those added by judicial decisions for fear of rousing the wrath of their constituents.

The leaders of the tax revolt hoped to go beyond merely cutting taxes and public spending in the short run and to permanently restructure the division of authority over budgetary decisions. Virtually all the tax and spending limitation laws enacted require special majorities of the electorate or legislative bodies to over-ride the mandated ceilings. This provision clearly elevates accountability in budgeting over flexibility, reflecting the frustration with elected officials that fueled the tax revolt. Believing that politicians could not be trusted, the tax rebels sought more power for the people. Barbara Anderson, executive director of Citizens for Limited Taxation, the organization that led the drive to pass Proposition 2½ in Massachusetts in 1980, expressed the populist impulse this way: "Our fight is not mainly about money. It's about control. *They* have to learn once and for all that it's *our* government" *(11)*.

California
The tax rebels in California fired on all the main targets, slash-ing both state and local taxes and imposing a limit on public spending. Proposition 13 passed by a two-to-one margin after two years of debate in the state legislature had failed to produce a program for property tax relief. The Jarvis-Gann Initiative lim-ited property tax rates in the state to one percent of assessed val-uation, rolled back assessed values to 1975-76 levels for proper-ties that had not changed hands since then, limited annual increases in assessment to two percent, except upon sale, and barred new property taxes *(12)*. Proposition 13 also prohibited local governments from imposing new taxes without the approval of local voters, although the California Supreme Court's decision in the Farrell case has circumvented this requirement.

The State Department of Finance has estimated that between 1978-79 and 1983-84 Proposition 13 will have saved taxpayers (and cost local treasuries) almost $51 billion *(13)*. And this is a conservative estimate of the revenues lost to local governments, calculated on the basis that in the first year after the passage of Proposition 13, 1978-79, property tax collections fell by $6.6 bil-lion and that this shortfall, modified slightly by a factor that takes account of growth and inflation, occurs annually. A less conservative estimate is possible. If we assume that by 1982-83 the result of Proposition 13 was that taxable property in the ag-gregate was underassessed by 50 percent, then the approximately $6 billion in property taxes collected in 1982-83 under Proposition 13 rules would have been $30 billion if "fully" assessed and taxed at the pre-Proposition 13 statewide rate of about 2.5 per-cent. On this calculation, the hypothetical loss to local govern-ments in 1982-83 alone amounted to a staggering $24 billion *(14)*. Whether even the most creative officials could have found politically acceptable ways of spending this sum is doubtful, of course, but the above exercise does underscore the potency of California's tax structure before the recent restrictions were im-posed.

Soon after the passage of Proposition 13, the state legislature, burdened with an embarrassingly large surplus of almost $11 million, cut state taxes by more than $1 billion by providing a one-time income tax credit, increasing tax relief for renters, re-ducing certain business taxes and partially indexing personal in-come taxes. These reductions were partly designed to head off Howard Jarvis's proposal to cut state personal income tax rates by half, and a ballot initiative to this effect was defeated by a margin of 60 to 39 percent in June 1980. But this is the lone de-feat for the tax rebels in California. In June 1982, again by a ma-jority of about two-to-one, the voters passed initiatives that fully indexed the state's personal income tax, overriding then-Gover-nor Brown's veto of similar legislation, and repealed the state's inheritance tax, going beyond the reductions previously enacted by the legislature.

The effect of indexing is cumulative, so its impact on revenues increases over time. The Legislative Analyst has estimated that the passage of the initiative to fully index income taxes will have cost the state $210 million in 1982-83 and $420 million in 1983-84, years of dampened inflation and slight economic growth *(15)*. Taking into account the effects of prior indexing legislation be-tween 1978 and 1982, it is estimated that over the period 1978-79 to 1983-84, this form of a tax cut will have reduced California's personal income tax revenues by $12.1 billion, or more than 22 percent of what would have been collected without indexing *(16)*.

The combined effect of Proposition 13 and subsequent tax cuts was to lower the overall state and local tax burden for California by more than 25 percent in just four years. In 1978 California's taxes were 24 percent above the national average; by 1982 its state and local tax burden stood at about the mean for all other states *(17)*. The fall in property taxes was much more precipitous. In 1978, just before the passage of the Jarvis-Gann Initiative, property taxes in California were 51 percent above the national average; in 1981 they were 22 percent *below (18)*. Whatever the unanticipated consequences of the tax revolt in California, the promise to slash taxes has been kept.

What might be called an "Inflation Security System" is another result of the successes of the tax revolt in California. The high rate of inflation of the late 1970s, particularly in that state's real estate values, was a critical factor in the escalation of state and local taxes that stimulated the voters' protest *(19)*. One motive for supporting Proposition 13 was defensive; it provided permanent insurance against inflationary increases in assessed valuation of property, while it furnished predictability and stability in one's future property tax bills. Indexing constructs a shield against uncertainty in the other main component of the individual's state and local tax burden, and the repeal of the inheritance tax means that heirs are spared from the impact of inflation on the value of what they are left.

In November 1979, amid the flurry of tax-cutting activity described above, voters in California approved with little fanfare a measure designed to prevent state and local expenditures from rising, in real terms, above 1978-79 levels. Proposition 4, the so-called "Spirit of 13" initiative, amended the California Constitution to place a lid on the annual growth in tax-supported appropriations of state and local governments and to forbid the retention of surpluses by requiring any *unappropriated* balances at the end of a fiscal year to be returned to taxpayers within a two-year period. But, unlike Proposition 13, which had an immediate and powerful impact on state and local budgeting, the spending limit is yet to act as a direct constraint. Indeed, the State Department of Finance has estimated that there is a gap of approximately $3 billion between the constitutionally imposed appropriations limit ($20.4 billion) and the 1983-84 budget appropriations subject to the limit ($17.4 billion) *(20)*.

This large gap developed because in the base year for setting the limit, 1978-79, the state had a large surplus and appropriated more than it collected in ongoing revenues or could sustain under existing tax laws. Moreover, because of the recession from 1980 to 1982, the state's tax revenue grew more slowly than the year to year allowable increase in the appropriations limit. The resurgence in tax collections which has enabled the 1984-85 budget to increase state appropriations greatly has also narrowed the gap to an estimated $1.6 billion *(21)*. But unless this reversal persists for several consecutive years, the state will lack the money to spend up to what Proposition 4 would allow. Until now, then, the popular endorsement of a formal *spending* limit has influenced budgeting in California only indirectly, by underlining the message of Proposition 13 that the growth of government should be braked.

National Patterns and Trends

Heeding the public's warning to cut back helped officials in most states outside California to escape the imposition of truly restrictive new budgetary rules, but the tax rebels did hoist their flag at a number of significant outposts. As of January 1, 1983, twenty states had enacted constitutional or statutory limits on either the taxing or spending authority of state government. More than half of these measures were the result of successful grass-roots campaigns in eleven of the twenty-three states that allowed voters to place initiatives on the ballot. The others, usually less severe, were referred to the electorate by legislators themselves or enacted by statute *(22)*. How much these institutionalized lids on taxes or spending contributed to the emergent fiscal discipline of the post-Proposition 13 era is another matter. It was the loss of revenues due to the national economic recession rather than formal limits on expenditures (which in any case could be evaded quite easily) that forced most states to make ends meet further down the ladder *(23)*.

Statistics compiled by the Advisory Commission on Intergovernmental Relations (ACIR) confirm that the enactment of limits on the fiscal power of local governments also has accelerated since 19789 and that these restrictions are more varied and comprehensive than their historical antecedents *(24)*. For example, until 1970 the limits on local authorities dealt almost exclusively with property tax rates. Between 1978 and 1982, thirty-four measures aimed at restraining local revenues and expenditures were passed, more than in the previous seven years. While twenty-eight focused on the property tax, still the *bete noire,* these included limits on assessment and full disclosure provisions as well as ceilings on rates, and six more global restrictions were enacted.

The protracted and diversified attack on their capacity to raise property taxes understandably has driven local officials to search for new sources of revenue. Almost everywhere—and certainly throughout California after the passage of Proposition 13—they have resorted to user fees and service charges *(25)*. This shift in the structure of municipal finance is already pronounced. Between 1978 and 1980, the proportion of municipal revenues nationwide derived from property taxes fell sharply from 42.7 percent to 35.3 percent, while the proportion contributed by user charges rose from 18.6 to 20.7 percent *(26)*. In California, local revenues derived from charges grew by 40 percent (over $1 billion) between 1978 and 1980 alone *(27)*.

Since polls have shown that the public prefers the imposition of service charges to higher taxes if additional funds are needed to finance local services, reliance on this instrument of revenue is almost sure to grow. Observers quarrel about the desirability of this trend, though few question its inevitability. Advocates of fees argue that charging directly for services as received is more equitable than subsidizing their consumption from general revenue sources because this reduces the number of "free riders," provides a more valid estimate of "demand" for government activity, and makes citizens more quality-conscious than if the service were provided free. Against these purported advantages are posed the regressivity of fees, the potential inability of the poor to pay the growing number of charges, and the danger that the movement to what has been called "pay-as-you-go" government will result in the withering away of services such as education or public safety that are less susceptible to pricing *(28)*.

Leaders of the tax revolt typically complain that many of the increased fees are unnecessary and devised to circumvent the popular drive to reduce the size of government. In California, Howard Jarvis has secured enough signatures for a constitutional amendment that would require the approval of two-thirds of the voters in a jurisdiction before any fee could be raised. Government officials naturally dread the prospect of such a regime, and are expected to mobilize *en masse* to oppose it *(29)*.

Compiling a comprehensive box score for the tax revolt is complicated because what should count as a win or loss is not always straightforward. For example, it seems reasonable to score as a defeat for the tax rebels their failure to obtain enough signatures to place an initiative on the ballot. But what if this occurs or their proposal is defeated largely because politicians reacted to popular pressure by cutting taxes on their own? Yet if one credits the tax rebels with a victory for every instance of a tax reduction after 1978, should not the recent proliferation of increases in state taxes be entered in the loss column?

The analysis that follows sets aside these ambiguities and only considers the results of statewide initiatives and referenda that actually were voted upon between 1978 and the end of 1983. The table on the following page classifies these measures according to the major type of change they proposed and the year they were decided *(30)*. Some nuance is sacrificed by ignoring the precise division of the vote and merely tabulating whether or not a proposal was adopted.

Until now I have concentrated on charting the onward march of the tax rebels. The data in Table 2, however, make clear that the relative severity of a fiscal limitation proposal strongly influenced its chances of success. Moderate restrictions tended to pass, but drastic reductions in taxes usually were rejected. So, for example, only four of thirteen of the property tax reforms closely modeled after Proposition 13 passed, compared to seven of eight relatively minor property tax relief measures *(31)*. Reductions in income taxes and other state levies were approved on eleven of nineteen occasions, whereas the proposal to impose a global limit on state or local expenditures, which typically had no immediate consequences, passed eight of ten tests.

The less stringent restrictions not only were less controversial but also had enough official support to come before the elector-

TABLE 2

Post-Proposition 13 Outcomes on Tax or Spending Limitation Measures (1)

Type of meaure (2)	1978-1979 Total	Passed	1980-1981 Total	Passed	1982-1983 Total	Passed	All Years Total	Passed
Jarvis "Clones," cutting and limiting property taxes	5	3	7	1	1		13	4
Lesser property tax relief measures such as exemptions, rebates	4	3			4	4	8	7
Cuts in other taxes, such as sales or income	4	2	7	5	8	4	19	11
State spending limits	8	6	1	1	1	1	10	8
Corporate Tax changes			4	2	4	2	8	4
Rules changes making tax or spending increases more difficult	5	3	2	1	2	1	9	5
Total	**26**	**17**	**21**	**10**	**20**	**12**	**67**	**39**

(1) These measures include both initiatives and referenda voted on at the state level between June 6, 1978 and January 1, 1984. A Tennessee spending limitation initiative passed in March, 1978 and is therefore omitted.
(2) Measures are classified according to one main provision they include.

ate as referenda rather than popular initiatives. All the Jarvis "clones" and seventeen of the nineteen proposals to cut state taxes were placed on the ballot as a result of grass-roots peti tions. That they passed less often than the officially sponsored referenda is another illustration that the tax rebels frequently could succeed in wresting concessions from the established order while failing to prevail when more fundamental transformations of the fiscal system were at issue.

An interesting footnote concerns the influence of voter turnout on the results of these elections. The more controversial and re-strictive grass-roots initiatives typically aroused more public in-terest and stimulated vigorous campaigns. This helps explain why fiscal limitation measures were more likely to pass when the rate of voting was low: fourteen of twenty-four propositions passed when less than 40 percent of the electorate cast ballots, compared to fifteen of thirty-three when more than 40 percent participated *(32)*. By mobilizing public sentiment, then, the tax rebels forced the issue of fiscal retrenchment to the top of state and local agendas. The threat of lost revenues, however, alerted defenders of the public sector to organize their constituents, some whom are infrequent voters. Thus, an enhanced level of turnout, while seeming to help Propositions 2½ and 13, is no cer-tain advantage for the anti-tax forces *(33)*.

The data in Table 2 also show that the intensity of the tax re-volt diminished after 1980. In 1978 and 1979, twenty-six fiscal limitation measures were put before the voters, and 65 percent passed. In the next four years, during which there were two gen-eral elections, scattered state electorates considered only for-ty-one such proposals, and the success rate dropped to 54 per-cent. This decline was especially notable in the case of the initiatives that imitated Proposition 13; after November 1978, only one of eight, Proposition 2½ in Massachusetts, won approv-al.

The targets of the fiscal limitation measures changed as the tax revolt progressed. In 1978 and 1979, property tax relief and the imposition of limits on state spending were the principal con-cerns. Later, voters were more likely to decide on reductions in income, sales or inheritance taxes, and on whether the tax burden should be shifted from individuals to business through the impo-sition of severance or other corporate taxes.

Precisely what and how many changes in government activity voters had in mind when supporting the tax revolt continues to be controversial, but no one disputes that lower taxes were the primary goal *(34)*. In probing the conditions promoting the chances of success for the tax rebels, therefore, a natural starting point is to compare the tax and spending policies of those jurisdictions which survived with those which succumbed to their attacks. It is generally assumed that popular approval of tax cuts is more likely where taxes are high, although there remains disagreement about whether the overall amount of taxes, the amount of *visible* taxes such as the property tax, or the rate of increase in taxes is the critical factor in spreading discontent *(35)*.

How does the tax burden affect support for the tax revolt? When the preferences of individual voters within a given jurisdiction are analyzed directly, self-interest does emerge as a powerful influence on how people acted. Surveys in California, Massachusetts, and Michigan have found that the belief that one was paying too much in taxes and the anticipation of substantial tax savings were strongly related to support for proposals to reduce state and local taxes *(36)*. Homeowners at all income levels have consistently favored the tax rebels' proposals more often than renters when the property tax is at stake, and the relatively affluent are the strongest supporters of cuts in income taxes, presumably because they would benefit more *(37)*.

But when one compares support for the tax revolt in different jurisdictions, the role of specific tax or spending policies is less clear-cut. For example, in Massachusetts a city's or town's property tax rate and its overall tax effort relative to the statewide norm were positively related, as expected, to its aggregate voter for Proposition 2½. But this measure fared relatively poorly in communities where property values, total revenues and per-capita spending were high *(38)*. In California, by contrast, Proposition 13 fared *worse* in counties with a high or rising property tax rate and better where assessed valuation per capita was relatively high *(39)*.

One possible reconciliation of these conflicting findings is that local tax rates reflect both a community's wealth and its preference for government services. Thus, counties with high tax rates may have been less enthusiastic about Proposition 13 because their residents on balance were more favorable to government spending and more willing to pay for it. The readiness to pay, however, has limits. In Massachusetts, the dependence of local government on property tax revenues was even more pronounced than in California, and the burden on poor communities which required high rates to finance services was thus heavy enough to override their stronger preference for public services *(40)*.

The search for the fiscal conditions that stimulated the tax revolt can be extended by comparing the levels of taxes and spending in states where the tax rebels succeeded and failed, respectively. Table 3 on the following page pursues this analysis by using several measures of a state's tax burden: the amount of all state and local taxes per $1000 personal income, the amount of local property taxes per $1000 personal income, and the state's tax *effort,* an index developed by the Advisory Commission on Intergovernmental Relations to compare a state's actual taxes with what they would be if a nationally uniform set of rates were applied to its tax base *(41)*. In each case the table reports a state's tax burden relative to the national average, which has an index value of 100.

Neither a state's relative tax burden nor its level of public spending influenced the likelihood that it would adopt a proposal to place a ceiling on state or local government expenditures or to provide minor property tax relief. These types of fiscal restrictions almost always passed and were as likely to appear on the ballot in states with a tax burden well below the national average than the opposite. Table 3 shows that this holds true for proposals to reduce state income or sales taxes too, so the discussion below concentrates on the so-called Jarvis "clones." A high property tax burden was important in spawning initiatives like Proposition 13: in ten of the thirteen cases (seven of nine states) where votes were taken, the local property tax burden in the fiscal year immediately before the election was higher than the national average—and in seven cases, more than 20 percent higher *(42)*. The role of high property taxes in energizing the tax rebellion is underscored by the fact that a state's *overall* tax burden was noticeably higher than the national average in just five of the thirteen tests for the Jarvis "clones."

What about the influence of high taxes on the adoption of initiatives like Proposition 13 once they appeared on the ballot? At first glance, the chances of success do not seem to improve if a state's tax burden is relatively high. Two of three "clones" won a

TABLE 3

Outcomes of Tax-Cutting and Tax Increasing Ballot Measures by State's Fiscal Context

Jarvis "Clones" (1)

State	Year	Outcome	Local* property tax burden (3)	Overall tax burden(4)	Tax effort(5)	State and local expendi- tures (7)
*National average = 100						
California	1978	Passed	142.8	123.4	117	109.6
Idaho	1978	Passed	82.9	91.5	89	107.8
Nevada	1978	Passed	81.9	98.9	62	110.2
Michigan	1978	Failed	106.4	99.7	109	101.3
Oregon	1978	Failed	124.4	97.8	92	121.4
Massachusetts	1980	Passed	182.0	119.7	135	105.4
Arizona	1980	Failed	117.6	113.3	117	107.0
Nevada	1980	Failed	72.8	90.6	60	106.1
Utah	1980	Failed	101.6	106.8	101	126.0
Michigan	1980	Failed	126.5	100.0	116	105.6
Oregon	1980	Failed	133.3	100.2	93	116.3
South Dakota	1980	Failed	138.2	91.3	88	112.0
Oregon	1982	Failed	N/A	105.0	101	120.2

State Tax Cuts (2)

(** = increase)

State	Year	Outcome	Overall tax burden(4)	Tax effort(5)	State and local expendi- tures (7)
North Dakota	1978	Passed	95.7	88	115.6
Arizona	1978	Failed	81.1	78	90.9
Louisiana	1979	Passed	100.7	82	108.0
Oklahoma	1979	Failed	82.3	74	92.5
Washington	1980	Passed	93.2	94	103.0
Montana	1980	Passed	109.6	02	121.1
Nevada (2)	1980	Passed	90.6	60	106.1
Utah	1980	Failed	106.8	101	126.0
California	1980	Failed	105.4	102	100.1
Missouri**	1982	Passed	77.7	81	83.9
Maine	1982	Passed	105.3		113
103.0					
California(2)	1982	Passed	101.8	100	102.3
Nevada	1982	Passed	90.9	62	103.2
Nevada	1982	Failed	90.9	62	103.2
Nevada**	1982	Failed	90.9	62	103.2
Washington	1982	Failed	89.0	92	107.7
Ohio	1983	Failed	81.5	89	88.5

(continued next page)

(Outcomes continued)

(1) All measures are initiatives.
(2) All measures are initiatives except Louisiana 1975 and Nevada* 1002. These two measures are referenda.
(3) Total local property tax revenue per $1000 of personal income expressed as a percent of the U.S. average. Source: Security Pacific National Bank.
(4) Total tax revenue of state and local government per $1000 of personal income expressed as a percent of the U.S. average. Source: Security Pacific National Bank.
(5) Tax effort is the ratio of a state's actual tax collection to its tax capacity expressed as a percent of the U.S. average. Figures for 1978 measures are from fiscal year 1977. Figures for 1982 and 1983 measures are from fiscal year 1981. Source: Advisory Commission on Intergovernmental Relations.
(6) For 1978 measures, figures represent change between FY 1975 and FY 1977; for 1979 measures, figures represent change between FY 1977 and FY 1979; for 1980 measures, figures represent change between FY 1977 and FY 1980; and for 1982 and 1983 measures, figures represent change between FY 1979 and FY 1981. Source: Advisory Commission on Intergovernmental Relations.
(7) State and local direct general expenditures in relation to state personal income expressed as a percent of the U.S. average. Figures for 1982 and 1983 measures are from fiscal year 1981. Source: Advisory Commission on Intergovernmental Relations.

majority when the local property tax burden was well below the national average compared to a two for ten batting average in the states which taxed residents more heavily. However, a closer look at the three states which ultimately passed grass-roots proposals to reduce property taxes drastically (California, Massachusetts, and Idaho) does suggest that there is a pattern of fiscal pressures which enhances support for the tax revolt.

In California before the passage of Proposition 13, both local property taxes and the overall state and local tax burden were far above the national average. Moreover, property taxes were escalating rapidly; had Proposition 13 failed, the homeowners' property tax bill would have almost doubled between 1974 and 1978 *(43)*.

In Massachusetts, property taxes in 1980 were virtually double the national average, and as a result the total state and local tax burden was also above the norm. And while there had been no increase in property taxes between 1979 and 1980, several weeks before the election on Proposition 2½ voters received the news that 1981 taxes would go up by 11.5 percent over what they had paid in 1980 *(44)*. This message sealed the fate of the opposition to Proposition 2½, much as the revelation of dramatic increases in Los Angeles property taxes had demolished the campaign against Proposition 13 in California.

When Idaho voted on its Jarvis "clone" in November 1978, its property taxes and overall tax burden were low compared to other states. However, residential property taxes had risen sharply over the previous decade because of a State Supreme Court decision that forbade the use of separate assessment ratios for different classes of property. This caused the homeowners' share of the property tax burden to leap from 24.5 percent in 1969 to 44.5 percent in 1978 *(45)*. Even where taxes are relatively low, then, a steep rise in visible exactions can fuel a revolt, particularly if the trend toward higher taxes is perceived as uncontrollable.

This suggests that political factors are important in translating favorable fiscal conditions into success for the tax revolt. Oregon's version of Proposition 13 was defeated three times, albeit by narrow margins in 1978 and 1982, despite the state's relatively high and rising property taxes. One reason for this outcome may have been that the total amount of state and local taxes paid by Oregonians was at the national average, but most observers believe that the existence of procedures that allowed voters to reject property tax increases and a program of property tax relief funded by the state were more influential *(46)*. In Michigan, the Proposition 13-like Tisch amendment was voted down in 1978 in part because dissatisfied taxpayers could support the less drastic Headlee amendment. (Property taxes in Michigan had been rising, but compared to other states the total tax burden in Michigan was not unusually high.)

With public cynicism about government prevalent, a failure on the part of elected officials to meet burgeoning complaints about high taxes at least partway was critical to the success of the tax revolt. The rebels won their greatest victories, in California and Massachusetts, where the political system was unresponsive to an obvious problem—in other words, where democratic processes broke down. The relative skill and resources of the opposing forces also has influenced the outcome of campaigns to impose fiscal restriction. For example, the success of Proposition 13 brought recruits, enthusiasm, and political allies to the tax rebels in other states, who sometimes rode to victory on Howard Jarvis's coattails *(47)*. On the other hand, the attempt to repeal Ohio's 90 percent increase in state income taxes was badly defeated in November 1983, in part because the opposition coalition led by the state's governor outspent the tax rebels by an overwhelming margin *(48)*.

To sum up, because voters must weigh their desire for lower taxes against their interest in maintaining a wide range of public services, they often have rejected proposals to cut governmental revenues radically. Success for "revolution" rather than "reform" appears most likely when taxes actually are both high and rising and when many voters come to believe that relief is unlikely under the prevailing political practices.

New State Taxes and the Future of the Tax Revolt

Proposition 13 ushered in an era of tax relief during which many states legislated reductions and others eschewed the increases that would have been required for government to continue to expand. Between 1978 and 1980 political actions resulted in a reduction of an estimated $29 billion in *state* tax collections alone *(49)*. In forty-four of the fifty states, there was a decline in state taxes per $1000 of personal income between 1978 and 1982 *(50)*. Ironically, the success of the tax rebels in inducing elected officials to relieve the taxpayer's burden made their subsequent proposals for fiscal limitation less compelling to voters.

The era of tax cuts abruptly ended in 1981 when many states reversed course and began to raise taxes once again. In the 1981 and 1982 legislative sessions, thirty-four states raised at least one tax, and in 1983 this happened in thirty-eight states *(51)*. Analysis of the specific changes made shows that both "sin" taxes on cigarettes and alcohol and the more broadly based personal income and general sales taxes, which together provide about 60 percent of state revenues, were affected. The measures to raise taxes resulted in a net increase in total state collections of $3.8 billion in 1981, $2.9 billion in 1982, and $7.7 billion in 1983 *(52)*. This growth in revenues represents less than 5 percent of state tax collections nationally, but there are nineteen states where tax revenues for fiscal year 1984 were more than 5 percent above their collections for 1982, even after one excludes the contributions of changes in the tax laws that offset other tax reductions or merely extended temporary surcharges *(53)*. California and Massachusetts avoided political actions that increased net state taxes on an ongoing basis, but in Idaho, the remaining state with a Jarvis "clone" on the books, state taxes rose by 17.4 percent between 1982 and 1984 *(54)*.

The rash of increases in state taxes does not indicate a new phase of steady growth in government or that the spirit of the tax revolt has faded away. As several analysts have argued convincingly, most states raised their taxes out of fiscal desperation, not choice. The deep economic recession sharply eroded revenues, and states were forced to confront this shortfall with accumulated reserves spent, commitments made to provide aid to local governments, and little hope of federal assistance *(55)*. Taxes were raised in order to sustain existing levels of services in a context of shrinking resources rather than to fund new programs. Indeed, expenditure policy tended to be very conservative. Moreover, new levies typically were imposed as part of a broader strategy to balance the state budget that included a wide variety of belt-tightening measures and cuts in expenditures. For example, a 1983 survey found that forty-one states had placed limits on hiring, thirty-seven had cut selected programs, thirty-two had restricted travel for their employees, fourteen delayed making payments, twenty-two adopted or proposed plans to lay off workers, and seven put workers on unpaid furlough *(56)*.

Political preferences shaped the mix of policies employed to close the budget gap, with Republican governors and legislatures predictably seeking more spending reductions and fewer tax increases than their Democratic counterparts. But in all cases, major tax increases were a policy of last resort and were approved only after substantial program reductions had been made.

The nature of the specific tax increases imposed also suggests that officials proceeded warily, always fearful of arousing the beast lurking within the electorate. The first taxes to be increased were those the polls showed to be most politically acceptable—taxes on cigarettes, alcohol, and gasoline. Increases in income or general sales taxes were adopted only when the fiscal crisis was truly severe. Of the ten states that increased either their personal income or general sales tax rates in 1981 and 1982, all but two had higher-than-average unemployment rates and were dependent on the ailing heavy manufacturing and construction industries *(57)*. Moreover, states forced to raise these unpopular taxes usually were below the national average in their current tax effort; all tried to hold down the required increase by also acting to collect more taxes from business.

Another indication of the continuing influence of the tax revolt is that most recent major tax increases are temporary, designed to tide states over until economic recovery refills their coffers. And it must be remembered that the impact of state tax increases on disposable income was offset by the reductions in federal income taxes that were going into effect at the same time. It is obviously easier to tolerate a specific tax hike if it is viewed as a short-term emergency measure and if one's overall tax burden is not increased anyway. J. Shannon and S. Calkins rightly interpret the events of 1981-1983 as showing that "a state government now extracts a major transfusion from its citizenry only when it is clearly apparent that the state is suffering a severe fiscal hemorrhage—due to the economic recession." *(58)* Making this apparent is necessary to keep the tax rebels at bay. Today, major tax increases must be carefully marketed; voters must be convinced that the new revenues are needed simply to keep the vital organs of state and local governments functioning.

This is not to say that citizens everywhere accepted higher state taxes with equanimity. Ohio's tax rebels tried and failed to overturn the increase in income taxes, while two Michigan legislators who had supported raising taxes were recalled in November 1983. A number of radical tax-cutting initiatives may be on the ballot in November 1984, including Proposition 1 in Florida, which would place a cap on all state and local revenues excepting federal aid, the fourth incarnation of Proposition 13 in Oregon, and Michigan's Voter Choice Initiative, which calls for a rollback of all state taxes to 1981 levels and approval of any future tax increases by the voters. Michigan and Oregon tax citizens at a rate somewhat above the national average and have increased taxes since 1981. Florida, by contrast, both taxes and spends at a comparatively low level. But, as noted above, political factors are likely to be crucial in determining the outcomes.

The durability of the national economic recovery, however, may have the greatest influence on the future course of the tax revolt. The recession not only necessitated state tax increases, but also resulted in a renewed reliance on property taxes by many local governments strapped by reductions in state and federal aid. Between 1981-82 and 1982-83 national property tax receipts rose by 14 percent, far above the rise of 5 percent in other state and local taxes, and the share of all state and local government revenues drawn from property taxes rose sharply from 30 to 31.7 percent, reversing a long-term trend. *(59)* Rising property taxes, of course, are the politically combustible material that touched off the tax revolt in California and elsewhere, and so a failure to limit their growth is likely to boost the chances of success for newly cloned versions of Proposition 13.

The resurgent economy promises to leave state and local governments with surpluses totaling an estimated $60 billion nationally. Rebuilding "rainy day" funds to protect against another economic downturn is an uncontroversial use for such surpluses, but once that is done the struggle between raising expenditures and cutting taxes is bound to be joined. Seared by recent experience, state leaders are unlikely voluntarily to limit their taxing authority or further shackle state revenues to local purposes. For example, Minnesota greatly expanded its program of local property tax relief and school aid and indexed income taxes between 1978 and 1980 only to have to abrogate indexing and raise personal income tax rates. No one wants to repeat this cycle.

Yet surveys indicate little enthusiasm for enlarging the public sector and continued frustration about the high cost of government *(60)*. The public appears willing to tolerate enhanced spending in some areas, such as infrastructure, that were severely cut back in the recent retrenchment and in public education, a widely used service whose quality is widely thought to be in decline. Beyond this, however, there is a rough consensus that the growth of government should be confined to the growth of the economy as a whole. The tax rebels who flourished in the late 1970s when stagflation squeezed personal incomes while govern ment treasuries swelled, are likely to resist recurrence of this pattern.

Because people are willing to pay more in taxes when their own incomes are rising, a robust economy gives the public sector room to grow. But as long as the widespread disenchantment with government which animated the tax revolt persists, officials must practice moderation if they are to fend off a new round of budgetary restrictions. In this regard, the lessons of the past five years are clear. If large surpluses accumulate, share government's wealth with the taxpayers. Justify a strong surge in spending by necessity, and if taxes must go up, start by closing loopholes and taxing first "sin" and then business rather than voters directly. In contending with the tax revolt, then, state and local leaders can influence their own troubled destiny. Having learned to cope with adversity in hard times, they also must develop a political strategy for managing prosperity. Although the tax rebels may lose electoral battles, their brooding presence remains a force for fiscal restraint.

COPING WITH FISCAL STRESS IN CALIFORNIA

The immediate fiscal consequence of the passage of Proposition 13 was to strip local governments in California of revenues amounting to 22 percent of their total budgeted expenditures *(61)*. Moreover, because the initiative limited annual increases in the assessed value of unsold property to 2 percent, it was virtually certain that the initial loss in property tax collections would grow each year. Proposition 13 did not cut directly into the state government's revenues, but political realities ensured that Sacramento's resources would not go untouched.

In adopting Proposition 13, the electorate had ignored the chorus of officials' warnings that economic and governmental "chaos," seriously "crippled" local services and "shocking" new taxes surely would follow *(62)*. The state's political leaders thus returned to the budgetary drawing board in June 1978, reeling from the blow struck by Howard Jarvis's "two by four" and deeply conscious that in a few months they had to confront the voters who had just repudiated their fiscal policies. Governor Brown and state legislators therefore had little choice but to swallow their preelection words and draw on the state surplus to try to prevent the realization of their own predictions of doom.

From the very beginning, political considerations dominated California's adjustment to life after Proposition 13. The state's leadership faced this acute dilemma: how to reconcile the victorious tax rebels' demands for retrenchment with the intense pressure from local agencies for aid and their own concern for maintaining the state's social programs. The strategic response evolved in the first three weeks between the passage of Proposition 13 and the adoption of the 1978-79 state budget, and has remained largely intact. Its guiding principle was to minimize disruption to established patterns of power and policy, in other words, to protect the status quo.

The following specific rules governed budgetary reactions to the fiscal challenge posed by the tax revolt. First, to keep the rebellion at bay, new taxes on individuals had to be avoided. In fact, even the state's liberal Democratic leadership bowed to the spirit of the times by enacting a preelection tax cut amounting to $1 billion in the summer of 1978.

Second, local government had to be kept afloat, and so the state greatly increased its level of financial assistance by assuming the costs of various health, welfare, and education programs and by disbursing block grants to local entities.

Third, when public spending had to be reduced, the cutbacks were tailored to the demands of both general opinion and bureaucratic self-defense. Accordingly, the budgetary pain has been doled out unevenly. Visible services that in principle are available to everyone have suffered less than those with specialized clienteles.

Within these broad parameters, partisan and intragovernmental differences over policy have persisted. When the state's fiscal circumstances truly worsened, Republicans pushed harder for lowered public spending, while the Democrats contemplated selective new taxes in order to sustain existing programs. Democratic legislators have also sought to preserve a redistributive cast in public policy, as evidenced by their protracted conflict with the Republicans over the size of the Cost of Living Allowance (COLA) for welfare recipients.

By increasing the financial dependency of local governments, Proposition 13 has intensified the competition among cities, counties, and special districts for their share of the state's largesse. The various units of local government have united to lobby their Sacramento banker to provide a statutory guarantee for the flow of aid and to allow broad discretion in its use. While not wholly unsympathetic, politicians at the state level understandably have been reluctant to make their own fiscal resources hostage to local purposes. In the continuing negotiations over how to stabilize the tangled fiscal relationships between state and local government, each party seeks to enhance certainty for its revenues and flexibility for its budgetary decisions.

A Smaller Government?

The steps taken to cope with Proposition 13 thus were intended to lessen its impact on the size of government. Indeed, it is often claimed that the public sector has managed to keep growing, a proposition that supporters of the tax revolt frequently take as proof that the prior level of taxation was too high and that officials have conspired to thwart the electorate's desire for retrenchment.

How one characterizes the post-Proposition 13 trends in taxing and spending depends on the yardsticks employed. In absolute terms, government is larger; more dollars are collected and spent today than in 1978. But if one adjusts for changes in the state's economy, inflation or population, compares recent trends with the rate of growth before 1978, contrasts events in California with the national pattern, or asks what would have happened in the absence of Proposition 13 and other tax reforms, the inescapable conclusion is that government in California has receded. Whether voters troubled by the size of the public sector think in real or nominal terms is unknown. Clearly, though, to trace changes in the share of people's income taken by government in what tax revenues buy, the proper approach is to adjust for inflation and economic growth.

The statistics of California's recent fiscal history are laid out in the Los Angeles Times articles that follow, and so only the highlights are summarized here. As already noted, the main consequence of the tax revolt was lower taxes. Between 1977-78 and 1982-83, Proposition 13 and other reforms "cost" state and local government in California an estimated $70 billion; state and local taxes per capita, once adjusted for inflation, declined by 26 percent *(63)*. The best measure of the tax "bite" on individuals is how much they pay per $1000 in personal income. This dropped by 15 percent for state taxes and by 49 percent at the local level, although there new fees picked up some of the slack *(64)*. Taken together, state and local taxes in California fell by 31 percent, or $48 per $1000 of personal income, between 1978 and 1983.

California's tax effort, the amount of actual collections relative to what would have been obtained by applying the national average in tax rates, declined by 14 percent between 1977-78 and 1981-82 *(65)*. No other state unflexed its fiscal muscles to the same extent. And there is evidence that the public has noticed that the tax burden is lighter and is appreciative. Polls show that compared to 1978, fewer citizens complain that their state and local taxes are too high *(66)*. In particular, the implementation of Proposition 13 has assuaged the intense dissatisfaction surrounding high property taxes that stimulated its passage.

The basis of the argument that Proposition 13 failed to stem the tide of governmental expansion is found in the statistics on public spending. Expenditures from the state's General Fund have increased by approximately $11 billion, or an average annual rate of 12 percent, between 1977-78 and 1983-84 *(67)*. In absolute terms, government is spending more. However, relative to the size of the state's economy, expenditures of both state and local government have declined. Second, Figure 1 shows that adjusting for inflation reduces the increase in spending to about $2 billion, spread over six fiscal years *(68)*. In addition, this increase was devoted entirely to replacing the property taxes lost by local entities. Spending on services provided by the state itself actually declined by 12 percent in real terms. And the massive influx of fiscal relief, even when added to new fees and charges, was insufficient to keep local spending from falling—by 10 percent *per capita* among cities and 8 percent per capita among counties *(69)*. Real spending of cities declined by 4 percent between

1977-78 and 1981-82, though counties registered a one percent increase *(70)*.

Figure 1 clearly demarcates two phases in California's adjustment to fiscal constraint: 1978-81, when the surplus revenues and a strong economy enabled expenditures to rise, despite yearly current deficits; and 1981-84, when the recession emasculated incoming revenues and reserves already were exhausted. During the first phase, most of the growth in spending occurred in the first year, 1978-79. To absorb the initial shock of Proposition 13, the surplus was used to underwrite an increase of 28.3 percent in *real* spending from the General Fund *(71)*. To provide this level of local fiscal relief, state government made a historic sacrifice and reduced real spending on its own staff and services by 6.2 percent in 1978-79 *(72)*. How far these cuts in spending have reduced the delivery of services, of course, depends on what was cut and changes in the productivity of government, but the over-all level of services is lower.

The tax revolt has made only a limited inroad into the size of the public work force. The number of state employees (in personnel-years) actually rose by roughly eleven thousand, or 5 percent, between 1977-78 and 1983-84, fueling complaints that the bureaucracy once more had evaded the guillotine *(73)*. Yet the number of public employees relative to the state's population fell by 6 percent. Moreover, much of the increase in staff is due to the need for additional personnel in the prison system required to police the ever-growing number of inmates. Spending more to control crime has widespread support, even among the tax rebels.

Local government has reduced its level of staffing since 1978 by about 4.5 percent, or 123,000 workers between 1977-78 and 1981-82 *(74)*. However, neither cities nor counties substantially dismantled the structure of personnel changes which had occurred as their activities grew over the past fifteen years. Instead, they cut jobs eliminating CETA positions rather than refunding them with local money and by reducing some administrative positions changed with the operation of federal programs that were being cut back *(75)*. Beyond this, attrition and hiring freezes were the tactics employed to protect the jobs of those already on the payroll.

Where the Money Goes

Did the tax revolt influence the shape as well as the size of government in California? At the state level, there were few changes in the mix of services provided. Figure 2 traces the trends in spending from the state's General Fund in the main categories of programs. The main shift recorded is the growth in the relative share of expenditures devoted to health, welfare, and education. In 1983-84, 84.1 percent of outlays from the General Fund went to these programs compared to 77 percent in 1977-78, the final pre-Proposition 13 fiscal years *(76)*.

This rise in the proportion of the state budget devoted to the so-called "people" programs occurred in the first two years of the new fiscal era and resulted from the assumption of the bulk of the cost of elementary and secondary schools (K-12) by the state. Spending for K-12 education consumed 22.1 percent of the General Fund in 1977-78, but an estimated 36.4 percent in 1983-84 *(77)*. The proportion spent on post-secondary education changed hardly at all, while the share spent on health and welfare programs fell from 36 percent to 33 percent, as indicated in Figure 2 by the flattening of the curve for this category of expenditure after 1981-82.

Within the health and welfare area, a significant recent change concerns the role of Medi-Cal costs. Between 1978 and 1982, Medi-Cal spending steadily increased in dollar terms and consistently took up approximately 35 percent of total state spending on health and welfare. However, a dramatic change took place in 1983-84 when, because of the termination of eligibility for medically indigent adults, other reductions in benefits and the establishment of hospital reimbursement rates on the basis of negotiated contracts, Medi-Cal spending actually declined *(78)*. The fiscal restraint imposed by these reforms should curb state spending for health on an ongoing basis.

Changes in the pattern of public spending at the local level have been pronounced and reflect the influence of political constraints on budgetary sources. Polls consistently show support for maintaining or increasing spending on police and fire services. Local officials have paid obeisance to public opinion and to the organized power of the police and firefighters' unions. The

Figure 1

Comparison of General Fund Revenues and Expenditures

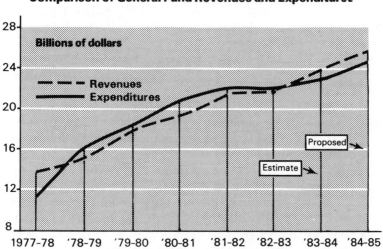

Annual Growth in General Fund Expenditures

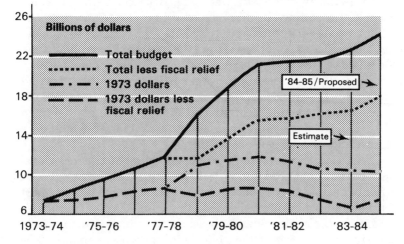

Figure 2

Trends in General Fund Program Expenditures

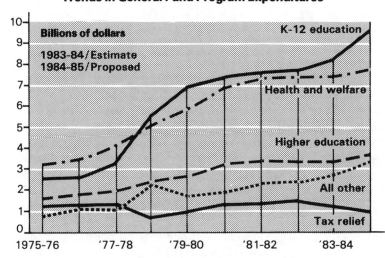

share of the local budgets devoted to public protection services rose by 6.5 percent among counties and 9.3 percent among cities between 1977-78 and 1981-82, the last year for which complete data are available *(79)*.

The advantaged position of police departments is confirmed by the inflation-adjusted figures reported in Kevin Bacon's chapter later in this book. The operating expenditures of the 114 police agencies reporting to the Los Angeles Times survey were 17.1 percent *higher* in constant dollars in 1981-82 than in 1977-78 and their per capita real spending rose by 8.9 percent. Local spending on health also increased, but public works programs and recreational agencies, where cuts would be made without an immediate visible impact on the quality of services, lost substantially in purchasing power.

Finally, local governments reduced spending on overhead and general administration, the "fat" about which the tax rebels complain, between 1977-78 and 1981-82. In the short-run at least, this increase in productivity has helped local government shore up activities that touch citizens in more directly perceptible ways.

As the economy goes . . .

Simply slowing the growth of government, let alone reversing this entrenched historical trend, is a notable achievement. Yet leaders of the tax revolt are dismayed, and most public officials correspondingly relieved, that California has managed to adjust to the constraints on its revenues without drastic changes in the size or structure of the public sector. True, a 10 percent decline in "real income" spread over five years is meaningful, but it is not, contrary to the familiar litany that blames any and all shortcomings in California's public services on Proposition 13, the end of the world.

How much of what has been cut and may be "waste" is a hotly debated issue that statistics alone cannot settle. The right "body type" for government ultimately is a matter of subjective preference; some see "fat" where others can only find finely sculpted muscle. So how one evaluates the reductions in public spending after Proposition 13 depends only partially on their difficult-to-measure impact on the quality of services. It also depends on how one feels about the size of government in 1978, the initial point of comparison.

California could reduce taxes more than spending because of the ingenuity of local government in funding new sources of revenues, the strength of the state's economy between 1978 and 1980, and the oft-mentioned surplus in the state treasury. The surplus had accumulated because during the middle and late 1970s the state's revenue base was larger than what was required to fund its services *(80)*. The size of the surplus was consistently underestimated by budgetary officials who incorrectly forecast economic growth and inflation in California and their impact on the state's revenues. Between 1973-74 and 1977-78, when the state's personal income taxes were indexed, the elasticity of General Fund revenues was 1.85 *(81)*. This means that tax liabilities rose by 1.85 percent for every one percent increase in personal income. For the ten-year fiscal period from 1971-72 to 1979-80, the average elasticity of revenues was 1.529 *(82)*.

Ironically, then, inflation both stimulated the tax revolt and helped provide the wherewithal to mitigate its immediate impact on government. The electorate's decision in 1982 to index California's personal income taxes permanently and fully and to repeal gift and inheritance taxes has drastically changed the relationship of personal income to tax liabilities. For example, in 1982-83 General Fund revenues grew less, in percentage terms, than personal income, and the Legislative Analyst estimates that this will be true even for income tax liabilities in 1985 *(83)*. In the past, when inflation exceeded economic growth, government benefited. To transform inflation into the enemy of government may be the most significant long-term effect of the tax revolt on the political process.

Unless the fiscal constraints imposed by the tax revolt are relaxed, therefore, the future expansion of the public sector in California depends on the performance of the state's economy. The vulnerability of government services to macroeconomic reverses became painfully apparent in 1981 when the impact of the national recession forced the state, already denuded of reserves, to make significant cutbacks. Yet the latest state budget's proposal to massively increase expenditures shows that even under the prevailing fiscal limits government can grow at least as fast as the private economy.

California is so large and rich and its tax system so potent that the revenues "lost" to the tax revolt could have been absorbed without reducing government spending in real terms if the economic growth of the late 1970s had continued. By the same token, the public sector would have weathered the recession of 1981-83 had Proposition 13 and the tax reforms it spawned been defeated. It required *both* major tax reductions and severe recession to create a fiscal crisis in California. The state's fiscal resources are less stable as a result of the tax revolt, but it is hardly enfeebled.

Increased uncertainty in the state's budgetary circumstances has led to heightened concern with accurately estimating tax collections. One reason for the accumulation of the politically embarrassing surplus in the years leading up to Proposition 13 was the persistent tendency of the Department of Finance to underestimate revenues. After the passage of Proposition 13, a new Commission on State Finance was established under the chairmanship of the State Treasurer and charged with preparing independent quarterly estimates of revenues. The Department of Finance and Commission have differed little in their forecasts, which consistently underestimated revenues during periods of economic strength but overestimated them during the recession *(84)*. For example, the difference between the receipts estimated in May 1981 and the actual receipts for the fiscal year from July 1, 1981 to June 30, 1982 was $1.6 billion, or 7.5 percent of actual revenues *(85)*.

During the recessionary period, these errors in forecasting contributed to the uncertainty of budgetary policies. Since decisions were contingent upon the availability of revenues, budgets had to be made and remade as the extent of deterioration in the state's fiscal position was revealed. In 1981-82, for example, when unfavorable new estimates of revenues were made early in the fiscal year, Governor Brown responded by ordering a 2 percent cut in all state operations and by calling for a delay in capital outlays. But these measures proved insufficient, and budgeting continued throughout the fiscal year as news of additional shortfalls in receipts mounted. To balance the budget, *ad hoc* measures that accelerated tax collections, raided special funds, and reduced assistance to individuals and local governments were negotiated.

When no one knows how much they have to spend, planning becomes problematic. And when there are no reserves to fall back on, a juggling act is required to accommodate the inevitable unanticipated expenditures for emergencies such as the Medfly crisis. To cushion such shocks, state officials are stressing the need for a substantial Contingency Reserve Fund. And they continue to be preoccupied with improving the management of cash flow and obtaining more accurate economic forecasts.

The recognition that the smooth flow of public services needs a strong economy has focused official attention at both state and local levels on how to foster development. Notwithstanding the utility of such efforts, federal decisions strongly influence the performance of California's economy. The tax revolt has coupled the financial fortunes of the different levels of government more tightly. Local governments rely on the state, whose ability to help in turn depends on the success of national economic policy.

Bailing Out the Local Government

The centralization of fiscal power at the state level was an unanticipated, and to many tax rebels an unwelcome, consequence of Proposition 13. Although the tax revolt initially aimed its fire on the local property tax, voters tended to view local agencies as more responsible and less wasteful than the state bureaucracy. Moreover, there was considerable justification for the complaint of local officials that they had been forced to raise taxes in order to pay for programs mandated but not fully funded by Sacramento. As noted above, it was quickly recognized that local services could not be allowed to shrivel, but how much aid to give, how to distribute it, and what strings to attach to it were less easily settled.

The emergency relief program enacted as S.B. 154 in the immediate aftermath of Proposition 13 required that police and fire services be maintained at previous levels and that all jurisdictions freeze local salaries. The first provision was eliminated from A.B. 8, the "permanent" bailout legislation designed to institutionalize the system of fiscal relief, and the second was declared unconstitutional by the State Supreme Court.

However, the *pro rata* formula developed to apportion state aid among the multifarious units of local government has been preserved. This principle of allocation has the virtues of being easy to explain and simple to calculate, as well as seeming fair on the surface. However, by ignoring differences in wealth among localities and variations in the alternative sources of revenue of cities, counties, and special districts, this approach solidified existing inequalities in the wealth of local jurisdictions. Once more, then, officials chose to minimize political contention and let pass an opportunity to reform and redistribute.

The state's long-term bailout law, includes a notorious "deflator" clause. This provides that if state revenues fell below certain target levels, state aid to local governments and schools would be *automatically* reduced by the full amount of the shortfall.

Schools and local governments would share equally in this cutback, should it be necessary. The deflator obviously was designed to give the state more flexibility in budgeting during hard times. By reducing what was owed to the local government, more money would be left to fund the governor's and legislature's own projects. In addition, state politicians sought to insure themselves against having to raise taxes to provide funds for a statutory level of support to localities. If more money would have to be raised, they wanted local officials to extract it from an unruly electorate.

The legislature therefore established a relatively high target level of revenues which was to be achieved if application of the deflator was to be avoided. The base figure included the remaining surplus as well as the 1979-80 General Fund revenues *(86)*. This meant that when the recession eroded the state's financial position, local governments theoretically faced Draconian reductions in aid. In fact, the operation of the deflator ultimately was suspended in the three years it technically came into effect— 1981-82, 1982-83, and 1983-84. When the chips were down, local governments possessed enough good will and bargaining power to escape with smaller reductions in aid than required by prevailing law. For example, for 1983-84 the Governor proposed to replace the $1.2 billion cut in aid to local governments that the terms of the deflator demanded with a reduction of only $400 million from the previous year's level of support.

Although the state's bark has so far proved worse than its bite, local governments clearly are unhappy with the present system of fiscal relief, which until the very end of the budget planning cycle keeps them guessing about what amount of assistance they can expect. Counties and school districts in particular are subject not only to the vagaries of the business cycle but to the outcome of the budgetary struggle in Sacramento.

The conflict over the 1983-84 budget between Governor Deukmejian and the Democratic-controlled Legislature has led to efforts to lessen the dependency of local governments on the state. The Governor refused to contemplate a general increase in state taxes and instead insisted on balancing the budget through cuts in spending and carrying over a projected deficit into the next fiscal year. Desperate to maintain spending for their priorities—health, welfare, community colleges, and environmental programs—the Democrats countered by proposing to allow the deflator to go into effect on July 1, 1983 and to give local governments the option of raising the local sales by one cent beginning October 1. This tax increase would have completely offset the effect of the deflator in 1983-84 and provided $750 million in additional revenues in 1984-85.

Local governments had a mixed reaction to a proposal that promised them increased financial independence but required them to take direct responsibility for a tax increase. In any event, the Governor flatly rejected this approach and ultimately had his way. He used the item veto to bring the budget sent to him by the Legislature into conformity with his original blueprint. The deflator was suspended and local aid cut by about $350 million, with the Democrats receiving no more than a promise that a permanent solution to the financing of local government would be a top priority.

The 1984-85 budget proposes a solution that entails repeal of the deflator, a constitutional guarantee for vehicle license fee and cigarette tax subventions, and restoration of local governments' access to the market for general obligation bonds, a market that Proposition 13 had closed. As the Legislative Analyst has pointed out, these proposals would improve the fiscal stability of local governments but not completely guarantee it. The state would still be able to adjust its manifold subventions in the light of its own fiscal circumstances. To become more fully financially independent, local governments require the authority to impose their own taxes and a statutory commitment that any new programmatic obligations imposed from above would be funded. The incentive to take these more fundamental steps, however, may be reduced by the improvement in California's economy.

It is often asserted that by concentrating financial power at the state level, Proposition 13 has resulted in the loss of local control over policy. By determining the amount of revenues available to local governments, the state obviously constrains their budgetary choices more than in the past. However, the passage of Proposition 13 has not led the state systematically to link monetary aid to the adoption of designated policies. It is true that the state's decision to fund only 70 percent of the health expenses of medically indigent adults forced counties to redirect local resources. And increased funding for schools has been tied, as in the past, to the implementation of specific reforms. For the most part, though, the tax revolt has not reduced the state's willingness to allow local governments to set their own priorities—provided the necessary funds are available. And the knowledge that they must be prepared to fend for themselves has forced local governments to adopt a more entrepreneurial style of management, both with respect to raising revenues and controlling costs.

THE POLITICS OF DECREMENTAL BUDGETING IN CALIFORNIA

In the years leading up to the passage of Proposition 13, government in California was blessed with enough resources both to continue existing programs and to undertake new initiatives. Under these relaxed conditions, budgeting was incremental in the sense familiarized by Aaron Wildavsky: decision-makers regard last year's budget as a sacred "base" and concentrate only on how to allocate this year's additions. *(87)* The unwritten rule in distributing the increment is that no major claimant is denied. Because nobody gets hurt and everyone gains a little, the conflict over who gets how much is muted. After all, the department that gets relatively little this year has a claim on a "catchup" increase in the next budget. And without a need to tighten belts, there is little incentive to evaluate the efficiency of ongoing programs. When times are good, the budgetary process can focus on planning rather than control.

But when resources are inadequate to cover the yearly rise in the cost of existing programs, let alone satisfy claims for new services, the rules of incremental budgeting lose their relevance. Since the "base" (last year's budget) must be cut, it can no longer be taken as given. How to allocate a *decrement* becomes the budgetary chore.

Adapting the strategy used in distributing growth is one approach to the problem of subtraction. In the decremental case, this again involves taking last year's budget as a satisfactory base rather than evaluating the worth of each of its component programs and putting together a new product from scratch. And every interest shares in the loss of funds, perhaps through the application of an across-the-board cut *(88)*.

California's initial bailout plan largely followed this decremental approach. There was no effort to review the merits of existing programs. Instead, the amounts of lost property taxes and available replacement funds were calculated. The allocation of relief then proceeded on the principle that all units of local government would be "held harmful" to about 10 percent of their projected receipts absent Proposition 13. Finally, spending on state programs also was reduced.

Nevertheless, the decremental and incremental situations are not symmetrical. Specifically, gaining general acceptance for this strategy of cutting back is more troublesome. In a decremental era, to grant legitimacy to the idea of last year's budget as the "base" is to admit that it includes non-essential items, that there are programs that can be cut without seriously damaging the public interest. No department will admit this willingly, and those relatively disadvantaged in last year's incremental settlement are bound to argue that since this was to be their "catchup" year they should be spared from the budgeting axe. The policy of across-the-board cuts is one way of evading such debates. However, this method of distributing losses penalizes smaller departments for which the specified proportionate cut constitutes a greater part of overall resources.

More generally, people prefer doing without a promised gain to surrendering what they already possess and are used to *(89)*. This psychological principle suggests that political competition will be fiercer in a decremental context. No department will volunteer to be the first to sacrifice, and politically advantaged interests should be less likely to acquiesce to a policy of sharing the pain. This makes it harder to negotiate a consensus about what to cut and implies that fiscal stress encourages the centralization of budgetary decision-making. This certainly held true in California where at all levels of government the tax revolt strengthened the hands of central executives against department heads, of accountants against planners, and of management against labor.

Because cutting expenditures risks disrupting established routines and disappointing political supporters, competitors for available revenues all strive to define their specific "base" in expansive terms. Each department naturally enough views the highest point on its historical expenditure curve as the proper "base." In California, the last budget before Proposition 13 has provided this conceptual standard. Cuts have been grudgingly accepted out of necessity, but the universal plea is that "we must get back to where we were before Proposition 13."

This helps avoid the selection of criteria for deciding what is essential. For another difference between incremental and decremental budgeting is the difficulty of using simple quantitative rules for cutting. Since giving less entails political risks, it is guided by political principles of selection.

In coping with fiscal stress, then, officials do their utmost to maintain the status quo, defined as much in political as in programmatic terms. This simply means that the twin commandments in decremental budgeting are to cut as little as possible, but, if one must cut, to concentrate reductions so as to minimize the threat of electoral retaliation. For threatened officials, the message is clear: look for political protection wherever it can be found.

California's adjustment to fiscal stress illustrates the strength of the imperative to maintain continuity. Innovations in budgeting, a systematic review of the effectiveness of existing programs, and reforms in the structure of local institutions have been rare *(90)*. Instead, the tactics of short-run preservation dominate decision-making. These have been directed at reducing the size of the decrement and its impact on current programs and staff. They include these sets of maneuvers:

1) *Collect More Now*

One example of this approach is the greater reliance of local governments on fees, charges, and leaseback arrangements to

fund their programs. Another is the array of accounting gim-
micks used by the state to boost revenues. When California's
economy soured, the state accelerated collections of insurance,
sales, income and corporation taxes, increased penalties on delinquent taxes, and transferred revenues from various Special
Funds to the General Fund. In 1981-82, contributions to the
State Personnel Retirement System were eliminated during May
and June. And in 1983, new legislation required that property
sold after March 31 in any calendar year be taxed at one percent
of the sales price in the upcoming fiscal year. Buyers would thus
lose the one-year period previously allowed.

2) *Pay Later*

Postponing the payment of bills and deferring new projects,
particularly capital developments, were tactics frequently employed to alleviate the fiscal pressure on existing services. The
neglect of capital infrastructure after the adoption of Proposition
13 is not surprising given that what voters can't see, they are less
likely to miss. Similarly, on the presumption that people more
willingly tolerate a gradual increase in the shabbiness of their
surroundings than the loss of entire facilities or programs, local
governments typically have allowed spending or maintenance to
suffer disproportionately.

Travel and purchasing restrictions were another common
technique to capture savings without striking at the core of government services. A final example is the relaxation of statutory
requirements to index the level of entitlements to designated
economic changes in preference to altering the underlying structure of the entitlement programs.

3) *Protect the Payroll*

Avoiding layoffs of regular staff was a paramount objective in
most jurisdictions and departments. Hiring freezes and the loss
of staff through attrition or retirement helped achieve this goal
in the short run. Lower wage settlements also contributed, as
public employees frequently chose, however reluctantly, to trade
off pay for jobs. One unanticipated consequence of the tax revolt,
however, may be to erode the morale and quality of public servants. Because of the seniority system, the first to be laid off are
the eager young recruits. Moreover, declining relative salary lev-

els make government a less attractive place to work for the talented and ambitious who have alternatives.

4) *Go Off-Budget*

Agencies especially vulnerable to budget cuts are tempted to make fiscal arrangements to secure themselves a more protected status. A possibility in California is to call on voters to approve a tax earmarked for a specific purpose, such as the maintenance of library services. One indication of the strength of the tax revolt is the tendency of local electorates to reject such levies. Between the passage of Proposition 13 and the end of 1982, 61 percent of the 89 proposals for "special" local taxes were rejected at the polls *(91)*. Community colleges, corrections departments, even the police have been spurned. As a result, officials of the community colleges, badly hit in the last two state budgets, have spoken of sponsoring an initiative to guarantee constitutionally that certain state revenues be allocated to them. Those who spend, it seems, also have learned the possibilities of plebiscitary budgeting.

More generally, local governments are seeking an assured level of fiscal relief from the state. They also have created special districts and developed innovative schemes of bond financing to obtain a stream of financing beyond the direct control of voters and outside the ordinary processes of budgeting. And, because the spending, debt, and payroll of the off-budget enterprises are excluded from the statistics of the political entities that form them, their growth means that the officially reported size of the public sector is understated.

A more important implication of a proliferation of earmarked funds and off-budget accounts is to lessen the comprehensiveness and accountability of budgetary decisions. Spending departments escape uncertainty, but central control of the appropriations process diminishes. And as the normal budget subsumes less and less of what is spent, the formal ability of taxpayers to constrain or reorient public spending increasingly loses its meaning.

Underlying the coping strategies adopted by governments in California was the fervent hope that fiscal stress would be short-lived, that economic recovery or a change in public atti-

tudes would bring salvation. Decremental budgeting in Califor
nia thus aimed at "muddling through" the crisis *(92)* without
much concern for the long-run rationality of the system that
emerged.

HOW MASSACHUSETTS LEARNED TO STOP WORRYING
AND LOVE PROPOSITION 2½ *(93)*

For the study of the consequences of the tax revolt, Massachusetts is a particularly suitable case to compare to California. In
both states, the tax rebels struck against a background of abnor-
mally high property taxes and triumphed over the liberal political coalition that had presided over more than a decade of sustained growth in government spending on health, welfare, and
special education. And the catalyst of fiscal stress was funda-
mentally the same in each case. Modeled on Proposition 13,
Proposition 2½ also slashed the revenues available to local governments by rolling back property taxes and severely limiting
their future growth.

When Proposition 2½ passed in November 1980, however, it
appeared that Massachusetts was in a weaker position to cope
with the shock to its fiscal system than California two years previously. The nation was in the midst of a deepening recession.
And officials in Massachusetts had to contend with intense demands for maintaining government services and employment
without the advantages of a highly professionalized system of
public administration, a well-diversified tax structure or, most
importantly, a large surplus in the state treasury *(94)*. Yet despite these seemingly unfavorable circumstances, Massachusetts
has adjusted to fiscal constraint without significant disruption to
the operations of state or local governments *(95)*.

How Massachusetts managed to absorb the tax reductions
mandated by Proposition 2½ and avoid drastic cuts in public
spending confirms the main lessons learned in the preceding
analysis of California's experience. The strength of the economy
in Massachusetts since the implementation of Proposition 2½
has provided the funds for a large increase in the amount of state
aid to localities. Massachusetts escaped the brunt of the national
recession; indeed, officials there were able to increase state
spending at precisely the moment that California was forced to

retrench.

The political logic of decremental budgeting also held sway in Massachusetts. Officials there, as in California, struggled to protect the budgetary "base," that is, to preserve core services and avoid layoffs. The by now familiar selectivity governed the allocation of cuts. Quantitative criteria such as across-the-board reductions were abandoned in favor of a more explicitly political approach. Public safety programs suffered less than education, recreation, and public works. Capital projects were deferred to save existing jobs. And in Massachusetts too, the tax revolt resulted in the centralization of budgetary decision-making.

A Short History of Proposition 2 ½

Proposition 2½ took its name from the provision that limited the amount of property taxes a jurisdiction could collect to 2.5 percent of the "full and fair" cash value of its tax base in the 1979 fiscal year. Communities whose property tax revenues exceeded this limit were required to roll back their levy by 15 percent a year until the amount collected was under the appropriate ceiling. After this, the tax levy could be increased by no more than 2.5 percent a year. As originally drafted, the initiative allowed no exceptions for inflation, population growth, or new construction, but the legislation required to implement Proposition 2½ relaxed this condition. The levy limit could be overridden only by a vote of the relevant community's electorate *(96)*.

Proposition 2½ also reduced the motor vehicle excise tax rate from $66 to $25 per thousand dollars of valuation. This immediately cost local governments statewide an estimated $150 million *(97)*. Finally, the initiative included several provisions aimed at enhancing control of spending. Unfunded state mandates—legislative or administrative—were prohibited; state subventions would have to accompany such directives for local action. The autonomy of local school committees was abolished, as was compulsory and binding arbitration of disputes with public employees.

Proposition 2½ passed by a margin of 59 to 41 percent, despite the strong opposition of state and local political leaders *(98)*. Much as in California, the victory of the tax rebels in Massachusetts reflected both unhappiness over high taxes and anger at the recalcitrance of the state legislature which for several years had refused to enact tax relief. Perceptions of government in Massachusetts as wasteful, unresponsive, and corrupt were widespread and significantly contributed to the vote for 2½ *(99)*. Given such a negative image of elected officials, the very restrictiveness of Proposition 2½ seemingly added to its appeal as a reform that imposed popular control over taxes and spending.

In 1980, property taxes in Massachusetts, including the motor vehicle tax, were 74 percent higher than the national average *(100)*. One reason for such high property taxes was that Massachusetts lacks balance in its use of taxes, ranking forty-second among all the states in this respect *(101)*. The state employs a flat-rate income tax that denies it the so-called "inflation bonus" and a sales tax that exempts many items of consumption and raised $26 less per person than the national average in fiscal 1981 *(102)*.

This heavy reliance on the highly visible had aroused public discontent long before the campaign for Proposition 2½. Historically, local officials had assuaged protest through a creative system of abatements and selective assessment procedures that protected residential property owners. However, beginning in 1974 court decisions ruled several such practices unconstitutional, and the informal "political" system of tax relief began to break down under the legal pressure to revalue, the increasing complaints of business organizations about high taxes, and the continued growth in public spending.

The political history of Massachusetts before 1980 is strewn with failed efforts to reform the state's tax structure and provide property tax relief. The latest push to cut property taxes began in earnest after the passage of Proposition 13 in California. In November 1978, voters passed a nonbinding advisory resolution that directed the legislature to reduce property taxes and increase state aid to localities. Governor King and the legislature responded by adopting a loose "tax cap" that for the next two fiscal years only limited increases in the property tax levy to 4 percent of the previous year's amount. The limit excluded school budgets and was often overridden by votes of town meetings and

city councils. Thus, while temporarily slowing the rise of property taxes, the tax cap was not an adequate long-run solution.

In the legislative arena, then, liberal ideology, the resistance of
elected politicians to the idea of giving up control over tax policy,
and the entrenched influence of the pro-spending constituencies
prevailed. The consequence was an electoral uprising that transformed the rules of the budgetary game.

The Impact on the Size of Government

Proposition 2½ succeeded in lowering the tax burden in Massachusetts. Statewide, the property tax levy fell by 9.3 percent in
the first year following its passage, or 15 percent in real terms
(103). In 1982, property taxes, including the motor vehicle tax,
took a $46.60 bite out of every $1000 of personal income, as compared to $58.30 in 1980 *(104)*.

How these tax savings have been distributed is a matter of current debate. The previous system of assessment in Massachusetts subsidized homeowners at the expense of owners of commercial property. Proposition 2½ created an incentive to
reassess all property at "fair and full value," and this revaluation
has had a relatively greater effect on residential property. Critics
of Proposition 2½ argue that this has meant that the main beneficiaries of the tax cut have been utilities and owners of commercial and industrial property. Not only has there been a rise in the
residential share of the tax burden they claim, but many individual homeowners are paying more because the upward revaluation
of their property has more than offset the lower tax rate *(105)*.

Officials in the Department of Revenue, however, believe that
such increases in the tax liability of homeowners have been infrequent, and certainly less than would have occurred in the absence of Proposition 2½, since communities ultimately would
have had to capitulate to revaluation *(106)*. At any rate, in Boston, Proposition 2½, *as written,* lowered residential property
taxes by an estimated 15 percent in one year. *(107)*.

Officials in Massachusetts chose to bear the brunt of the required reduction in the first year after the passing of the initiative, in part because they believed politicians in California had
missed an opportunity to attribute the necessary loss of services

to the impact of the voters' decision *(108)*. The experience of Massachusetts further parallels that of California in that shrinkage of public spending has been smaller than the shrinkage of tax "revenues" as a result of Proposition 2½.

In fiscal 1982, local budgets statewide declined by 1.5 percent *(109)*. The state's expenditures for purposes other than local aid grew by 2.5 percent, which represents a sharp drop from the 9 percent annual increase over the previous three years *(110)*. But in fiscal 1983 and 1984, both local and state expenditures rose. Since the passage of Proposition 2½, then, state expenditures have risen 5 percent in real terms, and the 1984-85 budget proposes an 8 percent real increase.

Public sector employment in Massachusetts also slipped in the first year following the passage of Proposition 2½. The number of state employees fell by 6.2 percent, or 6,200 workers, and local employees by 11.8 percent or 30,400 workers *(111)*. About half of the local employees who lost their jobs were laid off; many, as in California, were CETA workers. The shrinkage of the local workforce was concentrated in the schools; two-thirds of the municipal workforce are school employees, and a similar proportion of those who lost their jobs were employed in education departments *(112)*. By contrast, police and fire departments lost fewer staff in proportion to their share of the total work force. The reduction in public employment, however, largely ended after 1982. In general, government in Massachusetts recovered quite quickly from the blow struck by Proposition 2½.

Drastic cuts in local services could be avoided in Massachusetts because several sources replaced the revenues lost to Proposition 2½. Revaluation of existing property, new construction, and increased fees added to local resources. Most important, however, was the increase of state aid. Although Governor King initially proposed that the state "bailout" in 1981-82 be limited to a trivial $8 million, the final amount of assistance for that year was $252 million, and this would rise to a proposed $550 million for fiscal 1984 *(113)*.

The political commitment to state assistance for local government in Massachusetts seems strong, if belated. The present governor, Michael Dukakis, has pledged to guarantee that 40 percent of any annual growth in state revenues would be allocated to state aid. And, despite the efforts of the education lobby, it has so far been agreed that this additional aid should be discretionary rather than earmarked for schools. However, the formula used to distribute aid among communities takes no account of their need in the light of the impact of Proposition 2½. As a result, once state aid has been distributed some towns and cities are better off than before the initiative passed. The equalization of revenues among local jurisdictions was largely ignored by state officials in Massachusetts as in California when they allocated bailout funds.

Allocating the Decrement

Several surveys of local governments in Massachusetts confirm that officials deviated from the criterion of proportional suffering when reducing expenditures. In deference to public opinion, police and fire departments were cut substantially less, despite evidence that they were staffed higher levels than their counterparts in other states *(114)*. Departments with smaller and less vocal constituencies, such as recreation and libraries, endured the deepest cuts in percentage terms. And partly because of the forced withdrawal of municipalities from the bond market in the first year following the passage of Proposition 2½, there were enormous cuts in equipment purchases, road construction, and building maintenance. As the fiscal situation improved in the second post-2½ year, however, there was less need to defer capital expenditures.

Schools and health departments were attractive targets for the budgetary axe because their expenses had been growing for many years and now constituted a large share of total local budgets. Since many educational, health, and welfare programs had been foisted upon local governments by the state Legislature, local officials preferred to concentrate reductions there in order to preserve programs of their own making.

Advocates of public schools have complained that education departments have been unfairly treated in the post-Proposition 2½ budgetary process. Other analysts claim that the decline in spending on schools should be attributed to the willingness, long overdue, to tie expenditures on education to enrollment. From 1974 to 1982, per-pupil spending in Massachusetts rose by 133.7 percent, while enrollment declined by 20.7 percent *(115)*. Even in 1982, when overall spending on schools declined, per-pupil expenditures rose because of the drop in enrollments. Moreover, in Massachusetts as in California, school officials tended to eliminate peripheral programs such as adult education and summer programs while preserving core activities and staff.

This is not to say that careful cost-benefit analyses played a large role in determining what reductions to make. Politics was usually more important. For example, faced with the need to cut back, fire department administrators in Boston recommended the closure of several district stations, pointing out that this would save jobs. This aroused a storm of civic protest, since the stations were apparently more popular than their occupants, and in the end the city of Boston used part of its state aid to keep the stations open *(116)*.

Sweet are the Uses of Adversity

Most politicians in Massachusetts awaited the implementation of Proposition 2½ with fear and trembling. Now that they have survived the initial threat to basic services and personnel so well, many local officials are finding unanticipated virtues in the initiative. Echoing statements made in California after the passage of Proposition 13, they claim that the fiscal crisis "gave us the political clout to do things to make government more productive that we've wanted to do for a long time" *(117)*.

Clearly, when money becomes scarce there is a greater incentive to collect and spend it more efficiently. With Proposition 2½ in place, local communities have an interest in making sure that properties are constantly taxed at "full and fair" value. Thus, one obvious need is for more professional assessment practices *(118)*. Ironically, by freezing assessments Proposition 13 made California's respected and efficient assessors redundant.

Local governments in Massachusetts have undertaken a variety of management reforms in the effort to increase their productivity. Among these are interlocal arrangements to share overhead, the contracting out of services, the adoption of self-insurance programs, computerized recordkeeping, and more modern cash management policies. It is too early to assess the net effort of these innovations, but at least one dramatic example must be reported. After Proposition 2½ passed, the City of Boston decided to "decriminalize" minor traffic violations and dispose of them through the administrative process rather than in the courts. The result was to increase the amount collected in penalties from $2 million to $30 million in the first year *(119)*. One senior Boston official acknowledged that Proposition 2½ should be praised for "nudging an antiquated system of government onto the road to modernity" *(120)*.

As a result of Proposition 2½, the process of local budgeting has changed in ways that considerably enhance the power of central executives. The loss of autonomy for school committees and the end of compulsory arbitration have increased their ability to control personnel costs, the major component of local budgets. Moreover, once budgeting became a matter of quickly deciding who gives up what rather than simply adding up the requests of departments and calculating the tax rate required to fund them, consultation with employee unions, client groups, and individual citizens diminished *(121)*. Particularly during the first, decremental year after Proposition 2½, central managers were able to formulate their own plan and make it stick.

In one important way, local entities have benefited from the impact of Proposition 2½ on their relationship to state government. In the past, local property taxes had to be raised to pay for policies established by state Legislature and administration. Now local services must rely on financial assistance from the state, but amply compensating for this increased dependency is the statutory prohibition against unfunded mandates from the state to do more. Local revenues may be less certain, but one important claim on them has been checked.

Indeed, frustration with Proposition 2½ seems most pronounced among officials at the state level. True, Proposition 2½ furnishes besieged legislators with a convenient excuse for saying no to incessant demands for more spending. But the diversion of revenues to localities is a barrier to the expansion of programs to which the liberal Democrats who control state government and their electoral constituencies are deeply committed.

This consequence of fiscal stress has intensified the desire of liberals to enlarge the state's fiscal base. In 1983 Governor Dukakis appointed a state Tax Study Commission with a mandate to recommend changes in the existing tax structure. The tax rebels may find that a consequence of their success is an increase in the state's sales taxes, which are now relatively low.

No one expects Proposition 2½ to depart the fiscal scene. Popular support for this measure remains strong. As of September 1, 1983, seventy-four of one-hundred attempts to override the 2.5 percent levy limit were defeated. And Citizens for Limited Taxation forced Governor Dukakis to beat a hasty retreat in the summer of 1983 when he proposed to allow city councils rather than the electorate to defer the third year of cuts in the property tax levy required to achieve the 2½ percent limit.

One reason for the resilience of Massachusetts' economy during the recent recession is that the state relies more heavily on high technology industries and less on declining industries such as metals and transportation equipment or construction, which are so sensitive to fluctuations in interest rates. State officials are therefore attentive to the positions of the Massachusetts High Technology Council (MHTC), the main financial backer of Proposition 2½, and to the threat of high taxes pushing easily movable computer companies into other states *(122)*. The fear of losing business to a neighbor with lower taxes extends to the local level. Many small communities have preferred not to use their right under the state's classification law to tax commercial property at a somewhat higher rate than residences.

To the extent that it is true, as many on both sides of the issue believe, that by improving the business climate in Massachusetts, Proposition 2½ has helped sustain the strong performance of the state's economy, the initiative also mitigated its impact on government spending.

In sum, Proposition 2½, like Proposition 13, is both a source of tangible benefits and a symbol of the "people's" victory over the "politicians." Barring a major economic crisis that maims the fiscal capacity of the state and slashes widely desired services, its status is secure.

THE MEANING OF PROPOSITION 13

The People's Verdict

When Californians voted on Proposition 13, public opinion held that taxes were too high, public expenditures excessive, and government grossly inefficient, but that the level of most specific public services should be maintained or enhanced *(123)*. People seemingly desired if not something for nothing, then more for less *(124)*. Since Proposition 13 has passed, public officials, once bitten, have been twice shy to conform more closely to popular sentiment. Fiscal developments in California thus have moved California in the direction favored by the tax rebels: taxes are much lower, the pace of government spending has slowed, and reductions in public services have been concentrated in areas with lower levels of public support. Despite a number of unanticipated consequences, these major outcomes of the tax revolt in California—and in Massachusetts for that matter—represent a successful translation of mass opinion into public policy.

Trends in public attitudes have tended to reflect the new fiscal realities. The most dramatic manifestation of public reactions to Proposition 13 is the drop in the proportion of the public's complaining about the level of their property taxes: In 1983 only 15 percent felt this way, compared to 60 percent in mid-1977 *(125)*. And 78 percent of homeowners credited Proposition 13 with reducing their property taxes. Opinions about the overall state and local tax burden have softened more slowly; in 1983, 59 percent said their taxes were "somewhat" or "much" too high compared to 70 percent in 1977 *(126)*.

Perceptions of the government as wasteful also have diminished. In May 1978, as Californians prepared to vote on Proposition 13, 38 percent believed state and local governments could be cut by 20 percent or more without reducing services. In August 1982, only 22 percent felt there was this much "fat" in state and local budgets *(127)*.

The syndrome of wanting lower taxes *and* more services continues to prevail. In March 1983, the California Poll once again asked California whether public spending in fourteen specific domains should be increased, held the same, or reduced. In only one instance, government regulation of business and professions, did preferences for less spending outnumber responses in favor of increases. More generally, those in favor of cutting back were always a small minority, and the proportion in favor of either the status quo or more spending had increased since May 1978 *(128)*.

Do people who say state spending should stay the same mean they are satisified with the cuts in services made in response to Proposition 13? The California Poll consistently has found that more people believe that the budgetary reductions have occurred in the "wrong" rather than in the "right" places, with the most common complaints that schools have been cut too much and "bureaucracy" too little *(129)*.

Five years after the passage of Proposition 13, 42 percent of Californians felt that the quality of state and local government services had declined, compared to only 6 percent who perceived improvement, with education, street maintenance, and libraries singled out as the areas of greatest decay. Interestingly, these were indeed among the areas that suffered most after Proposition 13. Thus these shifts in opinion are largely consistent with changes in the structure of expenditures, and current preferences concerning where government should now spend more come as no surprise.

As Table 4 shows, when asked about the specific impact of Proposition 13 on one's personal circumstances, opinions understandably vary according to whether the focus is on taxes or services. Even in 1983, a majority of Californians (53 percent) felt Proposition 13 had had no effect on the services their family received. Those reporting unfavorable consequences have gradually increased since 1980, however. The proportion of the public that perceives positive consequences for their taxes also has slipped a little, although whether this is due to the impact of new fees or because people have come to take the benefits of Proposition 13 for granted, one cannot say.

The recognition has spread, then, that Proposition 13 has forced a trade-off between tax relief and some loss in services. In

TABLE 4

Current Attitudes Toward the Tax Revolt

1. Impact on Proposition 13: "What has been the effect of Prop. 13 on you and your immediate family in regard to the (taxes you pay/services you receive)? Has it been favorable, unfavorable, or hasn't Prop. 13 had any specific effect?"

	Very favorable	Somewhat favorable	No effect	Somewhat unfavorable	Very unfavorable
Taxes	28.6	21.5	32.5	10.1	7.4
Services	4.1	9.2	53.7	18.5	14.5

2. Overall Impact of Prop. 13: "Taking into consideration the changes in taxes your household pays, the wages it receives, the fees you pay for government services, and the level of public services provided, would you say that your household is better off or worse off because of the passage of Prop. 13 or hasn't it had any effect?"

Better off	No effect	Worse off
30.6	45.1	24.3

3. Tax Burden: "On the whole, do you feel that the level of state and local taxes that the average citizen like yourself pays is much too high, somewhat high, or about right?"

Much too High	Somewhat too high	About right
30.2	31.6	38.2

4. Size of Government: "In general, government grows bigger as it does more and provides more services. If you had to choose, would you rather have a smaller government providing fewer services or a larger government providing more services?"

Smaller government/ Fewer services	Larger government/ More services
69.5	30.5

5. Deficit Reduction: "Some people feel that if state and local government face a budget deficit that we should not allow services to be cut back from their present level, even if this means raising taxes. Others feel that we should cut back on existing state and local government services rather than raise taxes. Which of these statements is closer to your view?"

Raise taxes/ Maintain services	Cut services/ Don't raise taxes
38.8	61.2

(continued on next page)

(Attitudes continued)

6. Quality of Services: "Would you say that during the past five years the overall activity of state and local services that you receive has improved, remained about the same, or declined?"

Improved	About the same	Declined
6.1	50.0	43.8

7. Satisfaction with Prop. 13: "As you know, in 1978 California voters approved Proposition 13, the Jarvis-Gann initiative, and property taxes were reduced. What's your overall feelings now about the tax and government spending changes that have occurred in California since the passage of Prop. 13? Are you extremely satisfied, somewhat satisfied, somewhat dissatisfied, or extremely dissatisfied?"

Extremely satisfied	Somewhat satisfied	Somewhat dissatisfied	Extremely dissatisfied
21.4	12.9	37.1	28.5

Source: The California Poll, March 1983

March 1983, 30 percent of the public felt that taking all changes into account, Proposition 13 had improved their *personal* circumstances; 24 percent believed, on balance, they had suffered; and 45 percent reported no net effect. When asked about the impact of Jarvis-Gann on taxes and spending in California as a whole, opinion was divided evenly between those expressing satisfaction and those expressing dissatisfaction.

The growing acknowledgment that Proposition 13 has brought problems in its wake is no indication that if given a chance the electorate would reverse its decision of 1978. It is, of course, unlikely that voters would be posed the question in such a stark way, but in any event polls have continued to show a majority saying yes when asked "Would you vote for Proposition 13 today?" Similarly, in early 1983, the most painful moment of California's fiscal crunch, 56 percent preferred cutting services to increasing taxes in order to meet a budget deficit. This, parenthetically, was the approach adopted by Governor Deukmejian. If taxes absolutely had to be raised, only 14 percent supported the idea of higher residential property taxes *(130)*. In-

creasing taxes on alcohol, cigarettes, gasoline, crude oil, or business was more acceptable, so here too policy has followed opinion. Clearly, there are areas of concern and dissent, but the majority verdict on the tax revolt remains favorable.

With the trade-offs posed by the tax revolt in California clear-
er, attitudes toward the tax revolt have become somewhat more
polarized on lines of interest and ideology *(131)*. Owners di-
verged more sharply from renters in 1983 than in 1978, as did
people over fifty-five from those younger and conservatives from
liberals. *(132)* Surprisingly, differences in outlook between public employees and those working in the private sector have actually narrowed.

Although it is commonly asserted that low-income families
and racial minorities have suffered disproportionately as a result
of recent reductions in public spending, complex statistical analyses show that in 1983 a person's race or income did not significantly influence his level of satisfaction with Proposition 13. But
being college-educated, particularly if someone in one's household currently was attending a public college or university in
California, strongly increased distaste for Proposition 13, over
and above the influence of other aspects of background and ideology *(133)*. The university milieu apparently breeds a commitment to the value of a large public sector and an accompanying
antagonism toward Proposition 13 as government's symbolic foe.

More Inequality?
It is possible to make a crude classification of groups as "winners" or "losers" from the tax revolt in California, but a precise
accounting of the distributional consequences of recent changes
in fiscal policy awaits further research. For example, the net effect of the incidence of taxation as a result of Proposition 13, the
indexing of income taxes and other reforms is unknown. The best
one can say is that indexing makes the tax system more progressive, whereas the growth in fees and the limit in annual increases
in assessed value to a flat rate of 2 percent increase its regressivity.

It seems plausible that reduced public spending disproportionately hurts the poor, who presumably find it more difficult to

pay for the market alternatives; but there is no systematic evidence concerning trends in the utilization of government services across social classes. Finally, it is clear that rich and growing communities are advantaged in the search for new revenues and that the distribution of state aid makes no attempt to compensate for this. Impressionistic evidence suggests greater inequality in the fiscal condition and services of local governments, but, again, the magnitude of such a trend, if any, is unmeasured.

The Quality of Services

Another element in the balance-sheet for the tax revolt is how the quality of services delivered by government has changed. Here, too, there are conceptual and measurement problems. What constitutes the "product" of governmental activity can be elusive, and this obviously complicates the task of linking inputs to outputs. The roads may be bumpier in the aftermath of Proposition 13, but has this increased the danger of accidents, or has it reduced it by encouraging slower driving? And what about the effect of unrepaired streets on the frequency and cost of automobile maintenance? Are mechanics unanticipated winners from the tax revolt?

The difficulty of measuring the output of various public agencies encourages a tendency to equate dollars spent and services delivered. This tempting approach, though, makes it easy to confuse quantity and quality. It should be possible, in principle at least, for government to do less but to do it more efficiently. (Indeed, officials in California claim that this has occurred as a result of Proposition 13, that of necessity all the "fat" in government has been trimmed away.)

In an absolute sense, the quality of some public services in California clearly has slipped in the past five years. Roads and sewage systems have deteriorated, university buildings are shabbier, park lawns are shaggier, and so on. But has quality per dollar invested, if such a concept has meaning, also declined? For example, the time it takes police to respond to calls has grown since the passage of Proposition 13, an apparent worsening of service. Yet, according to the Los Angeles Times survey, one cause of this was a decision of police departments to invest their resources more "productively." But, since the investment in response time has declined, the response time per dollar spent may be unchanged. As this suggests, an adequate assessment of the impact of fiscal constraint on the quality of government is yet to be made.

Business as Usual

In meeting the challenge of fiscal stress, the dominant response of governments in California was to try and maintain organizational continuity. Self-protection motivated all participants in the process of adjustment. For example, the legislature has sheltered state spending and employment more than those of cities and counties. Changes in the structure of California government have been minimal; the proposals of the Post Commission appointed by Governor Brown to recommend changes made little or no impression. Since the passage of Proposition 13, most innovation in government has centered on pinching old pennies and finding new revenues. The purpose of a "pay as you go" mentality, however, was to minimize change.

Still, the tax revolt has influenced the political process in California in a way that transcends the outcome of the variegated efforts to cut costs or safeguard programs. In one important and pervasive sense, business is no longer as usual. Proposition 13 has modified the culture of policy-making. Austerity and self-reliance have become new symbols of legitimacy. Politicians increasingly speak the language of trade-offs and constraint, rather than progress and social reform. In the earlier era, policymakers could think first of what programs they wanted to expand and feel confident that the revenues required were available. The current mood is different. Given popular sentiments about taxes and uncertain fiscal conditions, officials must revise spending priorities to fit fixed revenues *(134)*.

Fiscal constraint does provide a justification for politically difficult decisions. For example, legislators blamed the tax revolt in denying requests for additional funds from the powerful special education lobby. The stated need to spend less also spurred the successful effort to reform the system of reimbursement for hospitalization under Medi-Cal. But these benefits provide little solace to the many liberal legislators who entered politics with an activist vision. One legacy of Proposition 13 is to encourage a marketing orientation toward budgeting. New programs must be "sold," since they either take money away from ongoing activities or necessitate raising fees or taxes. That disaster is at hand is a compelling argument in this contest for the taxpayers' acquiescence. When vivid examples make the need obvious, even those sympathetic to the tax rebels' cause will support more spending. This process may not make for orderly planning, but in stops and starts expenditures still can climb.

No More Incrementalism?

The accession of Governor Deukmejian is another influence on the future of the tax revolt in California. The governor's first budget, for 1983-84, was prepared in the context of a cash shortage so severe that the state had to resort to issuing "warrants" (IOUs). Adamant that taxes would not be raised, he dealt with the crisis by using his veto power to cut expenditures in a politically selective way. This naturally angered the governor's legislative antagonists, but his actions at least fell within the implicit rules of decremental budgeting.

Once economic recovery prepared the ground for renewed growth in government, a return to the incremental mode was possible. The 1984-85 budget disappoints those who expected the traditional norms to apply. The governor indeed proposed a large increase in spending, rather than a new reduction in taxes, but refused to apportion funds on the principle that everyone should get a fair share of the increment. Instead, his proposed allocation disproportionately increased expenditures on higher education (the University of California), highways, and prisons, thereby appealing to the middle-class constituency that provided his electoral support. To the dismay of Democratic legislators, the community colleges, environmental programs, and welfare services once again received short shrift.

Governor Deukmejian's approach therefore is to try and control the size of government by insisting on setting priorities even when growth is possible. His opponents, defenders of the incremental faith, are likely to counter by appropriating more for the programs spurned by the state administration. With the item veto on hand, the governor is likely to prevail; but whatever the outcome of this particular struggle, his decision to take fiscal limitation seriously intensifies the partisan and ideological conflicts in budgeting.

The Proper Size of Government

The tax revolt in California has constrained the ability of the public sector to grow. How one appraises this historic achievement in the end depends on his beliefs about the proper functions of government. This is a question of value, not fact. Comparing the relative tax burden in California and other states cannot answer what the size of government should be: depending on one's philosophic stance, everyone's tax burden might be too high or too low. And the connections between the level of government spending, let alone specific tax-cutting measures, and the widely accepted goal of economic growth are too murky to serve as the basis for evaluation.

Government in California has proved resilient enough to stretch, though not to tear, the fabric of restrictions woven by the electorate. With this in mind, another criterion for judging the tax revolt is one's degree of confidence in the capacity for self-control among both citizens and elected politicians. The human impulse to feel entitled to something for nothing is strong. And officials have an incentive to agree to the distinct demands of every constituency, however small. But when taxes have to be raised to pay for these decisions, satisfaction with the separate parts of the budget may coexist with disapproval of the whole.

Do sirens enchant those who sail the seas of democracy to spend and spend and spend *(135)*? And, if so, is it wise to use fiscal limits to lash our helmsman, like Ulysses, to the mast and put wax in our ears? These are the enduring questions raised by the tax revolt, and they have been brought to a new clarity in the Los Angeles Times report on the revolt. As we shall see in the pages that follow, the search for answers goes on at every level of American government as well as among the taxpayers themselves.

ACKNOWLEDGMENTS

This essay benefited greatly from the comments of Judith Gruber, Martin Levin, Frank Levy, and Aaron Wildavsky. I am grateful too to the many "actors" in California and Massachusetts who were so generous with their time and material. Finally, my thanks to Ann Ben-Porat, Donald Green, and Tony Kenney for assistance in data collection and analysis and in the preparation of the manuscript.

NOTES

1. State of California, *Governor's Budget 1984-85*, p. 5. This refers to both General and Special Fund expenditures. The proposed increase in General Fund spending is 10.8 percent.

2. The term is used in contrast to the idea of incremental budgeting developed in A. Wildavsky, *The Politics of the Budgeting Process* (Boston: Little, Brown, 1964). For an early discussion of decremental budgeting, see W. H. Lambright and H. Sapolsky, "Terminating Federal Research and Development Programs," *Policy Sciences,* vol. 7, no. 2, June 1976.

3. As did Luca Brazzi in "The Godfather," Part I. A similar metaphor is used in R. Stanfield, "The Taxpayers' Revolt is Alive or Dead in the Water—Take your Pick," *National Journal,* December 10, 1983.

4. The lineup opposing the tax revolt obviously varied from state to state and issue to issue. Interest group organizations representing business in particular, presented a less monolithic front, sometimes adopting a neutral stance and in some cases supporting the tax rebels. The Massachusetts High Tech Council, for example, are important backers of Citizens for Limited Taxation.

5. Data on taxes are reported in California Legislature, *The 1984-85 Budget: Perspectives and Issues,* p. 140. Spending and employment data are taken from ACIR (Advisory Commission on Intergovernmental Relations), *Significant Features of Fiscal Federalism: 1981-82,* Washington, D.C., 1983. Other indicators of the size of government share the same trend.

6. J. Shannon and S. E. Calkins, "Federal and State-Local Spenders Go Their Separate Ways, " *Intergovernmental Perspective,* vol. 8, no. 4/vol. 9, no. 1, Winter 1983, p. 25.

7. G. E. Petersen, "The State and Local Sector" in J. L. Palmer and I. V. Sawhill, eds., *The Reagan Experiment* (Washington, D.C.: The Urban Institute Press, 1983), p. 184.

8. The fall in California was much sharper because of Proposition 13. See ACIR, *op. cit.,* p. 44.

9. Petersen, *op. cit., p.* 184.

10. *Ibid,* p. 161.

11. Personal interview with the author, August 23, 1983.

12. The full text of Proposition 13 is reprinted in *Cal-Tax Research Bulletin,* June, 1983, p. 5.

13. For a summary of tax reductions in California since Proposition 13, see *Cal-Tex Research Bulletin,* June 1983, and State of California, *Fiscal Year 1983 Budget Summary.*

14. I owe this example to David Doerr, Chief Consultant to the California State Assembly Revenue and Taxation Committee. The actual statewide property rate in 1977-78 was about 2.7 percent. Of course, the amount "saved" or "lost" varies depending on one's assumptions concerning the level of under-assessment.

15. California Legislative Analyst, *The 1983-84 Budget: Perspectives and Issues,* p. 81.

16. *Ibid.*

17. C. Jamison, *Taxes and Other Revenue of State and Local Government in California,* Report of Public Affairs Department, Security Pacific National Bank, 1982, pp. B13-B17, and ACIR, *op. cit.,* p. 39.

18. Jamison, *op. cit.,* p. A4.

19. For a full account of the events leading up to Proposition 13, see D. O. Sears and J. Citrin, *Tax Revolt: Something for Nothing in California* (Cambridge, Mass.: Harvard University Press, 1982).

20. California Legislative Analyst, *op. cit.,* p. 37.

21. California Legislative Analyst, *The 1984-85 Budget: Perspectives and Issues,* p. 37.

22. Stanfield, *op. cit.,* pp. 2568-2571.

23. For a fuller discussion see R. Cline and J. Shannon, "The Intergovernmental Picture for the 1980s—Do-It-Yourself Fiscal Federalism," unpublished manuscript, ACIR, Washington, D.C., November, 1982. Available on request.

24. R. Cline and J. Shannon, "Municipal Revenue Behavior after Proposition 13," *Intergovernmental Perspective,* vol. 8, no. 3, p. 23. These figures were updated by the present author.

25. *Ibid.,* p. 27.

26. *Ibid.,* p. 23.

27. Jamison, *op. cit.,* p. 11.

28. See G. Petersen, "The Allocative, Efficiency and Equity Effects of a Shift to User Charges and Benefit-based Taxes," The Urban Institute, 1982.

29. "Jarvis III," as this proposal is referred to in Sacramento, would also reverse the effect of the Farrell Decision which held that local legislative bodies could increase taxes for general as opposed to "earmarked" purposes without voter approval.

30. These statistics were obtained from compilations provided by Steven Gold, National Council of State Legislatures; Sue Thomas, National Center for Initiative Review, and *Public Opinion* Nov/Dec 1978, Nov/Dec 1980, Feb/March 1982. I have chosen to be comrephensive; therefore, the list includes some relatively minor changes.

In addition, many proposals referred to more than one type of change—for example, both taxing and spending limits, so the classification involves judgments that could be debated. The rule applied was to select the element in the proposal that dominated the campaign or differentiated it from other initiatives on the same ballot.

31. It should be noted that one "victory" for a Proposition 13 "clone" was in Nevada in 1978. However, that state requires a constitutional amendment by initiative to pass at two successive elections. Nevada defeated its Jarvis "clone" in 1980, and so the measure was not adopted.

32. These figures on turnout were provided by Sue Thomas, National Center for Initiative Review. It should be noted that they are incomplete, with data on participation missing for fifteen referenda and two initiatives.

33. For Massachusetts, see E. P. Morgan, "Public Preferences and Policy Realities: Proposition 2½ in Massachusetts," unpublished paper presented at Northeastern Political Science Association, Newark, N.J., 1981, p. 11. For California, see R. Attiyeh and R. F. Engle, "Testing Some Propositions about Proposition 13," *National Tax Journal*, vol. 32, no. 2, June 1979.

34. For an overview of the arguments about what Proposition 13 meant, see R. Novak, "What's Happening Out There?", *Public Opinion*, September 1978; and Sears and Citrin, *op. cit.*, ch. 1.

35. See M. J. Boskin, "Some Neglected Economic Factors Behind Recent Tax and Spending Limitation Movements" and G. F. Break, "Interpreting Proposition 13: A Comment," in *National Tax Journal*, vol. 32, no. 2, June 1979.

36. On California, see Sears and Citrin, *op. cit.* On Michigan, see P. Courant, E. Gramlich, and D. Rubinfeld, "Why Voters Support Tax Limitation Amendments: The Michigan Case," *National Tax Journal*, vol. 33, no. 1, March 1980. On Massachusetts, see H. Ladd and J. B. Wilson, "Proposition 2½: Explaining the Vote," John F. Kennedy School of Government Research Report No. R81-1, and Morgan, *op. cit.*

37. See Sears and Citrin, *op. cit.*, ch. 5, for a full discussion.

38. Morgan, *op. cit.*, p. 11.

39. Attiyeh and Engle, *op. cit.*, pp. 129-130.

40. For a similar discussion, see P. Shapiro, D. Puryear, and J. Ross, "Tax and Expenditure Limitation in Retrospect and in Protest," *National Tax Journal*, vol. 32, no. 2, June 1979.

41. This is explained in ACIR, *1981 Tax Capacity of the Fifty States*, Washington, D.C., 1981, pp. 14-15.

42. There is double counting here because Oregon voted three times, Michigan and Nevada twice each on Jarvis "clones."

43. See S. Gold, "State Tax Increases of 1983: Prelude to Another Tax Revolt?" National Conference of State Legislatures, Legislative Finance Paper 40, p. 20. Gold's excellent paper informs much of the discussion that follows. For comparative state data see ACIR, *Significant Features of Fiscal Federalism, 1981-82*, Washington, D.C., 1983.

44. Personal Communication from Edward Collins, Deputy Commissioner, Department of Revenue, State of Massachusetts.

45. See R. Palaich, J. Kloss, and M. F. Williams, *Tax and Expenditure Limitation Referenda,* Denver, Education Commission of the States, Report F80-2, pp. 50-51.

46. *Ibid.*

47. For example, Barbara Anderson of Citizens for Limited Taxation in Massachusetts insists that the passage and successful implementation of Proposition 13 was critical in building support for Proposition 2½.

48. Gold, *op. cit.,* p. 21.

49. ACIR, *op. cit.,* p. 45.

50. S. Gold, "Recent Developments in State Finance," *National Tax Journal,* vol. 36, no. 1, March 1983, p. 10.

51. For 1981-82, see ACIR, *op. cit.,* p. 48. For 1983, see Gold, "State Tax Increases for 1983: Prelude to Another Tax Revolt?" National Conference of State Legislature, Legislative Finance Paper 40, p. 20.

52. *Ibid.,* p. 11.

53. *Ibid.,* p. 14.

54. *Ibid.*

55. Shannon and Calkins, *op. cit.,* p. 23.

56. Cited in G. H. Miller, "Remarks," *National Tax Journal,* vo. 36, no. 3, September 1983, p. 392.

57. Petersen, in Palmer and Sawhill, *op. cit.,* p. 191.

58. Shannon and Calkins, *op. cit.,* p. 24.

59. These are Bureau of Census figures, reported in Stanfield, *op. cit.,* p. 2568.

60. See, for example, *Gallup Opinion Index,* December 1983.

61. J. Kirlin, *The Political Economy of Fiscal Limits* (Lexington, Mass.: D. C. Heath, 1982, p. 57). This book provides an excellent account of the state legislature's response to Proposition 13.

62. These are the words of the official ballot argument prepared by opponents of Proposition 13.

63. California Legislature, *The 1984-85 Budget: Perspectives and Issues,* p. 140.

64. *Ibid.*

65. *Ibid.,* p. 141.

66. The Field Institute, *California Opinion Index,* vo. 3, April 1983.

67. California Legislature, *op. cit.,* p. 27.

68. *Ibid.*

69. Legislative Analyst, *Trends in Public Finance: What is Happening to Government Taxes and Services,* December 1982, pp. 22-23.

70. *Ibid.*

71. California Legislature, *op. cit.,* p. 27.

72. Kirlin, *op. cit.,* p. 59.

73. California Legislature, *op. cit.,* p. 155.

74. Legislative Analyst, *op. cit.,* p. 25.

75. F. Levy, D. Shimasaki, and B. Berk, "Sources of Growth in Local Government Employment: California, 1964-78," *American Economic Review,* vol. 72, no. 2, May 1982, pp. 282.

76. California Legislature, *op. cit.,* pp. 48-50.

77. Since local spending from its own sources declined, this does not refer to an equivalent increase in the overall share of government expenditures devoted to education.

78. California Legislature, *op. cit.,* p. 51.

79. Legislative Analyst, *op. cit.,* p. 25.

80. A succinct account of the rise and fall of the surplus appears in the Legislative Analyst's report on the 1982-83 budget.

81. A. Rodda, *California Fiscal History, 1958 to 1983 and Prospects for the Future,* unpublished report for the Commission on State Finance, October 1982, p. 12.

82. *Ibid.*

83. California Legislature, *op. cit.,* p. 86.

84. *Ibid.,* p. 73.

85. California Legislature, *The 1983-84 Budget: Perspectives and Issues,* p. 55.

86. I owe this point to Kevin Bacon.

87. A. Wildavsky, *op. cit.* See also R. D. Behn, "Cutback Budgeting," *Working Paper,* Institute of Policy Sciences, Duke University, 1983.

88. Behn, *op. cit.,* p. 3 explains the appeal of this strategy.

89. D. Kahneman and A. Tversky, "Prospect Theory: An

Analysis of Decision Under Risk," *Econometrica,* vol. 46, no. 2, March 1979.

90. This conclusion is confirmed by N. Caiden and J. Chapman, "Budgeting in California," *Public Budgeting and Finance,* vol. 2, no. 4, Winter 1982.

91. This is the box-score compiled by *Cal-Tax Research Bulletin.*

92. In the sense of C. Lindblom, "The Science of Muddling Through," *Public Administrative Review,* vol. 29, no. 2, Spring 1959.

93. This account of the coping process in Massachusetts relies heavily on L. E. Susskind, ed., *Proposition 2½, Its Impact on Massachusetts,* Oegleschloger, Gunn and Hain Publishers, Inc., Cambridge, Mass., 1983.

94. L. Susskind and C. Horan, "How the Most Drastic Cuts Were Avoided," in Susskind, *op. cit.,* p. 263.

95. This is a summary conclusion that masks the obvious variation in the degree of difficulty experienced by particular communities.

96. For a summary of measure's provisions see Susskind, *op. cit.,* p. 9.

97. Massachusetts Municipal Association, *Report on the Impact of Proposition 2½,* January 1982.

98. See the account by S. T. Davis, "A Brief History of Proposition 2½" in Susskind, *op. cit.*

99. H. Ladd and J. Wilson, *op. cit.*

100. Massachusetts Tax Foundation, *A Massachusetts Primer, Economics and Public Finance,* p. 28.

101. *Ibid.*

102. *Ibid.,* p. 29.

103. E. J. Collins, Jr., "Proposition 2½: Impact, Challenge and Response," in University of Massachusetts Institute for Governmental Studies: *State-Local Relations,* p. 38.

104. Massachusetts Tax Foundation, *op. cit.,* p. 28.

105. This argument is made in L. D. Segel, "Property Tax Classification in Massachusetts: A Summary," in L. Susskind, ed., *Status Report: The Impacts of Proposition 2½,* a report of The Impact of 2½ Project.

106. Interview with E. Collins, Jr., Deputy Commission of Revenue.

107. *Impact 2½ Newsletter,* no. 21, March 1, 1982.

108. This was a recurrent theme in interviews with officials and interest group leaders in Massachusetts, regardlees of their stance on Proposition 2½.

109. Massachusetts Municipal Association, *op. cit.*

110. Massachusetts Taxpayers Foundation, *State Budget Trends 1975-1984,* p. 4.

111. Massachusetts Municipal Association, *op. cit.,* p. 5.

112. *Ibid.*

113. Massachusetts Municipal Association, *The Governor's Budget Fiscal Year 1983,* Table IV.

114. Massachusetts Tax Foundation, *op. cit.,* p. 18.

115. D. Soyer, "The Quality of Public Services" in University of Massachusetts, *op. cit.,* p. 61.

116. This incident was vividly described in interviews with several participants in the drama.

117. This quotation comes from a survey of local mayors conducted by the Massachusetts Municipal Association.

118. A leading expert on assessment practices in Massachusetts, Raymond Torto, describes them as "primitive."

119. This huge increase, of course, is a one-time again.

120. He was referring to the multiplicity of small units of government and the domination of administration by politics.

121. Susskind and Horan, *op. cit.*

122. Massachusetts Tax Foundation, *op. cit.,* pp. 30-31, suggests New Hampshire has gained at Massachusetts's expense because of a lower tax burden for business.

123. See Sears and Citrin, *op. cit.,* ch. 3.

124. *Ibid.*

125. *California Opinion Index,* April 1983, p. 1.

126. *Ibid.,* p. 2.

127. These data were calculated from the relevant California Polls and made available by the State Data Program, University of California, Berkeley.

128. *California Opinion Index,* April 1983, pp. 3-4.

129. Opponents of Proposition 13 complained about the dam-

age to schools, and its supporters about the failure to cut bureaucracy.

130. *California Opinion Index,* April 1983, p. 3.

131. These are the results of the author's analysis of the March
1983, California Poll. Full results will be provided on request.

132. The first group in each pair of names was more favorable
to Proposition 13.

133. This emerged from a multiple regression analysis which
employed social background variables, measures of political ideology, and reports about the personal impact of Proposition 13 to
predict overall satisfaction with the initiative.

134. This point is made also in Kirlin, *op. cit.,* p. 100.

135. See T. C. Schelling, "The Intimate Contest for Self-Com-
mand," *The Public Interest,* no. 60, Summer 1980.

1

A Look at the Revolt

The California Tax Reduction Movement is stirring with new life these days. In the organization's cluttered Wilshire Boulevard office, phones jangle and an overworked photocopier grinds as the "tax rebels" of 1978 gear up to put a new property-tax reduction initiative before the voters. "It's time to go back to the public," declares Howard Jarvis, group chairman and author of the landmark tax-cut initiative Proposition 13. "For five years now, the courts and the bureaucrats have done everything they can to undermine the will of the voters."

The California "tax revolt" has transformed state and local government since it erupted June 6, 1978, with two-to-one voter approval of Proposition 13. But as the tax group's new campaign suggests, the rebellion has not "worked" as its advocates hoped. Nor has it brought the dire consequences forecast by its opponents, who included most of the state's political establishment. A look at California's state and local governments five years after the beginning of the tax revolt shows that, indeed, nobody called it right:

■ The 25-year growth of state and local government has slowed dramatically but not reversed, as tax-cut foes predicted. California was below average among states in 1980-1981 in the share of personal income it spent for public schools, roads and health. But it was still far above average in spending in as a share of income for welfare, higher education, police, fire, parks and prisons.

■ Proposition 13 made local governments more dependent on state financial aid—and thus robbed them of decision-making power—to a degree that few had guessed. Counties and school districts in particular are now vulnerable when financial trouble threatens the state government, as it does today.

■ Proposition 13 has not caused widespread government lay-offs, as opponents forecast. The number of non-federal public employees has shrunk by 26,000, or 2%, since 1978. But the state and special-district levels of government have grown, and average government pay is still far higher here than in most states.

■ Court rulings have sapped the initiative's power to restrain spurting property taxes. Local officials can now raise property taxes for several purposes without running afoul of Proposition 13. And as Los Angeles Mayor Tom Bradley's tax-hike proposal shows, officials are increasingly willing to take political risks to do so.

The noisy beginnings of the tax revolt are now fading from memory, but its consequences are still felt and debated. The tax rebellion brought abrupt and lasting change to the state political scene. It centralized power and complicated local taxation in a way that has local officials increasingly clamoring for change. The tax revolt forced painful cuts in public services as it combined with recession and federal-aid reductions to slash the revenues available to once-flush California governments. Community colleges, parks and libraries were quickly singled out for spending and staffing reductions; more recently, public health and welfare programs have come under the budget-cutter's knife. In its effects on public schools, the tax revolt aggravated problems created by declining enrollments, court-mandated financing rules and other complications. And the rebellion has left a visible legacy: Public grounds, buildings and other structures across the Golden State have lost some of their luster as officials cut back spending for maintenance and repairs.

The tax revolt was a massive stimulus to the state's economy, boosting corporate profits and putting cash in the pockets of individuals. Economists believe these effects endure, although they cannot be precisely measured because the revolt occurred amid the larger economic events of recession and rising interest rates.

The tax revolt has consisted of three tax cuts—enactment of Proposition 13, the phase-out of the gift and inheritance tax and indexing the state personal income tax. In one swoop, Proposition 13 chopped $7 billion from property taxes, once the biggest and most dependable source of revenues for cities, counties and school districts. Proposition 13 rolled back local property taxes to 1% of assessed valuation, limited annual assessment increases to no more than 2% and barred new property taxes. It prohibited local governments from imposing new taxes without two-thirds approval of local voters, as it prohibited the state from raising them without a two-thirds vote of the Legislature. In its tax-cut passion, the Legislature also in 1978 trimmed gift and inheritance taxes, and began adjusting personal income tax brackets to offset the effects of inflation. Two initiatives adopted in June, 1982, repealed the gift and inheritance tax, and made income tax indexing permanent.

The impact of this massive revenue loss on local governments was delayed by a multibillion-dollar state surplus. It had been accumulating since 1975, as inflation and a superheated economy drove up collections of income, sales and corporation taxes. The state eased the impact of Proposition 13 in 1978 by doling out $4.4 billion in aid to local governments. As part of a deal that became permanent by law in 1979, the state provided local governments yearly transfusions of cash and picked up the local costs for some health and welfare programs.

The so-called bail-out of local governments swelled to $5.85 billion at its peak, in the 1982 fiscal year. But in 1983 it dropped 2.2%—or 7.1% in inflation-adjusted dollars—as a smaller surplus, declining federal aid and a poor economy plunged the state into financial trouble. By June, 1982, the mighty surplus had dwindled to $116 million. And the worst recession in 50 years had halted growth of state sales, personal income and bank and corporation taxes for the first time in more than a decade.

Meanwhile, state and local governments were increasingly pinched by a four-year decline in federal aid, which accounts for about one-sixth of their total revenues. Between 1978 and 1982, U.S. aid to state and local governments across the nation fell 25%, when adjusted for inflation and population growth. In the past two years, recession and declining federal aid have been the most visible reasons for the looming financial problems of the state and many local governments. But the tax revolt has had a role, too, because it created a persistent mood in which public officials were—and largely remain—reluctant to raise taxes.

At the state level, for example, the lingering spirit of tax rebellion has been evident all year, as the Legislature and the new Administration struggled to close a yawning budget deficit. Rather than impose a permanent tax hike, legislators voted a standby 1% increase in the sales tax—to be offset by a temporary sales-tax reduction next year. The tax revolt "cut revenues, then made it hard for us (in government) to do something constructive to handle the recession," says A. Alan Post, who was the state's nonpartisan legislative analyst for 30 years, and who headed a commission that recommended ways for government to adjust to Proposition 13.

On their face, government spending figures give no clue to the financial pressures that have gripped the state and local governments. Total expenditures of state and local governments have marched to $66.6 billion in fiscal 1983 from $43.1 billion in 1978, the Assembly Office of Research recently estimated. That climb represents an increase of 55%. But this growth has not been sufficient for government to even keep up in its ability to purchase services for a growing number of Californians. On an inflation-adjusted, per capita basis, state and local government spending has actually fallen 3.9% in the last five years.

The trend in tax collections illustrates the fiscal squeeze even more dramatically. Combined collections of state taxes, local property and local sales taxes grew 21% between fiscal 1978 and 1983, to $31.8 billion. But they would have had to grow 61%, to $42.4 billion, just to maintain government's purchasing power in the face of inflation and the state's 10% population growth over the five-year period.

The effects of financial distress have fallen unevenly on the state and local governments. Because of the surplus, the state was flush—and acted like it—for the first three years after Proposition 13. Beginning in fiscal 1982, however, recession and three years of deficit spending forced the state to begin cinching its belt. Adjusted for population growth and inflation, spending by the state grew a robust 12% between fiscal 1978 and 1981, ac

Growth in California Taxes

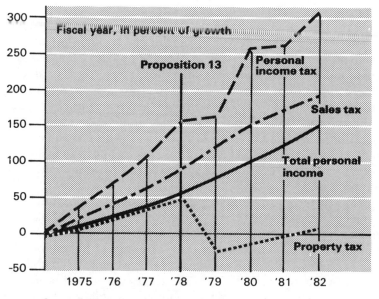

Source: California Taxpayers Association

cording to a recent estimate by the Assembly Office of Research. But revenues from major taxes, licenses and other governments grew only 3.9% on a per capita, inflation-adjusted basis. In the past two years, spending has declined 7% on the same basis, as revenues have fallen 6.3%.

Cities have taken advantage of their financial independence. After losing 51% of property taxes in the first year after Proposition 13, cities jacked up fees they charge the public, and began to rely more heavily on the sales tax, which had become cities' biggest money-maker. Between fiscal 1978 and 1981, revenues from such fees and charges as library fines, sewer-service and garbage-collection fees rose 48.4%, or 18% more than inflation, state controller's figures show. In fiscal 1981, fees and charges still accounted for only 12.5% of all revenues, however, up from

8% in 1978. (Fiscal 1981 is the last year for which complete state controller records are available.)

Sales tax revenues, meanwhile, grew 38.5%, keeping ahead of inflation by 6.5%, during the three-year period. Yet population growth and inflation have eaten away the cities' buying power. Between fiscal 1978 and 1983, the revenues that cities can spend as they wish (rather than at the orders of state and federal governments) fell 13.8%, in per capita, inflation-adjusted basis. Many cities have been forced to use cash reserves to maintain services. Even so, city spending fell 6.1% in five years on a per capita, inflation-adjusted basis.

California's 58 counties have fared even worse. With little sales tax revenue and limited ability to raise fees, they never enjoyed cities' independence from the state. Proposition 13 threw them into greater reliance on state and federal aid to carry out their principal duties of running health, welfare and jail programs. County revenues fell 19% between fiscal 1978 and 1983, on a per capita, inflation-adjusted basis. County governments also turned to reserves; still, counties' per capita, inflation-adjusted spending slipped 6.6% between 1978 and 1983.

California's public school districts have become most dependent on the state government. This increased dependency was a result of the 1979 law that restructured financial relationships between state and local governments to ease the impact of Proposition 13. Under the law, the state pays the lion's share of local school costs, while it takes property-tax funds formerly intended for the schools and allocates them among all local governments. This year, for example, the state has provided 62% of school revenues. The new financing scheme left the schools with almost no ability to raise money independently, and also gave the state greater say in how the districts spend their funds.

The five years since Proposition 13 have had sharply different effects on special districts, the unusual governmental creatures that are organized to perform government services that existing local governments cannot or will not perform. The period has had little financial effect on the so-called enterprise districts. They are run like businesses, relying mostly on fees to operate harbors, airports, water and electric power systems and similar enterpris

How California Compares with U.S.
in State & Local Tax Burden

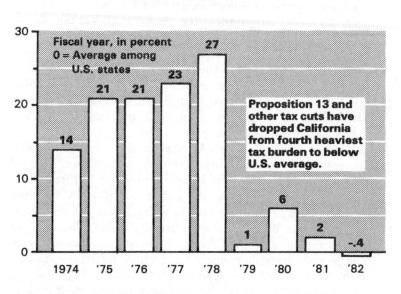

Fiscal year, in percent
0 = Average among
U.S. states

Proposition 13 and
other tax cuts have
dropped California
from fourth heaviest
tax burden to below
U.S. average.

Source: Security Pacific National Bank

es. Because they have little reliance on tax funds—and are thus largely beyond the reach of tax-cut fever—their combined revenues grew 4.5% faster than inflation between fiscal 1978 and 1981. The past five years have been more difficult for the non-enterprise districts, which provide flood control, mosquito abatement, fire protection, parks and other services that do not lend themselves to support by fees. Adjusted for inflation, their combined revenues shrunk 10% between fiscal 1978 and 1981.

Massive layoffs of public employees predicted in 1978 by Proposition 13 foes never came to pass. Yet the public payroll has declined in California in five years, as government agencies frequently have not replaced departing employees. The growth rate of the public work force has fallen substantially behind that of California's private sector since 1978. And California has

How California Compares
With U.S. in State & Local Spending

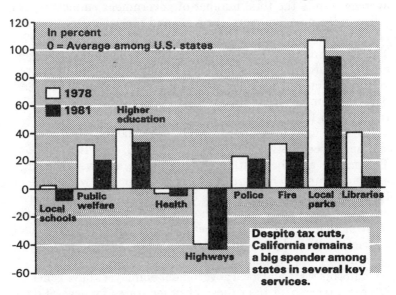

In percent
0 = Average among U.S. states

□ 1978
■ 1981

Higher education

Public welfare

Local schools

Health

Highways

Police   Fire   Local parks   Libraries

Despite tax cuts, California remains a big spender among states in several key services.

Source: U.S. Census

dropped below average among states in the size of its government work force in relation to state population. The number of full- and part-time employees of state and local governments dropped by about 26,000, or about 2.2%, between 1978 and 1982, according to figures from the state Employment Development Department. Some of the reduction occurred because of the phase-out of the federal Comprehensive Employment and Training Act program, which enabled local governments, and cities in particular, to expand their staffs with federal aid. No precise figures are available on the number of persons who have lost CETA jobs.

Because the state's population has grown 10.2% since 1978, the ratio of government workers to Californians has dropped 6.4%, and is now below the U.S. average, Census Bureau figures show.

The ratio was 3% above the U.S. average in 1978 but fell below it immediately after Proposition 13 and is now about 4% below the average. While the total number of government employees has fallen in the past five years, the state and special-district sectors of government have more employees today than they did in 1978. The special districts have grown the fastest, again because their greatest source of revenue has been largely unaffected by tax revolt, recession and declining federal aid. The number of full- and part-time employees of special districts swelled 20% since 1978, to 83,000 in 1982, state figures show.

The state work force grew by 5.5%, or 12,000 full-time equivalent employees, between 1978 and 1982-1983, state figures show. The prisons and the health and welfare programs were the largest contributors to that growth. City governments' work force of full- and part-time workers has fallen by 4.4%, or 12,300 workers, since 1978, state figures show. CETA workers account for most of that figure. As school enrollment has declined, school districts' full- and part-time work force has fallen 4.4%. County government employment has fallen by the same percentage.

California state and local government employees have generally been higher paid than those of other states for several decades—and the tax revolt has so far done little to change that. Pay levels have been higher in part because of California's higher cost of living. And Californians have traditionally paid civil servants better on the theory that it will allow them to attract and keep more able employees. California was second-ranked in the country (after high-cost Alaska) in average earnings of state and local government employees in 1981, figures from the Census Bureau show. The state had the same ranking in 1978.

Earnings of the average government worker in California grew 33.7% to a monthly $1,869, between 1979 and 1981, according to the agency. By contrast, the earnings of state and local workers through the United States advanced 28.5% during the three-year period, to $1,464.

Thus, the average California public employee's earnings were 28% above the U.S. average in 1981. That represents a widening of the gap since 1978, when earnings of the average California worker were 22% above the average. However, an 18-month-old state pay freeze may have brought the average California public employees' earnings closer to the U.S. norm, analysts note. Allan Burdick, lobbyist with the County Supervisors Assn. of California, said earnings of local government employees may have remained relatively high since Proposition 13 because of choices made by employee unions since 1978. In many cases, he said, employees asked for agreements involving some layoffs but providing salary increases for remaining employees, rather than agreements with no layoffs and no pay increases.

—PR, PB

WINNERS IN THE TAX REVOLT

One of the biggest winners in California's tax revolt, it turns out, was a tax-gobbling bureaucracy of just the kind the late 1970s "tax rebels" loved to denounce. Uncle Sam may have claimed as much as $12.5 billion of the estimated $50 billion that Californians have saved from a tax uprising that was widely intended to curb government's revenue appetite. The money flowed to the federal treasury as cuts in property, state income and gift and inheritance taxes swelled personal and corporate income and reduced itemized income-tax deductions.

"Our own reverse revenue sharing program, you might call it," said David Shulman, an economist with the UCLA Business Forecasting Project.

Uncle Sam's windfall is but one of several strange wrinkles in the story of how the savings from the biggest state and local tax cuts have been distributed among taxpayers. The middle-class homeowners who led the rebellion have been big winners in the tax-cut sweepstakes—particularly those who still live in the homes they owned in 1978 and have fast-growing incomes. Yet in treating themselves to a feast of tax cuts, these middle-class Californians also dished out vast sums to others, including Uncle Sam, non-Californians, businesses and the wealthy. What's more, the landmark tax-cut measure Proposition 13 created a glaring and growing inequity in the property taxes paid by the homeowners themselves.

Consider:

■ Proposition 13 has given 63% of its estimated $41.1-billion

tax savings to business, including landlords and agriculture—
though many business groups opposed the initiative. Homeowners have received 33% of the tax savings.

■ The wealthy are probably the biggest winners from repeal of
the gift and inheritance tax, though the campaign for its aboli-
tion focused on the hardships it was said to place on lower- and
middle-income survivors.

■ The burden of property taxes is distributed more unfairly
each year, because Proposition 13 taxes recent home buyers more
heavily than those who have owned their homes for a longer period. Homeowners who bought in Los Angeles County last year, for
instance, shouldered 13% of the total homeowners' property tax
burden—though they accounted for only 6% of such taxpayers.

■ About 47% of the first-year savings from Proposition 13 was
"exported" to non-Californians, two economists calculated in a
recent study. They say these benefits took the form of higher
federal taxes on Californians, tax cuts to non-resident property
owners and lower prices for out-of-state consumers of California
products.

■ Most tenants face fast-rising rents and a dwindling apartment supply, although Proposition 13 advocates pledged that the
initiative would restrain rents and stimulate apartment
construction.

Unquestionably, the revolt did accomplish its advocates' goal
of drastically cutting the total burden of state and local taxes.
Savings from the three principal cuts have totaled about $50 bil-
lion, the state legislative analyst has estimated—enough, for instance, to buy a $5,400 subcompact car for each California house-
hold. The cuts ended California's standing as a top-taxing state,
which it had been for 25 years. Between 1978 and 1982, California's state and local tax burden dropped from 27% above the average among states to 0.4% below it, Security Pacific National
Bank estimates.

Academics and government researchers still argue over how
the benefits of tax-slashing have been distributed across income
classes. They note that there was little public discussion during
the five-year tax-cut spree of how the reductions might shift the
total tax burden from one income class to another. Yet scholars

agree that every Californian was a "winner" in gaining something.

These benefits show up directly, as lower taxes on property, personal income and estates. And some economists maintain that they also show up indirectly, as lower prices on consumer goods, higher dividends and capital gains from public companies that reaped tax savings, and, over a period of many years, as slower-growing rents. The tax revolt's "losers" are those Californians who lost public services in the government cutbacks that followed the rebellion.

California's tax revolt was ignited in part by a feeling that government spending was out of control. But inflation also played a key role, as it drove up revenues from property, personal-income and estate taxes and convinced Californians their tax burden was far too heavy.Property-tax collections surged an average 12% a year between 1975 and 1978, as housing values exploded.

Meanwhile, as cost-of-living pay raises pushed Californians into ever-higher tax brackets, personal-income tax collections roared ahead 22% between 1975 and 1976, and 26% between 1976 and 1977. Inflation's impact on home prices and personal income worked together to increase the tax bite on estates. Inheritance tax revenues grew 300% between 1970 and 1980, making California the leader among states in the share of personal income claimed by the tax.

Critics said the framers of Proposition 13 were law-making with a meat-ax in their effort to scale back taxes. Indeed, estimates of how the relief was distributed show that if the goal was to aid aggrieved homeowners, the initiative was a crude instrument. For every $1 that the homeowner gained in gross tax relief, he gave nearly $1.75 to businesses, landlords and owners of agricultural property. Still, homeowners have won too—particularly those who have stayed put.

Proposition 13 calls for homes that are built, bought or substantially improved after 1978 to be assessed to full market value. Homeowners who bought their house in 1978 or earlier continue to pay the same property tax they paid that year, with an annual increase of no more than 2%. This assessment system means that two homeowners with identical properties can pay wildly differ-

ent property taxes. For example, county records show that a
Lakewood homeowner who bought a 1,021-square-foot home in
1981 paid $840 in taxes that year. A neighbor who owned a nearly
identical house in 1078 paid a 1981 tax of $280—or one-third of
what the new home buyer paid.

The system also means that as the years pass, the taxpayers
who have owned their homes longer pay an ever-smaller share of
total homeowner property taxes. This shift of the burden toward
more recent home buyers is accelerated by the fast growth in
home values. The average assessed value of a single-family home
in Los Angeles County, for example, soared to $120,434 last year,
from $34,688 in 1975. In Los Angeles County, as a result, home-
owners who have not moved since June, 1978, accounted for 60%
of homeowners in 1982. But they paid only half of homeowner
property taxes that year. Homeowners who bought, built or improved homes in 1982, by contrast, represented 6.3% of homeowners, but paid 13.2% of property taxes. "These inequities are
actually less than what I expected," said Los Angeles County Assessor Alexander Pope, a longtime critic of the post-Proposition
13 assessment system. "You would have seen new home buyers
pay even more if the home market wasn't suddenly frozen" by
high interest rates and recession.

Proposition 13 benefited homeowners in two ways: It slashed
their tax bills, and, by lowering taxes, it increased the amounts
they could get for their home if they chose to sell. Economist
Shulman offers the hypothetical example of a house that was
worth $100,000 in 1978. Proposition 13 would have cut the prop-
erty taxes on such a house from about $3,000 to $1,000. Because
of that cut, a buyer could afford $2,000 more a year in mortgage
payments. With a 10% mortgage, the price could be bumped up
as much as $20,000. In this way, says Shulman, those who owned
homes in 1978 were able to further increase the value of assets
that had already been skyrocketing in value as Californians
bought homes as a hedge against inflation. Shulman believes
that, for this reason, Proposition 13 has played a major role in
forcing up California home prices since 1978. In effect, "Proposition 13 was a case of homeowners getting together to vote themselves a capital gain," Shulman says.

State and Local Spending

At first glance, state and local spending figures suggest that 1978 brought no change in the rapid growth of public expenditures in California. But the figures tell a different story when they are compared to 1972 dollars to account for inflation, or expressed in per-capita terms to account for California's 19% population growth of the past 10 years.

Total state spending

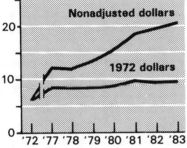

Total local spending

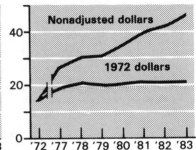

Per-capita 1972 dollars

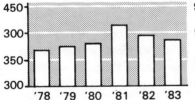

Per-Capita 1972 dollars

Inflation adjusted figures show that state spending grew slightly in the first three years after passage of Prop. 13, but turned downward in the past two years. The pattern is more pronounced when the figures are put on a per-capita basis.

Overall local spending has grown negligibly when the effects of inflation are taken into account; it has declined since 1978 when population growth is also considered.

Source: Assembly Office of Research Estimates

Of course, the homeowner's gain was the homebuyer's loss. Yet even homeowners who have moved since 1978 have saved considerably over what they would have paid in the absence of the initiative. The Lakewood family that paid $040 in 1081 taxoo would have paid $2,077 that year had the community's property tax rate remained at its pre-Proposition 13 level of 3%. Proposition 13 advocates argued that the property tax posed its greatest threat to elderly homeowners, who, they said, were being forced to sell because they could not afford the taxes. It is likely that the elderly have done well under Proposition 13, since they are more likely to own their own homes, and less likely to move, than most Californians. But tax officials say there is no way to tell if Proposition 13 reduced the number who have been forced to sell.

The facts are obscured because in foreclosures, it is always a combination of mortgage payments and tax bills that make a homeowner unable to meet his financial obligations. Public sales of homes with unpaid tax bills have been rare before and after Proposition 13, tax officials say. This is because the homeowner has five years to pay back taxes. The homeowner almost always pays off the debt in that period, sometimes by selling the home, they say.

Opponents of Proposition 13 predicted that the measure would penalize homeowners in one way that has yet to materialize.

They forecast that the initiative would shift an ever-greater share of property taxes to homeowners, because homes sell more often than commercial properties, and thus would tend to be assessed at the higher, market value. Advocates of this view have argued for a "split" tax roll, in which business properties would be taxed at ahigher rate. In 1982, backers of the proposal collected more signatures than were needed to put the proposal on the ballot but failed to submit them in time.

Four years of data from the state Board of Equalization, which oversees property tax collections, shows that such a shift has not yet occurred. The board's statistics show that homeowners' share of the total property tax burden was 33% in 1979 and 32% in 1983. The difference is so slight as to be statistically insignificant, says Jeff Reynolds, of the board's research staff. Predictions were incorrect, he said, for several reasons. Homes have not sold as fast as expected because of high interest rates and the recession. And forecasters failed to recognize how often owners of small businesses buy and sell property, or buy major new equipment that would require reassessment.

California tenants have won far less than homeowners from Proposition 13—and certainly far less than they were promised in the Spring 1978 campaign. Howard Jarvis and others wooed the state's renters by promising Proposition 13 would stimulate an increase in the apartment supply that would in turn restrain the growth of rents. Neither has happened, for two reasons: High interest rates slowed all housing construction, and the tenant uprising brought rent control to 11 cities and counties when renters failed to see rent reductions after passage of the initiative. Rent control made lenders less willing to make loans for apartment buildings.

Tenants in communities with the toughest rent control laws came up winners, however. And housing analysts say that over the long run, lower property taxes should translate to some increase in the availability and lowering of the price of rental housing.

There is no doubt about the federal government's winnings, which are estimated at between 15% and 25% of the total tax reduction. The federal treasury claimed its share as Proposition 13 lowered the amount of taxes that could be deducted on itemized federal income-tax returns. And as the initiative helped increase the earnings of individuals and businesses, it increased their income-tax liabilities.

Uncle Sam has taken a bigger bite from those better able to afford it. The wealthy tend to have higher property tax deductions, tax analysts note. And when their deductions are cut, the remaining earnings are taxed at higher rates. Lower-income taxpayers are more likely to use the standard income-tax deduction and thus forfeit none of their savings. About 40% of California taxpayers use the standard deduction, the Legislative Analyst's office has estimated. The net savings from Proposition 13 was also reduced as the initiative's benefits flowed out-of-state. Economists Howard Chernick of the Department of Health and Human Services and Andrew Reschovsky of Tufts University es-

timated that Californians kept only $3.89 billion, or 52%, of the
first-year savings from Proposition 13.

If Proposition 13 favored the stable middle-class homeowner,
state income-tax indexing offered the biggest share of tax relief
for the upwardly mobile, middle-class Californians. In its absence, taxpayers in the middle brackets—by far the largest
group—are bumped quickly upward from bracket to bracket by
cost-of-living pay increases. This "bracket creep" acts as a sort
of unlegislated tax hike to claim a larger and larger share of their
additional earnings. Indexing's savings to higher-income taxpayers is smaller as a share of total tax liability. This is because
these taxpayers have a larger share of income in the maximum
11% tax bracket, which began at $48,400 for joint-return tax-
payers in 1982. Indexing has no effect on income in this bracket.

Data from the state Franchise Tax Board, which collects state
income taxes, shows that the largest portion of benefits from indexing accrue to taxpayers with an annual income of between
$30,000 and $50,000. The federal government takes a cut here
too, as indexing's savings reduce the amount of state income tax
that taxpayers can deduct on itemized federal tax forms. Federal
taxes claim up to 30% of indexing's savings, the legislative analyst has estimated, with the largest share of that coming from the
higher-income taxpayers. "If Proposition 13 benefited the es
tablished folks, indexing is the tax cut—the only tax cut—for
people who are moving up in life," Shulman said.

Tax analysts say that each of the tax cuts was enacted in an
atmosphere of "tax cut fever," with little research or public discussion of how savings would be distributed among rich and poor,
business and other groups. "The public's attention was focused
on how much money they personally would get," said Jeff Reynolds, researcher with the Board of Equalization. "If people were
concerned about the equity (of tax reforms), I don't think we'd
have the tax structure we have."

Bob Leland, budget director for the City of Sacramento, studied the gift and inheritance tax as a consultant to the Assembly
Revenue and Tax Committee. According to Leland, most attention in the 1982 campaign for inheritance tax's repeal focused on
the emotion-charged claims of opponents that the tax burdened

survivors in low- and middle-income families. Those claims were made despite a 1980 law that exempted surviving spouses and that raised exemptions for all other beneficiaries from 200% to 1,000%. And, says Leland, they were made although nobody could point to examples of low- and middle-income survivors losing their inheritances to the tax collector. Researchers disagree on how the tax revolt shifted the total burden of state and local taxes among income classes.

A 1979 Rand Corp. study concluded that Proposition 13 had the immediate effect of shifting more of the state and local tax burden on upper-income Californians. The shift came about, the researchers said, because the initiative made California's tax system more reliant on the personal income tax, which taxes the wealthy more heavily than does the property tax.

But researchers Chernick and Reschovsky concluded that over the longer term—six to 10 years—low- and high-income Californians will reap a larger share of benefits, relative to their income, than Californians in the middle class. They believe that over this period, the economic competition will force landlords and businesses to pass on a portion of their property tax savings in lower rents and prices.

They said the wealthy would reap a relatively large benefit from Proposition 13 because they have a disproportionately large share of income from rents. The wealthy tend to hold the largest share of company stock and own more real estate too, and would benefit disproportionately from lower property tax bills, they said. Proposition 13 eventually will give the poor a large benefit, relative to their income, because the poor tend to live in urban areas and pay a large share of their income in high rents, Chernick and Reschovsky said. The two economists assumed that over a period of years, landlords will pass along 20% of tax savings to tenants.

"So over this period, it looks like the middle class—the big champions of 13—actually gained the least," Reschovsky said.

THE EFFECT ON INDIVIDUALS

To learn how Californians reacted personally to the onset of the tax revolt, The Times interviewed people throughout Southern California who represent diverse living situations. Many reported that they were satisfied with their tax savings, many reported that they wanted government to tighten its own finances more. Still others suggested that the changes wrought by the tax measures had altered their decision-making.

■ "I bought my house in 1974; in 1975 the house was worth $110,000," said Harold L. Katz of his Westwood home. "I was paying approximately $3,400 in property taxes, and as a result of Proposition 13, I paid $1,022. The house is worth now about $400,000. Without Proposition 13, I would be paying about $13,000 (in property taxes)." Instead, Katz, a 50-year-old senior partner in a Century City accounting firm, paid about $1,100 in 1982. He has thought about moving but the combination of low property taxes and an 8% mortgage has kept him where he is. "It would have cost me thousands and thousands of dollars a month to move a couple of blocks," he said. With an income in "the neighborhood of" $150,000 a year, he added that fee increases, such as for beach or Music Center parking, affect him little. He also termed his 1982 savings from income tax indexing, calculated by the Franchise Tax Board as about $1,020, "insignificant." But he has noticed, he said, "The streets are falling apart. They're just never going to fix them. Probably the biggest single expense to everybody is what's happening to their cars. . . I think its disgusting that I'm paying $1,100 in property taxes but I think it would be just as inequitable for me to be paying $13,000."

■ Because Proposition 13 passed, 75-year-old Thelma Perkins says she was able to save enough to have the peeling white paint on her bungalow redone this spring and can afford cable television, a $33-a-month luxury that once would have been unthinkable. A white-haired grandmother living on a $214 monthly pension from Crocker Bank and her Social Security checks, Perkins saw her property tax reach $610 by 1977. After Proposition 13, that dropped to $215. Without Proposition 13, her property tax could have been $2,640 last year rather than $247. "How could I have paid $2,600?" she asks now. "It took four years to save $1,200 to paint the house." Had Proposition 13 not passed, she said, "I'd probably have had to start taking boarders in. But then you'd have to start back with income taxes. The way it is now my pension is low enough I don't have to pay income taxes." Perkins and her husband, whom she later divorced and who is now dead, built the house for $3,500 in West Los Angeles in 1939. Once she counted up all the property taxes she had ever paid, she said: "I figured I've paid for the house six times over, just in property taxes." "When I heard about Proposition 13," she recalled recently, she immediately became a volunteer for Howard Jarvis. One thing Proposition 13 did not do as she hoped was make government more efficient. "The point of 13 was to take the fat out of government," she said with a laugh, "or as Jarvis said, the pigs feeding in the trough. But they didn't do that. Where they should have started to cut is at the top. I'm sure Mayor Bradley doesn't need all those people he has in his office."

■ A divorced mother of four, Linda Briceno collects $800 a month in child support, $64 in food stamps and whatever she can make from a part-time job as a substitute waitress. Her monthly mortgage payment on the El Monte home where she lives, still jointly owned with her former husband, is $180 a month. The property taxes of $415, or $35 a month, are included. Without Propostion 13, her projected tax would have been $3,036, or $253 a month. Her Medi-Cal eligibility changed, and she was notified that if she wanted to use that service for her children, she would have to pay a $180 deductible. "I couldn't afford it," she says simply."Luckily, my children aren't sick." About the same time, her food stamp eligibility changed, too, and she was reduced to $64 a month, from $108. "I went down and told the lady, I had a hard enough time with the $108," Briceno, 34, said. "I assume they've got to cut something back, I guess. I figure I'm the type of person the government's going to do with what they want to do, you know. They say every vote counts, but I don't think I count."A particular recent hardship involved increased costs of recreational programs in a nearby El Monte park. "The boys both play baseball," she said. "Last year baseball was $15 each,

but now for the oldest I had to pay $45 and the other one was $35.
I had my daughter in ballet (also at the park). Last year that was
$15 but that went up too, to $25. And I have to buy the body suit,
the shoes, and the costumes for any shows. We couldn't afford it.
She gave that up. I didn't think I could get the boys to baseball
but luckily I was able to work to earn it."

■ Carolyn and David Konow, who own a graphics firm in Bur-
bank, bought a $128,000 house in Granada Hills in 1980, knowing
their 1% property tax would be higher than that paid by neighbors who bought therebefore 1978. Proposition 13 "allowed us to
move into a bigger house. We have half an acre. We couldn't have
afforded that at the (1978) tax rate, even if we could have afforded the house."

■ What Virginia Jimenez remembers most about Proposition
13 were the campaign promises aimed at LosAngeles renters like
herself. "I remember them saying rents would go down, there
would be more housing available, " she recently recalled. "But it
happened exactly the reverse." A divorcee who raised six children, she has received the state renters tax credit, which the Legislature increased from $37 to $137 for a head of household with
dependents. But Jimenez does not notice the extra $100, she
says. In 1978, she was paying $140 a month for a two-bedroom
apartment in the Pico-Union area. Now she pays $458 a month
for a smaller apartment a few blocks away. If a Proposition 13
vote came up today, she says, "Not only would I vote against it, I
would campaign against anything Howard Jarvis said." When Jimenez, 45, looks at the budget cuts made over the last five years,
she notices the reductions in manpower training programs such
as CETA (Comprehensive Employment and Training Act),
which she credits for getting her off welfare. Indeed, her earned
income rose from $3,362 in 1975 to $35,474 last year, working an
11 p.m. to 6 a.m. shift as a lithographer. According to the Franchise Tax Board, because of income tax indexing, she paid an estimated $795 less in state taxes than she would have in 1977.

■ Jon and Tina Crowell have two children in college and one
still at home in Pasadena, soon to go to high school. The couple,
whose own property tax dropped 78%, or $1,620, between 1977
and 1978 because of Proposition 13 have seen museums deterio-

rate and fees increase for Music Center parking, fishing licenses, and dog licenses. They are also paying $100 more in tuition for one son to attend the University of California, Riverside. Though their net property tax savings grew over five years to a projected $5,898 in 1982, the Crowells were not aware of how much they had saved. Nor were they aware that according to Franchise Tax Board estimates, they paid $1,101 less in state taxes in 1982 than in 1977 because of income tax indexing. At times, Crowell, 47, said that "money did build up in our checking account. A couple of times we'd take a check and put it in savings."

■ An apartment renter in Hollywood, Charles Robinson did not vote for Proposition 13 in 1978, although he says he was "very much in sympathy with doing something about property taxes." That was a year before his son, Sterling, was born with cerebral palsy. Robinson, 34, and his wife, Shirley, kept the child at home instead of institutionalizing him and have undertaken much of his physical therapy themselves. At a time when budget cuts threaten the handicapped along with other public programs, Robinson says, "We need those public services. They are our only hope." Until 1981, Robinson, who is black, had his own folk art and jewelry store in Hollywood, but it closed, he said, because of the recession. Though Robinson continued his business as a mail order operation, and took a second job as a greeting card salesman, his income dropped from $24,000 to $18,000, he said. According to the Franchise Tax Board, Robinson saved $213 in state taxes in 1982 through income tax indexing. Robinson was not aware of it and called it negligible. Local cutbacks in library hours have hit hard because he and his wife depend on libraries to educate themselves about their son's illness. In addition, they have found the changes in hours confusing and hard to fit in with working hours. Robinson is also bothered by the new or increased fees in the city and county, especially for beach parking and admission to the zoo. "I think most people think, what's a few dollars here, a few dollars there," said Robinson. "But we don't have any way to make that up. And we are talking about things that are important for Sterling. And we can't leave Sterling with a regular baby sitter, we can't go to a restaurant and do regular things . . . . But we can take him to the beach. These are the only things we can do."

■ Homes on the 2100 block of East Quincy Avenue in Orange haven't changed much since they were built 22 years ago. Many still have the standard yellow glass window on the front door, the standard plastic light-switch door bell, the standard three bedrooms. It's a conservative, working class neighborhood, the type whose residents revolted against rising property taxes five years ago, pushing Proposition 13 into law. As a result, neighbors with nearly identical homes find their tax bills range from $308 to $1,376. Without the measure, the bills could be nearing $3,000.

If there had been no Proposition 13, Melba Schroth, 54, said she would have to go back to work as a factory inspector. In 1977 the tax bill on the home she and her husband, Gunther, 46, have owned for 15 years was $946.66. If their tax were based on the 1977-78 rate and current market values, they and other long-term homeowners on the block would be paying roughly $2,929. But since 1978, their bill has dropped and last year they paid only $316.34. As it is, they can live on and make mortgage payments from his hourly salary as a tool maker. With the money they saved, the Schroths, who have no children, were able to accomplish their first major repairs to their home: a $2,000 fence, $3,800 in brickwork and $3,550 for new carpeting. She has noticed that some public services, such as a mosquito abatement program, have been curtailed. And she's seen fishing licenses go up from $4 to $14.10.

"What gripes me," said Fred Shepherd, "is that you work to get it passed and government works to get around it." Shepherd, 50, is a grocery truck driver. His wife, Norma, is a salesperson at Sears. When they voted for Proposition 13, they were living in a less expensive neighborhood in Orange. Their $265 monthly house payment, which included property taxes, was cut by $30, he said. "I don't remember what we spent it on," he said. Despite the property tax bill of $1,376, they bought a new house on Quincy for $130,000. Although Shepherd would vote for Proposition 13 again, he is disheartened, because government "keeps trying to find out ways to get more tax money out of you." When the license for his pick-up truck went up to $75 from $47, Shepherd said he was told that a new "weight fee" had come into being, but that he could get around it by putting a shell on his truck and claiming it as a passenger vehicle. "I don't think that's right," he said.

Five years ago, when Robert Johnson was retiring from the gas company, he knew his $900 monthly pension plus Social Security would have to see him and his wife, Ruth, through inflation and rising taxes. The 1977-78 property tax on the house they'd bought new for $19,900 was $960.26 and "jumping 10 or 15% a year." They voted for Proposition 13. The next year, their tax rolled back to the 1975 level of $357.72; last year it was even lower: $319.34.The tax money they saved went into a savings account for doctors' bills. "We carry our own insurance, so to speak," said Johnson, who believes Proposition 13 has allowed them to enjoy their retirement. Without Proposition 13, they fear they would have to sell the house and move, or he would have to find some sort of work. They would both support the tax cut initiative again. Not only have they not noticed decreased public services, they think service is better than ever. "I'm proud of this city's services," said Johnson. "They still clean the street every Monday."

As far as John Satterthwaite is concerned, politicians have not yet gotten the message voters sent them in the Proposition 13 election: "Start cutting the fat out of their own organization." Satterthwaite, 53, is an industrial designer. His wife, Janet, who was a vocational educational teacher in 1978, is now a school nurse in the Los Alamitos Unified School District. They voted for Proposition 13 for tax relief. It worked, for their bill plummeted from $1,007.90 to $376.80. Last year, they paid $347.72. They put the savings from taxes in a bank and now that they're both making "good salaries" and their three children have left home, they feel secure financially. Governmental funding cuts most visible to the Satterthwaites are in education. "Other districts are beginning to lose their nurses and counselors," said Janet. "Nursing services are at the top of the list, as far as making cuts in a district. "They haven't cut programs or anything in the district I work for. But what happens next year is another story." She is unsure whether to blame the cuts on Proposition 13.

—PM,LS

A WORD FROM THE EXPERTS

It is interesting to note the comments of some of those who were involved at the time of the Proposition 13 battle with what appears to have resulted:

Howard Jarvis, Proposition 13 co-author: "For 90% of what it was designed to do, Proposition 13 has worked perfectly. It has cut taxes. The retired people who were losing their homes aren't losing them any more. In lowering the size and cost of government, it was a total flop. I just underestimated how the bureaucrats and the courts could block the will of the people. Without Proposition 13, rents would be 30% higher. A lot of these renters think they can pay $100 rent and live on the water. But the renter is the biggest beneficiary of Proposition 13. He tends to be poorer and minority. So therefore, with Proposition 13, you've helped the poor and minority."

Jarvis believes that there is more than enough money to provide good schools, roads, parks and other public services. "But the bureaucrats have squandered it. These cutbacks are because of bad management, incredibly bad management."

Paul Gann, Proposition 13 co-author: "It hasn't worked the way I expected. I didn't anticipate the courts would read decisions in Proposition 13 that weren't there. As for its intent—to save people's homes from (being overtaxed and, hence, to protect homeowners from losing their homes)—to that extent it has been very successful. It has saved taxpayers literally billions of dollars. Even today, I never go out but somebody always says, 'If it hadn't been for Proposition 13, I couldn't have remained in my home.' That's gratifying."

Gann is helping lead the effort to "patch the holes" left by court decisions. He criticizes the Legislature for failing to cut expenditures further. "The bureaucracy has blamed Proposition 13 for everything in the state, whether it's Proposition 13's fault or not. It's become a whipping boy."

William G. Hamm, Legislative Analyst: "The legacy of Proposition 13 is not so much the loss of revenue but the transfer of fiscal power from cities and counties to Sacramento. It worked for residential homeowners. It certainly has reduced the cost of maintaining residential property in California. If you had asked me (just before it passed), 'Could the state give up $7 billion without cuts in services?' I would have said no. But in retrospect, (the answer is) yes. We could have given up (the $7 billion) and continued to finance services that were then being provided. But what we couldn't do is give up that $7 billion plus another $3 billion in income-tax relief (indexing)" plus the loss of additional revenue through the elimination of the inheritance and gift tax and the business inventory tax. There is "a serious inequity" in the higher taxes that property owners who bought their homes after the measure passed must pay. But, he added, "the tax system is so replete with inequities that to single one out without recognizing the others" is not thoughtful. I continue to believe that once the economy rights itself, as we know it will, the tax system that we have in place right now is capable of generating enough money without an increase in tax rates to fund the current level of services. But it may not be enough to give education a major new infusion of funding. . . ."

A. Alan Post, former Legislative Analyst: "Proposition 13 provided property tax reduction which is generally needed and wanted. But it brought also with it some flaws," including the required two-thirds vote for substitute revenues and the problem of unfair home assessments. "There's no free lunch on Proposition 13 . . . It changed some economies too much. It made it impossible to increase other revenues."

Post sees the state looking to "a combination of reform and some new taxes both for local government and the state," including a "better distribution of sales taxes (the present local sales tax is distributed back to point of collection) so that small communities that used to rely on property taxes" can get some fiscal help.

Larry J. Kimbell, UCLA economist: "If people were given a chance to vote on it again today, I think they would do what they did in 1978. So in that sense I think it was a success. But that doesn't mean that if given a chance to change it, they wouldn't. Specifically, Kimbell, director of the UCLA Business Forecasting Project, believes that those who voted for the amendment had no desire to shift a greater share of the property-tax burden to those who have recently purchased homes or businesses. Kimbell's forecasting unit predicted in May, 1978, that adoption of the initiative would lead to the loss of 451,300 public- and private-sector jobs in California. In fact, very few jobs were lost.

The economist said that his prediction was wrong only in its timing, because the forecast did not take into account a multibillion-dollar state surplus. Now the surplus is spent, and the public and private sector work forces are about 450,000 jobs smaller than they would have been in the absence of Proposition 13, he said.

Lt. Gov. Leo T. McCarthy: "(Proposition 13) protected residential property as it should have done. (But) by taking away from local government and the schools . . . it made local government more dependent on Sacramento. Keeping independence in cities and counties is very important. Proposition 13 had the greatest impact on schools, he said. The state part of the school budget (before it passed) was 39%-40%, and now, he said, it is double that. But if Proposition 13 is to be modified, he said, "it will have to be done by the voters" because of the overwhelming original mandate of passage (66%). It would be somewhat arrogant to suggest that the voters didn't know what they were doing. I was against it then and I still have the same conviction that owners of large office buildings shouldn't be taxed the same as homeowners."

Alexander Pope, Los Angeles County assessor: "Proposition 13 did the job as far as lowering property taxes; and property taxes have stayed down. (But it also) shifted the power and responsibility for determining the level of spending and services (from local government to Sacramento). I think we overshifted. We now have a property tax system that has very large differentials (for those who have bought homes since the measure passed). I think it's unfair. He also thinks that it is unfair that Proposition 13 did not take into account that businesses change hands much less." He also thinks that it is unfair that Proposition 13 did not take into account that businesses change hands much less frequently than residential property and, predicts that residential property will eventually shoulder an increasingly higher propor-

tion of the property tax burden. He supports "periodical reap-
praisal of business property" in an effort to equalize the tax burden.

Peter H. Behr, former GOP senator who sponsored legislation
to head off Proposition 13: "(Proposition 13) worked out almost
as precisely as I had predicted, perhaps a year or so later than I
would have expected . . . Proposition 13 is plainly unconstitutional" because it violates the equal-protection clause of Constitution when it allows lower property taxes for those who had a
home before it passed. Clearly local government became less and
less independent (since Proposition 13 passed). . . . (Local governments) lost a major part of their tax base."

2

How Local Government Responded

Of the measures that launched California's tax revolt, Proposition 13 and the Gann initiative were aimed directly at the financing of local government, and it is among local governments that change can be seen most visibly. The change has affected the politics of raising public money, the ability of local government to deliver services and the quality—and price—of government services that consumers can expect. The Times surveyed a sampling of cities and counties about their specific response to financial pressures. Reporters used city, county and state financial and budget documents and spoke with scores of public officials and financial experts from around the state.

Proposition 13 has brought California a new, confused and often unfair system of government and taxation, with business, labor and public officials battling over how to repair a haphazard structure of laws thrown together after Howard Jarvis forever changed the state. At stake is the future shape of state and local government, and whether it can provide a fair and rational system of taxation and a distribution of political power that gives a voice to all Californians.

Not since Gov. Hiram Johnson wrested political power from the Southern Pacific Railroad in the early 20th Century or Governors Earl Warren and Edmund G. Brown Sr. created the state's generous public higher education and welfare systems has California witnessed such a turbulent shift in political power. Then it was government on the march. This time it is government in retreat. The Proposition 13 revenue cuts, combined with a faltering state economy and increasingly tight budgets, have caused government to begin squeezing many of the social and educational programs pioneered by earlier political leaders. Beyond the visible results of cutback—the potholes, increased class size, reductions in money for parks and libraries—something more ephemeral has resulted: There is concern about how the state's political structure is changing and what it means to the lives of Californians.

"What has taken place throughout the state during the past few years is nothing less than a radical restructuring of our system of taxation," the San Diego Taxpayers Assn. said in a report this year. "What is beginning to emerge is unquestionably a local government unlike that of the past. But whether the new form will be a more efficient system or merely an emaciated version of its former self remains to be seen." Said state Senate Majority Leader John Garamendi (D-Walnut Grove): "What the nature of government will be in the next 50 years."

Immediately after Proposition 13, power was transferred from city halls and county buildings to the state capital. That was because the measure limited local government's ability to increase its main source of revenue, the property tax. "Whoever has the gold rules," said Orange County Supervisor Bruce Nestande. Or as Oakland City Manager Henry Gardner put it: "You certainly aren't regarded as very powerful when your streets are falling apart and you can't pave them or when your sewers are backing up every time it rains."

That loss of power in itself was a revolution in government. Then, to the dismay of Proposition 13 advocates, a series of state Supreme Court decisions restored some of the cities' taxing power. That returned some of the lost power. But only some. In all but a few cases, county taxing authority was not restored by the the court. That means that the Legislature continues to make fiscal decisions for California's 58 counties, which run the civil and criminal courts, the jails, public hospitals and social welfare services. The once stable structure is in turmoil. Cities are trying to determine the extent of their newly restored taxing power and to beat back expected attempts to take it away. Counties remain deprived of power. Legislators are trying to sort out the mess. Gov. George Deukmejian has created a task force of state and local officials to do the same.

And special interests are trying to fill the resulting political vacuum. Big business and big labor are trying to keep power centered in the Capitol, where they have to deal with only two legislative houses and a governor instead of hundreds of often unpredictable local government bodies. Business—represented by the California Chamber of Commerce, the California Taxpayers Assn., the Business Roundtable of 86 executives from the biggest manufacturing, banking, agricultural firms—fears returning to a system which could legislate a state tax increase and which could give local governments additional taxing power. The Chamber and Cal-Tax favor action to repeal the court decisions that took some of the steam from Jarvis, to keep taxing authority centralized. Cornell Maier, chairman of the the board of Kaiser Aluminum, said that because his company has installations in Oakland, San Jose, Los Angeles and Rancho California, " I think the bulk of our taxes should be raised on a statewide level." The unions have found they have more clout in Sacramento to push through state legislation benefiting local government employees. Laws strengthening peace officer retirement and firefighter disability compensation have shown how unions can get what they want in Sacramento after being turned down at City Hall or the county building. "It's a lot easier to come to one place and have 62 votes up here or more; it's a lot easier to put things through or kill things here," said Sen. Ed Davis (R-Chatsworth), author of a government restructuring bill.

Things were simpler in 1851, when the Shasta County Court of Sessions, the board of supervisors of the day, levied its first small property tax, which, along with a $2 poll tax and a $25 license for each of the many saloons in the rowdy, gold rush area, was enough to pay government expenses. In a community where the balance was tipped heavily on the side of law enforcement, the county paid a court appointed attorney only $50 to defend two murder suspects and the sheriff $100 to hang them. Over the years, the tax laws got more complicated and the property tax grew to a burden, in the eyes of many.

In 1972, the Legislature attempted to impose some controls in a bill that government experts said was a one of the first steps in centralizing political control in Sacramento. In a package bill— SB90—the Legislature set revenue limits for school districts, set limits on city and county property tax rates and said the Legislature should provide money for any programs mandated for local government. For a time, property tax rates did drop in many cases, but property values and, therefore, assessed valuation, increased. And the Legislature began to ignore the obligation to provide money for mandated programs. In any case, sustained efforts to control the property tax failed, and by 1978, the voters, taking matters into their hands, approved Proposition 13. To the voters, it was a simple tax limit. But by limiting local tax power, voters actually had given the Legislature the opportunity to impose more conditions on local government in return for state aid suddenly needed to replace lost property tax revenues.

Less than three months before the Proposition 13 vote, the California Taxpayers Assn. raised this question: "What would happen to local control of local government under Proposition 13? Is there any way to prevent greater state control?" Five years later, another business-oriented group said it believed the Cal-Tax fears had been realized. "There is a growing dissatisfaction with the lack of fiscal independence and thus home rule . . . ," a chamber report said.

Now the question is how much of that fiscal independence did the cities actually recover when the state Supreme Court interpreted Proposition 13's vague words. Upholding a Los Angeles County Transportation Commission half-cent sales tax, the court ruled that the levy, approved by a majority of county voters, was not subject to the Jarvis requirement of a two-thirds approval for special-district tax increases. The commission, the court said, was not a special district. It defined the vague term "special district" as one with the power to levy a property tax, and before Proposition 13 the commission had no such power.

In the San Francisco Farrell case, Justice Stanley Mosk, writ-

ing for the majority, made another crucial definition, this time
dealing with the vague Jarvis term, "special taxes." Jarvis said a
"special tax" required a two-thirds vote. The City of San Francisco, with a 55% majority of voters, established a payroll and
gross receipts tax and contended it was not a special tax. The
court agreed. "We construe the term 'special taxes' . . . to mean
taxes which are levied for a specific purpose rather than, as in the
present case, a levy placed in the general fund to be utilitized for
general governmental purposes," the court said.

In the Carman case, the court ruled that a San Gabriel municipal employee pension obligation approved by the voters could be
financed by a special property tax increase. Pension obligations
authorized by voters before passage of Proposition 13, the court
said, were included in the vague Jarvis word "indebtedness" and
Jarvis allowed special property tax increases to finance "any indebtedness approved by the voters" before 1978.

"For better or for worse, the Supreme Court . . . has restored
the power to the municipalities," said Mayor Larry Agron of Ir-
vine said. "That puts us in a position to do what we had been
previously able to do (before Proposition 13). If the people want
a higher level of service, new programs, they essentially have to
be funded at the local level. Federal revenue sharing is drying up.
The state bailout is dried up. So now we're in a position of pretty
much going it alone. Now we have the authority to do it, whereas
for a few years we did not."

But Don Benninghoven, executive director of the League of
California Cities, the big municipal lobbying group, said that city
officials will be reluctant to use their new power because they
believe voters still vehemently oppose tax increases. "They won't
do it because they won't be reelected at this point," he said. "I
don't think you can ever really expect local elected officials to
raise taxes unless the situation is so dramatic they have to—
(such as) a flood, the streets being almost unusable." In addition, the political reality is that cities will have difficulty achiev-
ing the required two-thirds majority for new special taxes.

That dilemma dominated Los Angeles City Hall this year
when, faced with a $142 million deficit, Mayor Tom Bradley and
the City Council decided to raise taxes. City Councilman Hal

Bernson, a Republican representing one of the San Fernando Valley districts where the Jarvis tax revolt was born, said his constituents "don't like it, but what are you going to do, let the city go down the drain?" Will his constituents understand? "I hope so," he said. But, having made the decision to raise taxes, Bernson and his colleagues found themselves hampered by the ambuiguity in Proposition 13's language.

Implementing Jarvis, a Legislature bewildered by his language merely picked up some of it word for word in writing a complicated formula for distribution of the countywide property taxes that remained after Proposition 13. That fateful decision resulted in complex disputes between cities and counties. Unaware of the severity of the problem, Bradley proposed a property tax increase, only to see it caught in the technicalities of the law.

Most counties, on the other hand, have no power to raise taxes without legislative approval or a two-thirds vote of the electorate on a specific spending proposal. They are dependent on property tax revenues limited by Proposition 13, plus state aid. "In order to have autonomy in local government you must have a revenue base and local government, through Proposition 13, surrendered its revenue base," Orange County Supervisor Nestande said.

That was a true revolution. County supervisors were famous for their power. Using their unlimited authority to boost property taxes, they showered their districts with courthouses, bridges, parks, swimming pools and roads, and payed a share of the cost of social programs mandated by the state. "The biggest area where we can't do things today where we could have prior to Proposition 13 is in the whole area of capital improvements," Nestande said. "That's a big, big category, you can't build a jail, roads, fire stations, all the infrastructure needed for orderly growth." That is because counties can no longer sell general obligation bonds, which before Proposition 13 were guaranteed by the counties' ability to raise the property tax. They still can sell revenue bonds—which generally are underwritten by money generated by the facility being built.

As a result, the signs of retreating government are most visible in the counties. In the county building in Yreka, just up from the old saloons where '49ers spent their gold, Siskiyou County Supervisor Norma Frey cannot get the money to build bridges or roads. She and her colleagues, deprived of money and power, worked on a dais decorated with a handwritten motto that captured their frustration. "To work below our capabilities creates a deep hunger within ourselves and an enormous waste in society." Santa Clara and Orange County supervisors, their jails crowded, cannot raise the money to build new cells without either asking the Legislature to approve a new tax or winning difficult-to-achieve two-thirds voter approval for such a special levy.

Garamendi's office across from the Senate evokes memories of an earlier California. He discussed the state's problems amid furniture from the late 19th Century, when the state government was dominated by railroad and mining barons. Garamendi's desk is the one used by Hiram Johnson, the reformer who changed California government more than 80 years ago when he curbed the power of those barons and put the state on a progressive course. The history of that period helps understand what is happening in the Capitol today. One of the fascinations of California is how powerful economic interests, such as Southern Pacific, jumped in and shaped the government, even before there were many people in the state. Today, there are more interests, the diversity of their goals reflecting the diversity of the state. Political leaders are trying to reconcile them. The result will determine the taxes Californians will pay and the power of their mayors, city council members, county supervisors and state officials. The obstacles they face would puzzle even Hiram Johnson.

—BB

PAY-AS-YOU-GO GOVERNMENT

California's cities and counties are moving inexorably toward pay-as-you-go government and Proposition 13 is the reason. A growing number of fees and other charges are either being increased or imposed for the first time to pay for services that government once provided at little or no direct cost to the user.

Despite the obstacles posed by Proposition 13, residents in some communities are imposing taxes on themselves for specific needs like street lights and better fire protection. Even taken together, however, these approaches cannot close the revenue gap left by Proposition 13 and subsequent tax-cutting measures. While still a relatively small piece of the revenue pie for local government—12.5% for cities, 8% for counties and 10% for special districts— fees seem to be the most popular source of extra cash for local governments. In part, this is because they are aimed at those who use specific government services, in part because politically they are easier to legislate than new taxes.

Cities in particular have aimed new and higher fees at developers and at users of sewers, parks and recreation facilities, according to a recent survey by UC Santa Barbara economics professors Lloyd J. Mercer and W. Douglas Morgan. And officials responding to a Times survey from jurisdictions serving more than half the state's population indicate that since Proposition 13 passed, most of them have set new fees or raised existing fees to pay for a variety of services involving police, fire, street and park departments across the state. Here are some examples:

■ POLICE: Some 86% of responding departments—both cities and counties—reported raising fees; every responding city or county of more than 500,000 population increased fees. And 66%—more counties than cities—said they have new fees. Most of these fees are not directly concerned with public safety—they are charges for copying police reports, obtaining photographs, fingerprinting or for getting permits to carry weapons.

■ FIRE: 36% of fire departments said they had raised fees, with more than half the increases in cities. About 44% of respondents said they had initiated new fire protection fees—half in cities, half in special fire districts and counties. Most of these fees were for paramedic service or fire safety inspections, others for actual fire protection.

■ PARKS: Some 90% of responding departments said they had raised fees while 74% replied that they had new fees. The increases were in cities and counties of varying size. Park fees include charges for such things as swimming pool use, team sports, and recreational classes.

■ STREETS AND ROADS: Approximately 74% of replying street and road agencies said they had raised a variety of fees; about 61% said they had enacted new fees. These fees included charges to utilities for breaking into a street to repair and maintain un-

Losing Savings from Proposition 13

Homeowners who itemize income tax deductions had to share their Proposition 13 savings with the state and federal governments because of lower property tax deductions and higher reportable incomes. Those who did not itemize saw no such reduction. Here are some examples*:

1979 income (4-person family)	1979 home value	Gross Prop. 13 tax savings	Higher state, U.S. income tax	Net savings	Net as % of gross savings
$15,000	$45,000	$496	$ 20	$476	96%
30,000	69,000	806	268	538	67%
50,000	100,000	1,214	598	616	51%

*These three examples from 1979 assume standard deductions for income, with home values derived from state Legislative Analyst figures and adjusted for inflation.

derground hardware and lines or charging a developer a fee for the right to hook a road up to a main arterial street.

Other revenue-raising options have been exercised as well. In particular, cities and counties have raised special taxes, inaugurated special benefits assessments, or resorted to some rather innovative ways of raising new revenues.

Despite a Proposition 13 stipulation that cities had to get a two-thirds vote of the electorate to raise taxes for specified purposes, the League of California Cities reports that 26 cities, five counties and 17 special districts have done so. They involve a variety of special taxes, ranging from special levies for municipal services to taxes to pay for police and fire services to business license levies. This trend is especially true for fire protection taxes, according to The Times' survey. Virtually all the tax hikes have been in smaller cities. Large urban areas, such as Los Angeles and Oakland, for example, have rejected post-Proposition 13 tax increase efforts to pay for police and fire protection. "There is a tax revolt going on, but if the people need a service they're willing to tax themselves for it," said one government source.

A corollary might be that those who need the service—and who can afford a tax hike—are more likely to vote for it than poorer communities. For example, two-thirds of the voters of Hillsborough, an affluent community on the San Francisco peninsula, approved a tax increase in 1980 to pay for municipal services. A notable exception to the two-thirds vote rule occurred in a 1980 election in San Francisco when 55% of the electorate approved a payroll and gross receipts tax hike. The state Supreme Court subsequently ruled in the much-publicized Farrell decision that a two-thirds vote was not necessary so long as the revenues flow to a local general fund and not into a specialized coffer. Several local officials interviewed said, however, they believed the Farrell decision would be used cautiously because the voters have not abandoned the tax revolt philosophy that made Proposition 13 an angry electorate's war cry.

The special benefit assessments, a trend that is not quantified, is increasing, report local officials. Fresno, like many other localities, is establishing special districts in which property owners pay for certain improvements which benefit their property. In Fresno's case, a district was established to pay for street lighting. Taxpayer tab: $75 a year.

Faced with the loss of property tax revenue and the sharp reduction of financial aid from Sacramento, some local governments in California in many cases have found sometimes imaginative ways to generate new revenue. Said James Hendrickson, Fresno assistant city manager: "We can't rely on any level of support from the state and the federal government in the future. We have to rely on our own devices."

Among the new wrinkles:

■ EXACTIONS. These are the streets, sewers, sidewalks, parks and fire houses that cities and counties demand from developers in exchange for permits. What they really are, said a 1982 report of the governor's Office of Planning and Research, "are the legal, legitimate equivalent of extortion." While this is not a new phenomenon, developers say the practice is growing. Exactions to finance new parks are required by approximately 69% of cities, counties and special districts responding to a Times survey. Approximately 86% of responding cities and counties said they required developers to put up cash for new streets before they would give the developer needed permits, although 82% said they did something like this before 1978 as well. To get the go-ahead to build Rancho Carmel, a development 12 miles east of San Diego, for example, Shapell Industries had to cough up about $85 million worth of improvements, including a fire station complete with fire engines, a freeway overpass, traffic signals and parks. "This is not blackmail or anything else," snapped George Simpson, San Diego's assistant director of engineering. What it comes down to, he said, was that "before Proposition 13, we had money" to underwrite many of the projects that tie into a development. "We don't have that now."

■ EQUITY. The Solano County community of Fairfield gets a cut of the profits from a shopping center, a stipulation the city demanded before it gave the developer the go-ahead. The Contra Costa city of Walnut Creek has a similar arrangement in a major downtown development. "Local government is getting smarter faster," quipped City Manager Thomas Dunne.

■ INSURANCE. Cities such as San Rafael and Mill Valley are partners with a private insurance carrier, Avco Financial Insurance of Newport Beach. In exchange for performing residential fire inspections, they get a cut of Avco's premium income.

■ LEASEBACKS. Oakland and the San Francisco Peninsula city of Sunnyvale sold public buildings (Oakland, its museum; Sunnyvale, its library), put the cash into general funds and then leased the buildings from the private investors who bought them. The cities will own them again in a couple of decades and, meanwhile, have a cash windfall. Monterey Park in Los Angeles County is considering a similar arrangement involving its city hall.

■ CONTRIBUTIONS. Rolling Hills Estates has created a nonprofit foundation through which citizens can contribute park benches and shrubs for local parks. Monterey Park has an adopt-a-park program under which businesses contribute to the city in exchange for being allowed to advertise in the local park.

■ CRACKDOWN. Oakland is cracking down on delinquent business license fees, an estimated $3 million in the current fiscal year. "Professionals—attorneys, CPAs—weren't paying business license taxes," said John Flores, assistant city manager. "They were saying, 'We'll wait until the city gets to us before we start paying.' " Now they're paying on time, he said.

■ ENERGY. La Habra, Palos Verdes, Los Angeles city and county and Ventura County are among those government entities about to produce, or producing, energy from their own plants, some of which will, in turn, be sold to private industry or utilities.

But it is in the area of fees and service charges where the change is most visible. Before Proposition 13, local governments' general funds, fed by rapidly rising property taxes, largely subsidized services ranging from building permit and dog license fees to court filing charges. An effort now seems aimed at recovering the full cost of services. Imposition of new charges suggests that, in effect, when people use something, they should pay for it—a big step toward what many local officials argue is increased government efficiency.

"Central to all the messages," wrote a Los Angeles County task force on Proposition 13 in 1980, "was a single clear belief: that government, if forced to act, could improve the efficiency and effectiveness of its operations." This effort has prompted UC Santa Barbara professors Mercer and Morgan to conclude that "if the goal of the proponents of Proposition 13 is efficiency in local government, they should applaud rather than decry rising user charges." Here's local government's record on fees and user charges as measured by the latest annual data produced by the state controller:

■ CITIES. Between 1978 and 1981, California's cities increased the amount of cash raised from fees and service charges by 48%. In 1978, 10% of city revenues came from fees; by the end of 1981, that was up to 12.5%. Much of this activity seems to have occurred in the state's largest cities, according to a just-published survey by the California Taxpayers Assn. (Cal-Tax) and The Times' survey. Cal-Tax found revenue from licenses and permits increased 87% in the 26 largest cities, but only 3% among the remaining cities in a survey of 50 of California's 434 cities between fiscal years 1978-79 and 1981-82. According to the state controller, city user fee collections in Los Angeles increased by 67% between the 1978-79 period and fiscal year 1980-81. Some other large cities—such as San Francisco (52%), Sacramento (73%) and San Diego (48%)—also showed big fee revenue jumps between 1978 and 1981, the controller's figures showed. If any one group has been a prime target for fee boosts, it has been real estate developers, said the Cal-Tax survey. Cal-Tax's John Sullivan said, "In some cases it looks like there were exorbitant increases on builders." Not so, countered an Assembly Office of

Research source, who sought anonymity, adding that the construction industry before Proposition 13 had not been "paying its own way."

■ COUNTIES. Between 1978 and 1981, counties increased their cash from fees and service charges by 50%. This amounted to about 8% of total county revenues, up from 6% in fiscal year 1978. Actually, said a spokesman for the County Supervisors Assn. of California, counties "had nowhere else to turn to" except to fees and service charges to raise additional revenue. "Either they raise fees or cut essential services like sheriff's patrols," said the spokesman. That's because, he said, unlike the cities, California's 58 counties generally do not have tax-raising authority and it was unlikely they would get any new taxing authority from the Legislature.

■ SPECIAL DISTRICTS, ranging from fire protection to mosquito abatement districts, were heavily dependent on property taxes. Consequently, they increased their take from user fees by 74% between fiscal years 1978 and 1981. This represents about 10% of their total revenues against a level of about 7% in 1977. Like the counties, special districts must turn to the state for new taxing authority or to increase fees beyond their authorization. Special districts "had to make up the gap between what they were cut back to (when Proposition 13 passed), to the point of the cost of providing the service," said David Nagler, executive director of the California Special Districts Assn., which represents about 500 different districts in the state. "They (the approximately 3,000 special districts in California) got hit the worst primarily because the political strength of cities and counties was much greater than the special districts," said Nagler. "They had a lot more money taken away (by Sacramento) than the cities and the counties." However, according to the state legislative analyst, bail-out funds to special districts suffered fewer cuts than did those to cities and counties.

Has local government raised fees too much? Between 1978 and 1981, revenues from fees increased 48% in cities, 50% in counties and 74% in special districts, according to the state controller. Inflation, conservatively measured, ran 39% in the same period. In part, revenues increased beyond inflation because California continued to add population—an estimated 8%—and there were new fees as well as higher charges. Some cash from fees ends up in communities' general funds, where it is used to pay for government services which have little or nothing to do with the service for which the fee was assessed. And localities that had allowed property taxes to subsidize fees now require fees to carry more of the load. This has led to sharp fee increases for serivces which had depended on a heavy subsidy from property taxes.

So the question of whether fees increased beyond the cost of service offered for the fee is almost impossible to answer because many localities do not apply uniform cost control standards in their bookkeeping. At one end of the spectrum is San Francisco, which requires individual agencies to monitor their fee revenues rather than dump the cash into a general fund, said Ray Sullivan, San Franciso's financial chief. That way, he said, the money "is not used for other general fund activities." But in Los Angeles County, the fee money goes into the general fund. Chief Administrative Officer Harry L. Hufford, said: "We're (the Board of Supervisors) imposing all of the fees that we can." He said there is a supply-and-demand brake on local government, but he suggested that fees are a product "of what the market will bear."

Richard B. Dixon, Los Angeles County's chief budget analyst, said that "You would expect (fees) to run ahead of inflation." Local government, he said, has been playing catch-up since Proposition 13 by raising fees to "full-cost recovery" levels. This would probably account to some extent for the fact, Dixon said, that Los Angeles County fee revenues increased by 86% between fiscal years 1978 and 1981, according to the state controller, more than twice the inflation factor. Douglas W. Ayres, a La Mirada consultant who advises cities on how to raise revenues, believes that the movement toward pay-as-you-go government is among the most important products of Proposition 13.

"Proposition 13 passed because people were paying a lot of taxes and they didn't have the foggiest idea what they were getting for it," said Ayres, former city manager of Inglewood and Salem, Ore.

A recent analysis by Ayres of 1,000 fees in 15 cities showed that, in his opinion, there was still little cost control over the col-

lection of fees and taxes. In many instances, services used by
people who could afford to pay fees were "being heavily subsidized by taxes (from general funds)," Ayres found, adding,
"What that means is that taxes are going to the wrong place."
Keith B. Comrie, Los Angeles' chief administrative officer, suggested that fee increases certainly can provide a quick dose of
medicine for a city—such as Los Angeles—currently facing a lot
of red ink. As an example, Comrie said that by charging $6 a
month for garbage collection, currently subsidized by taxes, $50
million or more would ultimately flow into city coffers each year.
(A $1.50-a-month collection fee for single-family homes, finally
approved by the City Council, would raise $10.1 million annual-
ly.)

—RLS

FINDING CUTTING DIFFICULT

When Proposition 13 forced government officials in California
to cut spending to match property tax reductions, they found a
variety of programs virtually off-limits. Political pressures, complex intragovernmental relationships and restrictions stemming
from the initiative itself all had a hand in limiting what cities and
counties could do. Ultimately those factors helped shape a system that today favors public safety at the expense of public
works, health, welfare and social programs. In some cases, the
limitations were of local government's own making. But more often, they were created by a Legislature determined to avoid the
kinds of tough decisions spawned by the property tax cuts. Ultimately options were limited because:

■ There were conditions placed on post-Proposition 13 state
aid. The Legislature, fearing that local officials would cut police
and fire services, conditioned its bail-out aid on a promise that
those services would be left intact. But even after that limitation
was eased, political pressure from voters and unions forced most
cities and counties to give top priority to public safety spending.
As a result, cities that had been spending 29 cents of each tax
dollar on police protection in fiscal 1978 were devoting an estimated 37 cents to that purpose in 1981. Although some of that
increase was the result of changes in the way government agen-

cies reported spending, a Times survey found that law enforcement spending, adjusted for inflation and population, increased
by 8.5%.

■ There were state-mandated programs that by law could not
be abandoned. The Legislature in years past had enacted hundreds of laws requiring an array of programs, particularly in
health and justice; few included reimbursement. The state legislative analyst estimates that these mandates have cost cities and
counties an additional $260 million over the last eight years.

■ The Legislature also forced counties to take over expensive
services once provided by the state, particularly in health and
welfare programs, which are the bulk of non-educational spending. Among recent cases: the state gave counties responsibility to
care for medically indigent adults, but agreed to pay only 70% of
the costs. For urban counties, absorbing the additional caseload
meant overcrowdings and longer waits. For smaller, rural communities, it meant some hospitals would close.

■ Cities and counties, as a result of decisions made during more
affluent times, had to set aside large amounts of money to retire
bonds, pay the skyrocketing costs of pension programs and finance employee wage agreements that, according to the County
Supervisors Assn. of California, hiked public employee pay an
average of 35% since Proposition 13. A study by the conservative
California Taxpayers Assn., for example, found that between fiscal 1979 and 1980, pension costs for cities and counties rose a
whopping 54% to an all-time high of more than $1.2 billion. Los
Angeles and San Francisco, which provide some of the state's
most generous pension plans, moved recently to trim their retirement costs, but are still forced to set aside as much as 70% of
their payroll to finance the systems.

The tax revolt affected communities differently. For most, the
worst was forestalled by state bail-out money and moves to raise
new revenues. Those blessed with an abundance of tax-produc-
ing industry or commercial centers and some so affluent that
they never needed a property tax were able to avoid the tough
choices altogether. But for the rest, particularly older cities
heavily dependent on property taxes and plagued by a deteriorating urban core, cuts were inevitable. "It was a switch away

What Jobs Got Cut in L.A.?

When Los Angeles was forced to cut positions, it did so through a combination of layoffs and attrition. In all, there are about 4% fewer job positions in 1983 than there were in 1978, excluding federal CETA workers. the city laid off 889, but because of a "bumping" procedure, only 410 employees acutally ended up with no jobs. This is a list of lost positions by department and job level:

City dept.	Management	Full-time supervisors	Working supervisors	Other staff	Total cuts	Ratio of supervisors to staff
Animal regulation	1	—	2	34	37	1:7
Building & safety	—	1	6	30	37	1:4
City administration office	1	1	1	12	15	1:6
City attorney	2	1	2	76	81	1:25
City clerk	—	—	5	47	52	1:9
Data services	—	2	5	53	60	1:8
Fire	5	—	—	90	95	NA
General services	—	2	37	333	372	1:9
City auditorium	—	1	—	4	5	1:4
Personnel	2	—	6	56	64	1:9
Planning	—	—	—	13	13	NA
Police	1	38	7	394	440	1:9
Public works	3	8	46	281	338	NA
Social services	—	—	—	4	4	NA
Transportation	—	—	6	59	65	1:10
Library	—	—	3	109	112	1:36
Recreation, parks	—	7	16	110	133	1:5
Total	**15**	**61**	**142**	**1,704**	**1,922**	**1:8**

from problem solving to a survival mode," said Jonathan Lewis, a former legislative budget expert, now a Sacramento lobbyist.

At first, communities deferred maintenance, pared secretarial help, left some high-paying jobs unfilled and drew on surplus funds. Some tried unconventional methods: The cities of San Anselmo and Fairfax combined traffic enforcement; Martinez and Larkspur agreed to share one city attorney and consolidated elderly and handicapped transportation programs; Petaluma continued with a major park development program after arranging to finance it with proceeds from sales through a city "gift catalogue." Conceded Ken Emanuels, chief lobbyist for the League of California Cities: "Proposition 13 gave us a reason to do these things that probably should have been done in the first place,"

Ultimately, those efforts were not enough to avoid tougher decisions. For Los Angeles County, spending figures mask the real impact. Although the county's budget ballooned to $5 billion from $3.5 billion in 1978, inflation actually reduced its spending power by 14%. At the same time, the county was forced to set aside more discretionary money to pay for bonded debt financed years ago. According to Chief Administrative Officer Harry L. Hufford, those factors caused a dramatic erosion in decision-making power that left the county with little ability to "respond to community needs." In fact, as a result of Proposition 13 and state and federal mandates, the county today has control over only 14% of the funds which flow through its coffers, as compared with 40% in 1978.

In an initial attempt to avoid deep cuts, the county spent its reserves. Surplus funds plummeted from $163. million in 1978 to $1.6 million this year. The county also encouraged private takeovers of public services, which, according to Hufford, saved nearly $30 million over the last five years. While that figure has been disputed, county officials concede that even if it is accurate, a $6-billion yearly savings means little in a $5-billion budget. The county also ordered a freeze on hiring, eliminated 3,300 full-time and temporary jobs, mostly through attrition, and ordered several top officials to assume additional duties. For a time, even Hufford was required to wear three hats, serving not only as chief administrative officer, but also as personnel director and head of animal control. Meanwhile, spending for sheriff, jail and court programs continued to grow. The few non-mandated health and sanitation programs were severely reduced as were recreation and cultural services. Spending on construction of new facilities was halved.

Even though the City of Los Angeles was saddled with fewer mandates and possessed more authority to raise fees and taxes, officials found themselves in a similar predicament. Los Angeles lost $239 million in property taxes in the first year after Proposition 13, only $80 million of which was replaced by the state bail-out. The following year, the bail-out was reduced to about $50 million yearly. At the same time, the $204-million yearly cost of maintaining the city's fire and police pension systems jumped

33% in one year alone. When it became clear that the gap could only be closed by program reductions, officials turned their attention to what was vulnerable. They found that 70% of their general tax-supported budget was devoted to public safety—police, fire and ambulance services—all considered top priority programs. As a result, there were deep reductions in the remaining 30%—particularly street maintenance, parks, recreation and libraries. Libraries and parks opened later and closed earlier, a number of public facilities were closed, and routine maintenance on street and city vehicles was scaled back. But even police staffing was reduced by 8%. "Probably the average citizen has a medium-sized lot, a camper, a swimming pool and buys his own books," said Los Angeles Chief Administrative Officer Keith B. Comrie. "But there are the other 50% who make use of the parks and the library and they have been hurt. I don't know what you do about that."

In the City and County of Los Angeles, officials found these cuts: Hours at the city's 55 branch libraries dropped from an average of 8 to 5 hours per day; 24 small city recreation buildings were closed and hours at 128 others in the city were reduced by 40%; many streets have deteriorated to the point where they require reconstruction rather than resurfacing. Normal standards require repaving every 40 years but the current level of financing would allow resurfacing of all city streets only every 120 years; weekly street sweeping of 3,300 miles of parking-restricted streets in high density areas has been reduced to once every three to four weeks. Frequency of night cleaning in the Central Business District and other commercial areas has been reduced by 25%; more than $300 million in projects has been identified, but annual financing available for the work is only $9 million. The city has no money to reconstruct 22 seismically unsafe police, library and other buildings; closure of six community health centers, a 10% reduction of personal health care at the county's comprehensive health centers, 10% reduction in hospital based services; closure of an adult mental health ward at Los Angeles County-USC Medical Center, closure of Hammel House mental health facility, loss of 31 inpatient beds and other general reductions that affected an estimated 1,441 patients, cancellation of a

20-bed skilled nursing care program resulting in a loss in services to an estimated 7,295 patients; elimination or reductions in several probation programs including the Lathrop Hall Family Treatment Program, the Detention Facilities Program, the Intenstive Narcotics Supervision School Program, closure of Camp Fenner Canyon as well as 7 community day care centers, general increases in caseloads, elimination of the camp aftercare services which provided intenstive supervision to serious offenders released from detention camps; closure of six public service welfare offices, cancelation of cost of living increases in 1982 required recipients to aborb an 8.8% increase in inflation, termination of a state-financed welfare program shifted some 4,000 recipients to general relief. San Diego County cut back on items like county health programs, retail store inspections, the number of polling places kept open on election days. The effects of streamlining procedures in county planning and engineering departments "will not be known for many years, because long-range planning has been affected the most, but many people feel this was not a negative development," Clifford Graves, county chief administrative. A newly constructed county jail at the county's new $37-million regional center in El Cajon has been standing empty because the Sheriff's Department, which runs the county's jails, does not have the manpower to staff it, a situation especially galling to the Sheriff's Department because it is under court order to alleviate crowding at its downtown jail.

The City of San Diego second in population in the state, but 20th in numbers of sanitation employees, 21st in sanitation expenditures; 21st in parks and recreation employees, seventh in parks and recreation expenditures (although without the money spent on San Diego Stadium, San Diego would rank 21st in this category as well); 23rd in street maintenance employees, 25th in expenditures; 25th in number of police officers, 18th in expenditures; 26th in firefighters, 22nd in expenditures; 22nd in sewerage workers, 17th in expenditures, 22nd in financial administration employees and expenditures. Taking all of these common functions together, San Diego ranks 25th in numbers of employees (San Jose is last) and 24th in expenditures. In 1978, when there were 8.15 city of San Diego workers for every 1,000 residents, there were 286 employees in the library department and 898 in parks and recreation. Now, with the overall ratio 7.04 employees per 1,000 residents, there are 240 library employees and 675 in parks and recreation.

The need to cut programs in many cases resulted from financial problems unrelated to Proposition 13. The tiny San Joaquin Valley town of Parlier, for example, was forced last year to disband its Police Department to save enough to avoid becoming the first California city to declare bankruptcy. "We don't want to mislead people," said City Manager Bert Wills. "(Proposition 13) was only one factor that added to our problems."

For newer, growing communities with diversified tax bases and a smaller percentage of poor residents, there were fewer hard choices to make. Anaheim, for example, which collect bed taxes, sales taxes and a variety of other revenues from the thousands of tourists who flock yearly to Disneyland and Anaheim Stadium, has been able to provide much the same level of services that it did before Proposition 13. While Oakland, for example, was eliminating street sweeping, disconnecting 900 street lights and reducing the Police Department's criminal investigations, Anaheim was busy building a new $14-million City Hall and undertaking a major expansion of its stadium.

The tax revolt really worked "to keep the poor cities poor and the wealthy cities wealthy," said Seal Beach City Manager Allen J. Parker. What happened in Orange County can be summed up in a tale of two cities with roughly the same land area and population—Westminster and Newport Beach. Between 1978 and 1981, Westminster's population grew by 3.2%, from 68,900 to 71,119; Newport Beach's population climbed by 1.5%, from 64,300 to 65,256. Westminster's total per capita revenues increased from $183 to $219 in that time, but per capita revenues would have had to increase to $236 just to keep pace with inflation or down about 7.2% in inflation adjusted dollars. Newport Beach's per capita revenues increased from $354 to $459 in the same period; when adjusted for inflation, the real increase was 1%. Broken down further, however, the figures show greater divergence in the respective share of per capita revenues from property taxes: Westminster suffered a decrease of 36%, while

Newport Beach showed a startling increase of 60%, even after inflation was taken into account. One possible explanation is that there was about twice as much building activity and property turnover in Newport Beach as in Westminster, swelling the property tax rolls in Newport Beach.

But even for the hardest hit, there were some things that didn't change. At the same time that they were ordering deep cuts in public services and administrative spending, lawmakers continued to preserve many of the traditional government "perks." County supervisors in Los Angeles, who have been struggling with huge budget deficits for the last several years, are still driven to work in chauffeured cars. State lawmakers still get a $350 weekly tax-free expense allowance during legislative sessions in addition to their salaries as well as tax-paid gasoline credit cards. And in Oakland, where cuts have been among the most brutal, the City Council voted to increase its elected members' automobile allowances at about the same time they were mailing notices threatening to lay off mnore than 1,000 employees. "There are some things you just can't justify," said Douglas W. Ayres, the former Inglewood city manager who now runs his own government consulting firm.

Proposition 13 left other inconsistences in the ways individual communities coped. Santa Clara County, for example, seat of the famed Silicon Valley with its strong business climate, should be among the Proposition 13 success stories. Nonetheless, it has faced huge budget deficits each year since Proposition 13 and was recently forced to begin cutting police protection. Now voters may be asked to approve a special levy so that the county can solve a severe jail overcrowding problem that has forced the courts to approve early releases for many inmates. Meanwhile, San Francisco, which was heavily dependent on property taxes and has large pockets of poor residents, appears to be doing fine. As a result of the decision to raise business taxes under a controversial Supreme Court interpretation of Proposition 13, the city's treasury is so full that at least one county supervisor has pushed to refund $150 million to taxpayers. In fact, in 1981 and 1982 alone, the state controller reported that four cities and three counties, including San Diego County, took the unprecedented step of rolling back their tax rates by nearly $15 million. In part, the unusual giveback occurred because they were collecting more money than allowed under the tax-cutting measures that placed a ceiling on how much money government could spend. However, more than $6 million of those rollbacks were purely voluntary.

—LW, TG, KL, JAP

3

The Public Services

Cutbacks in public financing can be measured in a variety of ways. As well as surveying cities and counties, The Times sought to examine the impact on specific areas of public spending. The state's tax revolt has, in many cases, started to change either the basic services being offered or the way in which institutions offering those services will finance their work. But in some cases, institutions reported that it was not Proposition 13, but other factors coincidental to the tax revolt, that are more responsible. Reporters used Times surveys of a sampling of special districts and of school districts, state controller's reports and other county, state and federal documents as a basis for visiting institutions, officials and consumers around the state.

COMMUNITY COLLEGES

The "open door" that community colleges have provided for Californians seeking public higher education no longer stands wide open. Proposition 13, compounded by several years of lean budgets, is forcing the nation's only remaining tuition-free community college system to abandon the "college-for-everybody" approach that flourished for at least a decade.

After growing steadily, sometimes explosively, since the end of World War II, many community colleges face retrenchment that has meant a loss of educational programs and faculty layoffs. Class sizes have grown larger, along with faculty teaching loads. Badly needed repairs have been postponed. For the first time, students face the possibility of tuition. As dollars grow scarce, the emphasis has shifted to traditional students who are taking a year or two of introductory courses before transferring to a four-year college or university, or who seek either two-year "associate in arts" degrees or vocational certificates of various kinds.

The so-called "casual student" who takes a course or two at the local community college to satisfy some intellectual curiosity or avocational interest, is fading. "The 'lifelong-learning' concept that you heard so much about a few years ago is fast disappearing," said Richard Moore, president of Santa Monica College. "We are leaving behind the grand scheme that education is for all people at all times, and we're returning to the old notion that college is a vaccination, a one-time fix that is supposed to last a lifetime." Some "continuing-education" programs have been retained on a pay-as-you-go basis, but many have been abandoned. There is also less emphasis on remedial instruction, even though large numbers of students arrive on community college campuses ill-prepared in basic learning skills.

These changes in educational philosophy—away from continuing education and remedial classes—did not result from public discussion and decision, nor even as a calculated policy of any governor or any Legislature, but, rather, as the inevitable result of continuing budget cutbacks. Proposition 13 was fundamental to the change because it shifted the basis of community college financing from the local property tax to the state general fund. Power went with the money. Middle-level officials in the legislative analyst's office, the Department of Finance and other state agencies decided that the activities and aspirations of the two-year colleges had to be trimmed back, even as money proportionately grew for the University of California and the California State University. Patrick M. Callan, director of the California Postsecondary Education Commission, said the reasons were varied: Because they had been dependent on property taxes, community colleges had not been as dependent on state revenue; they have remained "free" institutions, unable to raise fees, as the four-year colleges have done; state officials may be less willing to support recreational and personal development courses than local trustees.

Since they had not depended on state money, lobbying for community colleges may lag behind efforts on behalf of the UC and Cal State systems. "Like the auto industry, we are going through a 'down-sizing' process," said Leslie Koltai, chancellor of the nine-campus Los Angeles Community College district, by far the state's largest. "I applaud the change. The adult education, the continuing education, was taking a tremendous amount of effort away from the basic task of the colleges." The state general fund now provides about 75% of general financial support, while in the past, about two-thirds of the funds came from local taxes, especially the property tax. This year, well over $1 billion in state dollars are going to the two-year colleges, the fifth-largest item in the state budget.

Over the last five years, state and local tax support per community college student has declined by more than 20%, measured in constant dollars, according to a report prepared by the California Postsecondary Education Commission. At least half the state's 70 community college districts face potential deficits in the coming school year, and a dozen are "on the brink of insolvency," according to Gerald C. Hayward, statewide chancellor of the loose-knit community college system. Statewide, thousands of students were turned away from overcrowded classes this spring. Most of the colleges could double enrollments in such vocationally oriented subjects as computer science, data processing and electronics if they had space in which to offer the classes and instructors to teach them.

All of this is new for most community colleges, which flourished in relative affluence and anonymity until well into the 1970s. The state now has 106 community colleges in 70 districts, from Siskiyou County to San Diego. Total enrollment reached 1.4 million this year. Of these, about 300,000 are full-time students taking courses for credit (that is, carrying 12 units or more). More than 950,000 are part-time credit students, while another 175,000 are enrolled in non-credit courses.

Some community colleges have been criticized for building fancy or unnecessary campuses, for hiring too many administrators and for paying them too much money, for over-aggressive recruitment of students and for duplicating expensive educa-

Paying for Community Colleges

Proposition 13 forced a shift in the source of revenues to pay for California's community colleges from the property tax to state funds.

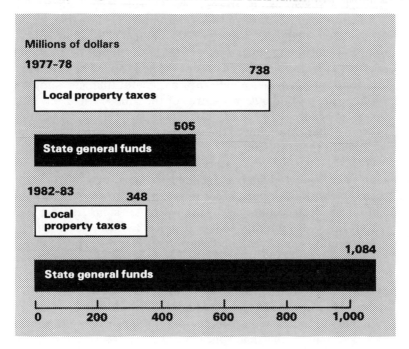

Millions of dollars

1977–78

Local property taxes	738
State general funds	505

1982–83

Local property taxes	348
State general funds	1,084

0   200   400   600   800   1,000

tional programs that were available at other nearby colleges. But for the most part, the local two-year colleges received strong support for their various missions of preparing students to transfer to four-year institutions, for vocational training or for an occasional course in archery or Shakespeare.

Some educators now say that they began to realize in the early 1970s that the bubble would burst, but the first clear evidence was an enrollment ceiling imposed by former Gov. Edmund G. Brown Jr. in fiscal 1976, during his first term as governor. The ceiling was removed the following year, but it proved to be a harbinger of things to come after voters approved Proposition 13. In fiscal 1978, the last school year before the effects of Proposition 13 were felt, community colleges received $738 million from property taxes and $463 million from the state. The next year this was reversed; the colleges received $785 million from the state and $331 million in local property taxes. Despite the state "bail-out" money that went to local governments in 1978-79, the first year after the passage of Proposition 13, funds for community colleges fell by 7% and enrollment dropped 12%. In fiscal 1981, the state fell about $50 million short of financing that year's enrollment growth. State officials blamed the community colleges for exceeding the enrollment limits contained in that year's financing bill, but college officials say that they were never told that such enrollment limits existed. Since 1979, the state has been pursuing a policy of "incremental funding," which means providing only two-thirds of the full rate for enrollment beyond the level of the previous year.

All of these steps were efforts to control what some state officials considered to be out-of-control community college spending. In the current school year, the state delivered three blows— no money for enrollment growth, none for a cost-of-living increase and a $30-million cut in avocational and personal development classes. For many years, some community colleges, responding to local wishes, had added such educationally questionable courses as belly dancing, pet care, toilet training and, a special target for former Governor Brown, "Macrame for Mama." Now these have been eliminated or have been placed in the "community services" category, where student fees support the full cost. The $30-million "hit list," as it has come to be called, struck especially hard at physical education, fine arts, home economics and real estate.

Some districts were more seriously affected than others.

■ The Coast Community College District, in Orange County, took a devastating $4.4-million budget cut, losing 162 courses and 300 class sections to the "hit list." This is a major factor in the district's financial problems, which have resulted in 93 layoff notices being sent to instructors, counselors and librarians at the district's three colleges—Orange Coast, Golden West and Coastline. Only 19 of those positions have been restored because of unexpected savings from a new early retirement plan.

■ Perhaps the hardest hit campus is Compton, which had to negotiate an extraordinary $750,000 loan from the state this year to balance its $11-million operating budget. Cuts were made in all phases of the heavily minority college's operations. Last year, 113 part-time faculty members were dismissed. Off-campus centers in Lynwood, Paramount and Willowbrook have been closed. Several roofs are leaking but will not be fixed because the district cannot come up with $100,000 to match a state contribution. Compton President Abell Sykes said the college probably will be unable to repay its state loan in the planned three-year period because an unexpected enrollment slump of several hundred students this year has cost the college more than $300,000.

■ In the tiny Barstow Community College district, several years of inept business management compounded troubles created by Proposition 13 and economic recession and, in early 1981, produced a deficit of $778,000 in an operating budget of $3.5 million. As a result, all salaries were slashed 12%. Part-time instructors were dropped and full-time faculty taught summer classes for nothing. Drama, intercollegiate athletics and field trips were eliminated and the college kept only one outside telephone line. These steps, plus a $500,000 loan from the state, enabled Barstow to balance its budget this year, but the situation remains precarious.

■ The huge Los Angeles district used $17 million in special construction funds to balance this year's budget. Facing a potential $28.6-million deficit next year, Los Angeles has instituted a hiring freeze and has offered special retirement incentives to teaching and non-teaching personnel. District trustees also are considering a 10% pay cut for all employees, forced work furloughs of 10 or 15 days, elimination or consolidation of academic programs and some administrative services, and a change from a two-semester to a trimester academic calendar. The calendar change would mean elimination of many part-time faculty positions and heavier use of regular faculty in the summer, for an estimated savings of $7 million next year.

Some districts moved quickly to offset the effects of Proposition 13 by imposing tight spending controls, but other districts did little, apparently hoping that the state would solve any problems that arose. At Pasadena City College, for example, the administration and board of trustees did little for four years. Now, facing an estimated $3.8-million deficit in next year's budget, they have sent layoff notices to 28 faculty members, librarians and counselors. Included were eight of the 30 instructors in the college's highly-regarded nursing program, as well as one out of six professional librarians. The college also eliminated 57 non-teaching positions and is still $800,000 short of making up its deficit.Why did the governing board wait so long? "I wish I knew," replied interim President Stuart E. Marsee, who has been in office only since February. "The trustees hopefully, wishfully, were hoping something would happen in state finance to alleviate the need for drastic measures . . . They should have acted five years ago."

Some budget decisions have been educationally unsound, administrators agree. Asked about the decision to eliminate the librarian, Steven A. Cerra, vice president for instruction at Pasadena City College and the man who ordered the cut, said, "None of this makes sense. We'll have a shell of a library, but it was done because libraries don't generate income." At Compton, President Sykes decided to remove faculty members from electronics and add them in remedial math, even though the loss of the electronics instructors means that students no longer can complete the program in the customary four semesters. "That was a very poor educational decision," Sykes said, "but I was forced to do it because we generate more ADA (average daily attendance, the measure that determines state payments) from remedial math than from electronics."

Some districts have been able to ride out the storm so far because they had accumulated substantial financial reserves before the passage of Proposition 13, but these reserves are fast dwindling. Only one community college district in the state—oil-rich West Kern, home of tiny Taft College, generates so much money from local property tax support that it requires no state assistance.

For those districts looking to the state, prospects for next year look no better. Gov. George Deukmejian's proposed 1984 com-

munity college budget once again includes no new money for enrollment growth or for a cost-of-living increases. In fact, the governor has proposed a cut of about $140 million in community col-
lege spending next year and has recommended that the colleges
make up $109 million of that by charging a tuition fee of $50 per
semester for students who take at least six units and $30 for those
who take fewer. Both the state Assembly and Senate so far have
rejected the idea of tuition. Even if the legislative budget includes substantial increases in community college funds, Deukmejian may well blue pencil the increase out of the final budget.
This would create the nightmare that many community college
officials fear—the governor's $140-million cut and no tuition in-
come to make it up. Should that happen, the budget cutting that
has taken place in most community colleges so far will seem like
child's play.

—WT

FOUR-YEAR COLLEGES AND UNIVERSITIES

By most standards, California's four-year public colleges and
universities have survived the state's tax revolt of the 1970s in
enviable shape. Campuses have not been shut, there has been no
mass layoff of professors, no dismantling of the state's dazzingly
array of teaching and research programs. Yet the 130,000 employees and 460,000 students at the University of California and
the California State University have seen worsening work conditions, declining pay and sharply rising fees as a result of the slowdown in government spending begun by Proposition 13.

UC and the Cal State systems show fewer direct effects than
community colleges or elementary and secondary public education because they have never depended on property tax revenue
for their support and did not suffer from the shift in financing
that followed Proposition 13. In fact, both are receiving a slightly
higher share of state funds. Nevertheless, there have been cutbacks in state funds and the effects are evident on any of the nine
campuses of the UC system or the 19 Cal State system campuses:
In many classrooms, paint is peeling, dormitories often are dirty
and cluttered, elevators are on the blink. Roofs need repair and
laboratory equipment is outdated.

Faculty salaries at UC and in the Cal State system, once among the most competitive in the nation, are keeping pace neither with inflation nor with pay scales at universities outside California. The latest survey by the independent California Postsecondary Education Commission shows that faculty pay at UC is running 9.4% behind that of other comparable public and private institutions in the United States and will drop more than 18.5% behind if substantial raises are not included in next year's state budget. At Cal State campuses, pay is now lagging by 2.4% and is projected to fall 9.2% behind.

While California is generally considered to be a tuition-free state, students do pay substantial fees. Those fees have been rising at a faster rate in the last five years than in most states. Between fiscal 1978 and 1983, student charges at UC grew from $710 to $1,294, a rise of 82%. At Cal State universities, fees climbed from $194 to $505, a whopping 160% jump. This year, for the first time, UC's $1,194 fee exceeded the national average of $979, according to a recent study by the College Scholarship Service. California has been unique, according to Patrick M. Callan, director of the California Postsecondary Education Commission, in increasing fees at the same time that it has cut state student aid from a high of $113 million in fiscal 1982 to a low this year of $105 million.

Despite warnings that it has been slipping in its support for higher education, California continues to rank 11th among states in per-capita spending for institutions of higher education, according to the U.S. Bureau of Census. A study by Security Pacific National Bank shows that, in the share of personal wealth it devotes to higher education, California was 21% above the norm in fiscal 1981, down from 35% above the norm in 1978.

And, the universities' budgets have grown throughout the tax revolt. Over the last five years, UC's budget increased 56%, from $737.5 million to $1.148 billion, while Cal State's rose 39%, from $666 million to $929 million. In the case of UC, the growth has been greater than the 52% rise in the Higher Education Price Index, the university's measure of how much inflation has eroded spending. Still, the 11% increase in spending for UC between fiscal 1981 and 1982 compares to a 13% increase for the University of Michigan, 18% for the University of Maryland, 40% for the University of Texas. In the Cal State system, appropriations growth varied from campus to campus, with a high of 19% at San Bernardino campus to a low of 4% at Cal State, Los Angeles. Comparable institutions in other states include the Texas State University system, which grew 20%; North Carolina State, which rose 23%, and Florida State University, which jumped 28%.

Predictions that the universities would lose ground to local school districts and community colleges for their share of state dollars simply have not come true. In fiscal 1969, before Proposition 13, UC got 3.4% of the state's general-fund and property-tax revenues. In fiscal 1983, that figure had risen to 3.9%. During the same period, Cal State's share rose from 2.8% to 3.1%. By contrast, the share of dollars to community colleges dropped from 5.3% to 4.9%. Part of this rise is a result of a growth in enrollment, although such growth has been limited in recent years. At UC, enrollment has risen 9% since 1977, from 126,500 to nearly 139,000 this year. At Cal State, the head count has increased about 2%, from more than 312,000 to nearly 320,000.

Most of these colleges had their biggest growth spurt between the late 1950s and the early 1970s, when hundreds of new dormitories, classroom buildings and laboratories were erected. Now, 20 years or so later, those structures are due for repair and renovation—at a time when money for such projects is unavailable. UC officials have put a $4-billion price tag above current spending on building and maintenance needs. Some estimates are more conservative, but there is agreement among analysts that the university will require, over the next decade, at least $1.6 billion more in capital outlays than it now has. Cal State system officials estimate that meeting the university's most pressing maintenance problems would require an immediate investment of somewhere between $30 and $45 million.

Changes in certain disciplines and shifts in student interest also have put new and unexpected pressure on the universities. In biology, for example, new discoveries and techniques in genetic engineering have meant a revolution in research, which, in turn, will mean substantial investment in costly new equipment. Students also have been changing what they study, according to a recent study by the California Postsecondary Education Commission. Students are moving from what, for universities, are relatively inexpensive programs—such as literature and education—and into high technology and business fields—such as engineering, computer science and management sciences—fields considered more costly to operate. In the field of business, the situation has become so urgent that two of the largest Cal State campuses—Cal State Long Beach and San Jose State—are threatened with losing their accreditation if they do not hire more faculty and improve programs within the next 12 to 18 months.

Since the Reagan Administration took office, federal aid also began to drop, putting yet another pressure on the universities. UC, which is heavily dependent on federal support for research, saw a $19-million drop in its $500-million federal budget in 1981-82, the latest year for which data are available. For the first time in three decades, there has also been a drop—about 9% between 1979-80 and 1982-83—in federal student-aid programs for low- and middle-income families who could not otherwise afford college costs.

In an effort to accommodate the slowed growth and the mounting pressure on their budgets, the universities have made substantial cuts in a few programs and numerous small ones in many others. At UC, reductions being phased in have been made primarily in the health sciences. Enrollment of medical students has been cut by 5% and dental students by 10%. In addition, the univeristy has cut 1,100 graduate students because of past over-enrollment that the Legislature would not finance. Those cuts have allowed the university to reduce teaching faculty. Typically, faculty and staff have not been laid off but have declined as a result of attrition. Students have been shut out of popular courses, in some cases delaying their graduation by as much as a semester or two. Travel to scholarly meetings and scientific conferences has been cut or eliminated.

"It's hard to say what are the major effects," said Anthony Moye, Cal State's assistant vice chancellor for education programs and resources. "What's happened since Proposition 13? It's been a slow deceleration. You go to get a pencil and it's not

there. The rooms aren't as clean because they don't have enough
people to clean them up. The equipment breaks down more often
and it takes longer to repair it. You don't get a raise this year but
your utility bill goes up. You don't get a raise next year but your
telephone bill goes up. Students are paying more and they're getting less. They're getting frustrated. There is a morale problem
that's developed among faculty. One of the problems that has
happened each year is that people have said it will turn around
next year. But it has not turned around . . . . "

—AR

PUBLIC SCHOOLS

The popular notion is that Proposition 13 devastated public
education in California after 1978. It is not so. In fact, California's level of spending for public schools has been sinking for
decades. Moreover, the most recent money crunch has as much to
do with declining enrollments, the state Supreme Court Serrano
ruling and the severe recession as it does with Proposition 13.

But whatever the cause, school spending has gone down so long
and so far that the programs and services once considered a vital
and necessary part of an education for previous generations of
California children are now fast disappearing. Since 1929, the
federal government has been collecting data on how much the
states spend on public education. Through the 1930s, the '40s
and into the '50s, the ranking of states typically read like this:
New York, California and New Jersey. For example, in 1940, California spent $142 per child, second to New York and far above
the national average of $88. But in the decades that followed,
California's ranking slipped steadily. By 1970, there were 14
states that spent more on public education per child than did
California, and in 1980, for the first time, California slipped below the national average.

"There has been a long and dramatic drop. It began well before
Proposition 13, but it has been even sharper since then," said
Gerald Kissler, vice provost for planning at UCLA who has ex-
amined California's school financing. "We were once considered
a leader in public education, but we're certainly not anymore."
School administrators and teachers union leaders typically refer

to any and all reductions in spending as "devastating" and "disastrous." And they have done so for so long and so often that they are regularly tuned out by those not directly affected. But the story of the tax revolt's effect on the schools is not one of sudden, devastating and disastrous spending cuts. Rather, it is one of years of squeezing, trimming and cutting corners: dropping elective classes ranging from dance to calculus; eliminating summer school for all but remedial students; not replacing worn-out typewriters or lab equipment; laying off counselors, nurses and attendance officers; deferring the maintenance and repair of school buildings; holding on to outdated textbooks, and holding down the pay of teachers and principals.

Whether the schools are in an affluent neighborhood such as San Marino or Palos Verdes or a more working-class community such as Montebello or Paramount, school officials can quickly tick off a long and nearly identical list of cutbacks. But as Hugh Cameron, superintendent of the South Bay Union High School District in Redondo Beach, noted: "You could drive by here every day and things would look pretty much the same. The kids still go to school for 175 days and leave here and go on to do well in college or in a job. But if you're here, you know how much it has changed. Education is a service industry, and we just can't offer the same level and quality of service we once did."

Still, while the decline in service is evident, it is less clear how much Proposition 13 is to blame. School enrollments have generally declined for the last decade, and state funds for local schools are sent out on the basis of the number of students. "If you had six children in your house and one graduated and left home, your costs wouldn't go down by one-sixth," said James Pierchala, financial analyst for the Los Angeles County Schools Office, but if you were a school district, your funds would decline by one-sixth. Besides the fixed costs of keeping open the buildings, schools must lay off the least-senior and lowest-paid teachers when enrollments fall, leaving behind a higher-cost work force.

In 1972, the Legislature established revenue limits, or caps on spending, for each school district in the state. Two years later, the Serrano ruling seeking to equalize spending said school boards and local communities could not spend more than their per-child limit. Property-tax collections soared through the mid-1970s, setting off the tax-cutting furor, but ironically, schools were not allowed to use the extra property tax money. Any amount collected above the district's spending cap was off-set by cuts in aid from Sacramento. School finance experts say the spending caps and the enrollment decline, followed by the severe recession and its shrinking of state revenues, did more than Proposition 13 to squeeze school spending. In any case, it has been squeezed. In the 1982-83 school year, a typical school had 7% less to spend in constant dollars for its regular program than it had in 1978, according to a Times survey of school districts. The Cal-Tax Assn., a nonprofit business-supported research group in Sacramento, calculates that schools lost 12% in constant dollars if only "general purpose" school aid is counted. And, school officials note, even if the funds per pupil had stayed even, they would have had to make cuts because of the higher per-student costs brought on by shrinking enrollments.

In the fiscal 1977 school year, before the tax-cutting measure, the Los Angeles schools had $1,372 for each enrolled student. In this school year just ending, city schools will spend an estimated $1,942 per student. But to have kept up with inflation over those six years, Los Angeles schools would have needed $1,999 per child. This means, for every classroom of 30 children, the school district has $1,710 less than it had in 1977.

How poor are California's public schools compared with those of other states? They do not rank 50th and never have. In its most recent rankings, the National Education Assn. said California stood in 31st place among the states in its "current expenditures for public elementary and secondary schools per pupil." In the 1982-83 school year, California's schools spent an estimated $2,727 in total per child, significantly below the national average of $2,952. At the top of the list are Alaska, New York, New Jersey, the District of Columbia, Delaware, Oregon, Rhode Island, Minnesota and Michigan. California's per-pupil spending places it with Indiana, Louisiana and West Virginia. In fiscal 1978, California ranked 22nd among the states in spending per pupil.

The education association research office also calculates how a state's spending for public education compares to its personal income. California's per-capita income is high, in fourth place among the states in 1980. Its school spending is slightly below average. In September, 1982, the California Department of Education, using incomplete numbers, estimated that the state had fallen to 50th place among the 51 jurisdictions of states and the District of Columbia in the percentage of its personal income devoted to the public schools. In fact, the education association said last month that California actually ranked 44th. This state spends an estimated 3.72% of its personal income on public education, kindergarten to 12th grade, as compared to a national average of 4.20%. In fiscal 1978, California ranked 45th by this measure. States that spend the most and the least are more difficult to predict. Some wealthy states, such as New York, Michigan and Minnesota, also rank high on this measure. Other industrial and reasonably wealthy states rank near the bottom with California, including Texas, Florida, Ohio and Connecticut. Over a 10-year span, from 1973 to 1983, California's spending per pupil rose 160%, less than the national average of 187%. When the states are ranked on how much they have increased school funding over the decade, California again sits in the 45th spot.

California does rank near the top of several education association charts—on average teacher salaries and in class sizes. In 1982-83, the state's teachers had an average salary of $23,935, sixth-best among the states. The national average was $20,603, according to the association. This rank has changed little, since California teachers ranked fifth in 1977-78 in their average salary. But that advantage is somewhat nullified by the fact that the state has the second-highest pupil-teacher ratio. In 1982, California had 23.1 children per teacher, well above the national average of 17.1. Only Utah had a higher ratio. Almost all classes are larger than this and typically include from 28 to 32 children. But special teachers—for example, those serving handicapped children or a music teacher who moves among several classes and schools—bring down the ratio. Although teachers' salaries have inched upward in the last decade, their purchasing power is down 16% from 1974, according to figures compiled by the legislative analyst and Cal-Tax.

The one area of real growth in the last decade has been in the "categorical" or special purpose programs—in particular, special education for handicapped children, compensatory education for low-achieving children, bilingual education and the School Improvement Program put together by former state School Supt. Wilson Riles. While total school spending per child in constant dollars was about level for the last decade, the categorical financing rose 113% in constant dollars from 1974 to 1983. Much of this increase stemmed from the federal government, which in 1975 required states to guarantee a "free appropriate public education" to all children with mental and physical handicaps. Since then, Cal-Tax Research calculates that state spending for special education nearly quadrupled, from about $180 million in 1974 to $727 million in 1983. Riles was a strong advocate for the special programs and succeeded during the mid-1970s in boosting their budgets. "Despite all crying and screaming, we did pretty well for several years in the mid-1970s," said Dick Caldwell, budget director for the Los Angeles school district.

But the categorical programs were envisioned as an addition to the regular education program. However, as funds have grown tighter, they have instead, in some cases, taken money away from the basic program. "They (legislators) pass all these mandates (such as special education for the handicapped and bilingual education for non-English-speaking children), but they don't fully fund them," said Paramount School Supt. Richard Caldwell. "Because of Proposition 13, we can't do anything to increase our revenue, but we still have to provide all these programs." As a result, California schools have been regularly forced to drop music and art teachers—because they are paid for from the general fund—while classrooms are well-stocked with a variety of teachers' aides and "resource teachers" who are paid for through special funds for bilingual education or special education of the handicapped.

Since 1974, the number of classified school employees, including teachers' aides, rose 37%, and the number of administrators went up 10%, according to Cal-Tax Research. But the number of regular teachers dropped 14% in those nine years—all during a time when enrollment dropped by 9%. The Little Hoover Commission, among others, has denounced the sharp growth in class-

room aides and program coordinators during a decade of declining enrollments. But local school officials are not permitted under state and federal law to use the special-purpose money for
the regular instructional program.

How have schools responded to Proposition 13 and the shrinking of revenues? By cutting around the edges.The Los Angeles
school system had a list of budget cuts made since Proposition 13
that runs, single spaced, for six pages. But most involve reducing
various formulas—for example, in the number of new books per
student or the number of custodians per school. "We always try
to cut as far away from the classroom as possible," said the Los
Angeles schools' budget director, a statement echoed by school
officials around the state. But they also note that trimming and
cutting around the edges can be done only for a year or two before
it starts to hurt the basic program. For example, how essential is
a school nurse? Or a guidance counselor? Or a school librarian?
Or a music and art teacher?

In The Times' survey of school districts, 74% said they had
reduced their staffs of counselors, nurses and psychologists.
Some districts have eliminated counselors. "We still have them.
But our ratio is 480 students per counselors. Can you imagine
trying to advise, even learn the names of, 480 kids?" asked Hugh
Cameron, superintendent of the South Bay High School District.
About 60% of the districts in The Times' survey said they had
reduced their spending on books, and 44% had cut back the
number of librarians. If the hallways are dirtier and the paint
chipping, it may be because 82% of the districts have reduced
their custodial staffs and dropped some regular cleaning of
schools and schoolyards. Another 85% said they had to put off
major maintenance or repairs.

Schools also have begun charging fees for various services that
had been free. "If you want a towel to dry yourself after gym
class, you bring one from home. If you need an apron in chemistry class, you bring one from home. Where we used to take kids
on field trips, we now do it after school and charge them. And if
you want to go to summer school, you pay for the classes," Cameron said. In The Times' survey, 46% of the districts said they
had begun charging fees for adult and recreational courses, 27%

said they charged students for extracurricular activities, including sports, and 18% said they had begun charging for transporting students. But the activity fees were declared unconstitutional last year by a Superior Court in Los Angeles, a case now on appeal before the California Supreme Court.

Sometimes the changes can be seen more easily by looking at a single school. Franklin High School in Highland Park is not the best or the worst in Los Angeles. Among city high schools, it differs little from the norm, except in one respect—Principal Morton Tenner has been at the school for 15 years, longer than any other city high school principal and long enough to observe great change. In the last five years, he has seen maintenance deferred, classes jammed into tiny rooms, morale among teachers fallen, and academic and elective courses eliminated. "For me, the worst impact of Proposition 13 was the loss of our academic summer program. We had a fantastic thing going—our kids came and took chemistry or algebra or a foreign language during the summer," Tenner said.

About two-thirds of the students went to summer school before Proposition 13 forced the school district to end it, he said. Now, only students who have failed a required course or the district's proficiency test may enroll. Don Palus, a chemistry and biology teacher at Franklin for 22 years, said the summer program had offered the best students tough courses. "For teaching chemistry, it was great. You went four hours, from 8:30 to 12:30. It gave the kids time to set up an experiment, write it up and we could talk about it," and that cannot be done in the standard 50-minute class, Palus said. Summer school now is "for the kids who goof off all year round and come to summer school to get a D so they can graduate," Palus said. "We've really punished the academically motivated students, the ones who are here to learn."

Among the courses dropped because of the loss of the sixth period in city high schools: modern English literature, speed reading, mythology, international relations, sociology, consumer education, urban ecology, drafting, European history, journalism, drama, commercial art and business education. "People complain that we're not pushing the kids hard enough, but how can we if we don't even have enough money to offer the courses?" Tenner asked. Stanford University Prof. Michael Kirst, who has just completed a study of 26 California high schools, said that the state's schools "lack real depth in their course offerings." Where high schools in other states can offer students advanced classes in math, social studies, foreign languages, science and industrial arts, California's schools have been forced to pare back to the basics, he said.

School facilities are deteriorating and students increasingly are being forced to pay for basic services—services that had been free. "We have about 50 windows that are broken right now. And (district repairmen) are just replacing some now (in early June) that we called in about last August," Tenner said. Elsewhere, there are typewritersthat need repair or replacement and a heating system in need of overhaul. Flowers planted in front of the building and painting of buildings were paid for by students.

In Los Angeles, as in most school districts, administrators sought to avoid direct cuts in the classroom. As a result, Franklin has maintained its student-teacher ratio, at 27 to 1 for 10th grade and 34.5 to 1 for 11th and 12th grades. Still, the most difficult question remains: How closely is quality in education tied to money? Don Palus, whom Tenner regards as "the best chemistry teacher in the city," continues to teach even though he cannot purchase the same quality of lab equipment he once did and even though cancellation of summer school has meant a pay cut of more than 10%. Principals note that it was the loss of summer income that has driven away many young teachers since 1978. Mary Curone, an English teacher at Franklin in her first year of teaching, a graduate of USC, spends a good part of her school day moving between rooms because of a shortage of classroom space. She teaches one class in a small converted room next to the girls' gym and another among stoves and sinks in what had been a home economics room. Despite it all, she says she likes the job, although "trying to teach composition to 39 kids is ridiculous," she said.

At the Vista Unified School District in San Diego County, reduced finances have meant increasingly outdated and worn-out equipment. Biology teacher Paul Bloom and many of his colleagues used his own money to buy magnifying glasses, razor blades and scissors. "We either make do with the broken stuff or we buy our own," Bloom said. "If you're going to do the job right, that means preparing the classroom. If you don't have it, you have to get it from somewhere."

Vista, a district becoming increasingly urban, with 14 schools and about 10,500 students, represents those communities which have seen a new, austere era following years of steady climb in enrollment—the key to higher state financing. By juggling temporary teachers and taking advantage of retirements, the district avoided laying off full-time teachers, but there are no more free buses or new lab equipment, few summer enrichment or remedial courses, no year-round use of school swimming pools. Student field trips are now scarce, student counseling has been pared. Teacher salaries are stagnant, administration jobs have been eliminated and maintenance lags. Supt. Gary Olson said a shortage of laboratory equipment may mean that scientific experiments will be performed before large groups, rather than by individuals. "Instead of having a laboratory approach, maybe we'll have a demonstration approach. Instead of the students learning science, they'll have to learn about science."

—DGS, DMW

PUBLIC SAFETY

If you are contemplating a life of crime, Proposition 13 may have made it safer for you to embezzle from your boss, but riskier to murder your spouse. If you get caught doing either, your chances of going to prison are higher, and don't look to your friendly probation department for help in getting out sooner. And if your neighbor's house catches on fire while you are behind bars, chances may be better that the fire will burn your house as well, depending on where you live. Cutbacks since 1978 have forced most public safety agencies to refocus priorities and to lower goals in some areas so that they can be raised in others.

Here are some of the most important changes:

■ Many police departments no longer investigate a wide range of crimes and have narrowed their efforts to are as where they think they can do the most good. That generally means police now concentrate more on violent crime and offer fewer services in such areas as burglaries, civil disputes and traffic accidents. One result: Overall arrest statistics are down, but arrests for the more serious offenses are up considerably in many jurisdictions.

■ There is a greater danger of fires spreading in some areas, including Los Angeles, because some fire departments have reduced the size of crews aboard pumper trucks from four fire-fighters to three. It takes four men to run two hoses, so the loss of one man means only one hose can be taken into the fire area. The backup hose, frequently used to contain the fire, cannot be deployed, thus increasing the chances of the fire spreading.

■ Efforts to rehabilitate felons after they have been returned to the streets have been severely limited through major cuts in county probation departments, the most heavily hit area in the criminal justice system. But while that sounds like a major change, there is serious debate over whether those costly efforts ever did much good anyway.

■ Prosecuting agencies have been forced to reduce their efforts in such areas as white-collar crime and consumer affairs so they can muster enough staff to go after violent offenders.

■ One area cut the most is research. Thus, at a time when agencies need to refine and streamline programs, they have lost the means of determining which are most effective.

■ Most prosecutors are forced to carry a heavier workload than most public defenders now, meaning that the publicly paid lawyers who are trying to keep defendants out of prison now have more time to devote to their efforts than do the lawyers who are trying to put them away. In Los Angeles County this year, the cost to the taxpayers for public defenders will surpass the cost for prosecutors from the district attorney's office for the first time. That change is the result of legal requirements that any criminal defendant who needs an attorney but cannot afford one must be furnished legal counsel at taxpayer expense. State law also requires the public defender to reject cases if he believes his attorneys cannot handle the additional workload. The court then must appoint private counsel, at taxpayer expense, and that is far more expensive than counsel furnished by the public defender's office.

This has come about, in varying degrees around the state, despite the fact that public safety agencies have fared far better than most other sectors of government. They did well partly because of strong anti-crime sentiment and partly because legislation stemming from Proposition 13 required a "maintenance of effort" in public safety. Nobody was quite sure what "maintenance of effort" meant: Some thought it prohibited any cuts, while others argued that it gave local officials authority to determine what constituted appropriate "effort."

Figures compiled by the state controller show that cities continued to increase police department budgets after Proposition 13, although much of that increase was eaten up by the rising costs of pensions. Excluding San Francisco and Los Angeles, which changed accounting procedures, the figures show an increase in real dollars statewide of slightly more than 12% for the three-year period ending June 30, 1981. Although the actual budget for the Los Angeles Police Department has increased nearly $90 million since Proposition 13, the purchasing power of the fiscal 1983 budget is from $10 million to $28 million less than the fiscal 1978 budget, depending on which adjustment is used for inflation. When population growth is factored in, many departments have lost budgetary ground. Nearly 64% of police departments responding to a Times survey reported a decrease in manpower in relation to population, and about a quarter said the decrease was more than 10%.

Since the crime rate also grew since 1978, big adjustments were necessary to meet the fundamental goals of the agencies. Cuts in one department sometimes had an effect on other departments because the criminal justice system consists of a series of interrelated agencies that depend on mutual support. As one prosecutor put it, "We are only as good in court as the evidence we have." And the quality of the evidence depends largely upon the quality of the police department.

Prosecutors and judges who handle criminal cases say that all too often today, the cases just are not as well prepared as they should be. "We have seen a gradual reduction in the quality of police investigations," said James A. Bascue, chief deputy district attorney for Los Angeles County, who thinks this is the most serious result of Proposition 13. Judge Ronald M. George, president of the California Judges Assn., said he sees "some evidence" that police work has suffered. "Sometimes they lack the basic supplies to do the job," said George, supervising judge of the criminal division of Los Angeles Superior Court. "Sometimes, they don't even have enough film to take pictures of all those arrested for drunk driving."

Many legal experts believe that even a slight decline in the quality of police work may end up costing the taxpayers a bundle. If a case is well prepared, the defendant may plead guilty, thus saving the cost of the trial. Conversely, even slightly flawed police work may lead a defendant to fight the case at much greater cost to the taxpayer. And the risk of flaws has increased because the workload for most officers has jumped dramatically, according to The Times' survey. More than half of the departments surveyed said calls for assistance had increased by more than 10% and, in many cases, the increase was substantial. Similarly, of the 86 departments participating in the survey, 59% reported more than a 10% increase in the number of arrests per officer.

Nearly all departments have delayed replacing equipment. In 1977, the Los Angeles Police Department's average patrol car was retired at 88,660 miles. By 1981, the average mileage at salvage was 115,126. Because of required time for maintenance, vehicle availability dropped from 95.1% to 90.9%. The Times' survey showed that many jurisdictions have eliminated services, including community relations programs and some anti-crime projects. Hardest hit have been juvenile delinquency prevention programs with 60% of the agencies reporting reductions and 20% eliminating the programs entirely. The other 20% never had them.

A significant development has been the almost universally reported trend toward "prioritization," meaning police departments now try to do the most important things first. As the priority declines, so does the effort. Many agencies around the state say they have eliminated investigations into "cold crimes"—crimes no longer in progress, such as past burglaries—and non-injury accidents. Newport Beach summed up the new philosophy in stating that it no longer investigates "routine reports of minor crimes not in progress and for which no physical evidence is apparent."

Police departments never were very successful at solving such crimes. But they were able to convince victims that they were trying to help. Statistics show that the length of time it takes an officer to reach the scene of a current crime has a direct effect on his success in building a case. If he can get there in time, he will find more witnesses with fresher perceptions, the evidence will be less tainted, and he may even nab the criminal in the act. The fact that response time will suffer if police departments try to answer every call is shown by the experience in Santa Barbara. That city has "dispatched officers on every call received for the last three years," according to The Times' survey, and that has had an effect on response time. In fiscal 1980, Santa Barbara's response time was 5.2 minutes. But by 1981-82, the city's efforts to deal with every call had lengthened response time to 7.3 minutes. Law enforcement officials regard an increase of more than a few seconds as serious. The San Diego County Sheriff's Department said that because of financial cutbacks, its average response time in unincorporated areas now is 9.2 minutes, an increase from 8.6 minutes in 1981-82.

Now, many police agencies are deliberately making a quick response only to the most serious crimes. About 47% of the departments in The Times' survey said they had changed their dispatching policy. And they are focusing most investigative resources on these crimes. In 1980, for example, the Los Angeles Police Department eliminated follow-up investigations on crime reports where there were no apparent leads. "We are putting the resources we have into major crimes—the ones that are more solvable," said Los Angeles Deputy Chief Barry Wade.

That, in turn, has led to a declining arrest rate for the lesser offenses and a rising arrest rate for the more serious crimes. And that sword cuts two ways, according to Wade. "It has prevented us from keeping up with the increase in (overall) crime," Wade said. "There is less of a deterrent now . . . a lot of burglars aren't going to jail. Crime pays and the government does not have the money to take some of the profit out of it."

However, this concentration of resources has enabled the

LAPD to enhance its performance in the areas that pose the greatest threat to public safety. There were 5.62% fewer sworn personnel actually deployed at the LAPD in 1982 than in 1977, although both the crime rate and the population increased significantly during that period. Like most departments, the LAPD absorbed some of the cut in its higher ranks. Staff officers of the rank of commander and above decreased 38% from 1977 to 1982, dropping from 37 to 23. Detectives dropped 4% and officers declined 5%. Nevertheless, adult arrests by LAPD officers for so-called Part 1 crimes—the most serious—increased 30% between 1977 and 1982, climbing from 29,906 to 38,928. But all other adult arrests decreased by 31% for the same period, dropping from 178,071 in 1977 to 123,717 in 1982.

Here is a more detailed account of how the LAPD, like other departments, has redirected its forces:

■ TRAFFIC ACCIDENTS In 1980, the department stopped investigating non-injury traffic accidents. "As a result, there really is no way to determine who is at fault," Wade said.

■ TELEPHONIC REPORTS The department now takes more crime reports by phone rather than sending officers to the scene. "People believe they aren't getting service and that really hurts our credibility," Wade said. "And once your credibility starts down, people say 'What's the use of calling.' " He also said that "when the public becomes disillusioned," there is less support for the department's budget.

■ REAL LOCATION The department has transferred many officers to areas where the problems seem most pressing. There are now "40 fewer people investigating drug charges," Wade said. "We had to decide the investigation of murder was more important." One result is that there is now "very little enforcement on the small pusher."

■ HELICOPTERS The department reduced its reliance on air support, decreasing flight hours by 25% between 1977 and 1982, due to "personnel cutbacks and anticipated major maintenance for the aging aircraft." Not all law enforcement officials embrace the concept of air support, primarily because of the cost, and Wade concedes that helicopters are expensive. "But I think they are cost-effective," he said.

■ CITIZEN CONTACT "A lot of times now we have to ask the citizen to come in rather than send an officer to the scene," said George Aliano of the Los Angeles Police Protective League. And today, he said, "you can't even spend time with the people. That's very detrimental to the public's perception of law enforcement."

Fire departments, like most police agencies around the state, continued to enjoy expanding budgets, but a growing demand for service, an increase in population and the high rate of inflation hacked away at the increases. According to the state controller figures, expenditures for city fire departments grew 8.7% in real dollars statewide in the three years after Proposition 13, excluding Los Angeles and San Francisco. In The Times' survey, 36% of 143 fire departments said they actually have smaller staffs today than in 1977, but more than 60% report a significant increase in calls for assistance.

If there is a major finding in The Times' survey, it is the unsurprising fact that poorer communities have done poorly, and richer communities have felt little effect. Oakland reported some of the most severe cutbacks. That city closed four fire stations, eliminated four engine companies, one truck company and one battalion and reduced training, administrative and fire prevention inspection staffs. By contrast, when wealthy Newport Beach was asked to "list the three most important actions your organization has taken since 1977-78 to control costs or to cope with limited revenues," it responded: "Not a problem." Most departments around the state, however, reported that they cut back severely on capital improvements, experienced some loss of manpower and expect to use their current equipment for a long, long time.

Donald O. Manning, Los Angeles fire chief, said that although his department's pumper trucks were designed for 60,000 miles, he now expects to overhaul them to boost that mileage to 180,000. Manning said his agency has been reduced by "roughly 300 people," leaving the department with "less people per capita than at any time in the past." Actual daily staffing has dropped from just above 900 in 1977-78 to slightly less than 800 today. Like a number of departments around the state, the Los Angeles Fire Department has absorbed its cuts in manpower partly by reducing the number of firefighters aboard its pumper trucks. That led to an immediate and dramatic jump in "exposure fires"—fires that extend beyond the area of original involvement.

The city had 819 exposure fires in 1977-78. The following year, that number jumped to 1,210, an increase of nearly 50%, where it has remained. Manning said the jump was a direct result of reduced manpower aboard the pumpers. One less firefighter aboard the pumper means one less hose to keep the fire from spreading, he said. Most fire departments have resisted the temptation to reduce manpower aboard pumpers, however.

One major change that many had expected simply has not come to pass. Only a handful of fire departments have consolidated with other agencies, largely because it is so "politically unpopular," according to Rand Corp. analyst Warren E. Walker, who studied public safety effects of Proposition 13.

When the ax began to swing, it took its deepest cuts in county probation departments, the agencies in the criminal justice system charged with the responsibility of helping those who have gone astray to get back on the right track. Although actual budgets are almost impossible to decipher because of the transfer of programs and responsibilities between various agencies, officials acknowledge that county probation departments have been hit the hardest among public safety areas.

Kenneth E. Kirkpatrick, chief of the Los Angeles County Probation Department, has watched his department drop from 4,563 employees in 1975-76 to 3,204 in 1982-83, a decrease of 1,358 for a net loss of just under 30%. That is a staggering cut compared to other agencies in the criminal justice system. One reason for the massive cuts, Kirkpatrick believes, is that "probation simply does not have a public constituency. That is more in the area of beefing up law enforcement."

In addition to supervising felons, the department runs juvenile homes and detention camps. It also provides the pre-sentencing report to help judges determine the sentence for convicted offenders. "Judges now have less information to base the sentence on," said Wilbur Littlefield, Los Angeles County public defender. The reports are "less complete," according to Judge George.

Somebody's past violations might not be detected, but some favorable material that might put the defendant in a better light
might also be omitted. "It can cut both ways," he said. Kirkpatrick points to the fact that detention is a very costly form of cor-
rective therapy. And he notes that while juvenile arrest rates are
down, detention rates are up. That is especially troubling in the
area of juvenile detention, where the "cheapest care is about $58
per day," Kirkpatrick said. "Juvenile Hall is $89 a day as op-
posed to $30 a month to supervise."

Among small cities around the state, the problems were more
acute, and solutions sometimes more unusual. Among the examples were these three:

Faced with steadily declining revenues, Imperial Beach closed
its Police Department after voters refused to approve a special
tax override by the required two-thirds majority. Although the
move was a blow to civic pride, officials decided that the only way
out was to abolish the department and contract with the San
Diego County Sheriff's Department for police services. The result, according to City Manager Sherman Stenberg, is better service at less cost. The contract with the sheriff will cost the city
about $100,000 less in the first year than the city would have
spent to keep its own department. And the city no longer has to
worry about equipment maintenance, training or recruiting.
"They are buying the finished product," said Sheriff's Lt. Lee
Landrum, who has moved into the old police station and, as commander of the Imperial Beach Station, serves, in effect, as the
city's police chief. Landrum said the sheriff fields an average of
nine units, compared with the city department's five. The city
also cut its five-member Fire Department by about 40%, contracting with a private ambulance firm to take over work done by
two paramedics—all at no cost to the city, since the firm received
an exclusive franchise to operate in the city in exchange.

In the Bay Area community of Brisbane, facing cutbacks requiring layoff of six of the 14 members of the Fire Department,
the city trained its police officers to fight fires. Firefighters and
police now belong to a Public Safety Department, which City
Manager Richard B. Kerwin said offers better service at far less
cost. When he proposed abolishing the Fire Department, the

city's largest agency, and reverting to a volunteer department, he found that "I was naive," Kerwin said. The volunteers, who were friends of the firefighters, warned that "if I touched a hair on one of their boys' heads, that would be it." A fight followed with the firefighters' union, but now Kerwin believes the city "actually has more trained manpower than before," with cost down at least 20%. Officers work 12-hour shifts, four days on and four days off. Some former firefighters have been rehired and sent to a police academy. Brisbane now appears ready to annex an adjacent industrial park and the city is building a marina in San Francisco Bay. Will prosperity and growth bring back the Fire Department? "That would be crazy," said Kerwin. "We'll stay with this program. It works."

In Cayucos, it took two tries, but this tiny community succeeded where so many others have failed, convincing voters to approve a special tax override that probably saved its Fire Department. In the year after Proposition 13 passed, revenues for the department—a "volunteer" unit that pays its firefighters a small stipend—dropped from $29,462 to $19,042. Loss of one-third of its income meant that the department could no longer maintain its equipment. And hopes vanished for the replacement of its 1948 fire truck. In 1980, the voters' resounding defeated of a small tax override, was enough to bring Harvey Hart, recently retired advertising manager of the Fresno Bee newspaper, into the fray. He set out to convince voters that the tax was needed, and put together a comprehensive list showing exactly what the money would provide. The items ranged from one "shovel—round point," at $10, to nine additional fire hydrants at $2,500 each. It would also create a reserve fund toward the eventual replacement of some major equipment. To raise the money, property owners would be charged $5 per year for each "unit of benefit." The number of units was determined by the use of the property. A vacant lot would be charged one unit; a single family home four units; and a bar, restaurant or self-service laundry would be assessed for 10 units. Hart put his best advertising instincts to work and last November the voters approved the measure overwhelmingly, 776 to 280.

Even among neighbors, there are different approaches. Seal

Beach in Orange County rejected a tax override measure and was forced to sell its two fire stations and its firefighting and para- medic equipment to the county, which now operates the fire sta- tions. In neighboring Stanton, police and fire departments also faced extinction, until the city became one of the few in the state and the only city in the county to have approved such a tax in- crease.

WELFARE

When voters knocked down local property taxes by approving Proposition 13, the government workers who ran the state's wel- fare programs believed that they were the target, according to Marion J. Woods, the man who headed the state welfare agency, the Department of Social Services, during Gov. Edmund G. Brown Jr.'s Administration. "Proposition 13 was intended to cut welfare costs," Woods said. "I thought that is what the people were voting for, and you could only do it two ways, either cutting grants and reducing eligibility, or cutting administrative costs." In the five years since adoption of Proposition 13 and other tax- cutting measures, state and county governments have used both approaches, and California's welfare system, still one of the most liberal benefit programs in the nation, has been pared back sig- nificantly:

■ Grants paid to recipients have grown, but more slowly than inflation, leaving welfare families with less spending power than they had before Proposition 13 was passed.

■ Changes in eligibility requirements have thrown large num- bers of recipients off the welfare rolls and sliced payment levels for many more.

■ The number of state workers coordinating welfare and social services programs has actually risen slightly, but less than the growth in welfare recipients. Meanwhile, the number of county workers has been dropping.

■ With caseloads rising because of poor economic conditions, county social workers have had to cut back on the services they can offer and have sharply curtailed visits to clients' homes, even though such visits can be vital to the health of the client and are important in identifying possible fraud or abuse.

■ Increased numbers of ineligible recipients have been success-ful in obtaining welfare benefits as caseworkers in county offices throughout the state make mistakes in their calculations or fail to catch clear-cut cases of deception. As a result, California now faces a substantial federal penalty.

The statewide welfare system, through its county-run offices, offers direct financial support to needy individuals as well as a variety of services, including housekeeping and cooking for the infirm and disabled, foster care placement for abused children and counseling services for distressed families. Financially, the system has been a partnership among federal, state and county governments. But with property tax revenues down because of Proposition 13, the state moved in immediately to help counties with their share of welfare costs. Before 1978, for example, coun-ties had paid 16% of the cost of family assistance grants, the state 34% and the federal government the remaining 50%. To-day, the county pays about 5% and the state 45%.

For a time after Proposition 13, a large state surplus seemed to promise that welfare and social service programs would be large-ly untouched, despite a brief moratorium on welfare benefit in-creases. But the surplus waned, and in 1981, even as the recession spurred demand for welfare aid, significant cuts were made by both the federal and state governments. Simply looking at the continued dollar growth of welfare programs tends to mask just how dramatic the effects of those cuts have been. Since 1978, the total cost of providing welfare grants to families has swollen from $1.8 billion a year to $2.9 billion—or $2 billion when adjusted for inflation, for an increase of 11%. But the number of individuals receiving family assistance has grown more rapidly, from 1.4 mil-lion recipients to 1.6 million, about 14%.

The payment increases have been kept in check by the budg-et-cutting measures in both Sacramento and Washington. These measures have reduced the real value of the maximum monthly welfare grant, dropped payment levels even lower for more than 200,000 recipients, and left another 120,700 individuals ineligible for welfare, according to Department of Social Services esti-mates. Today, those who are totally dependent on family assist-ance, primarily households of women and their children, are re-

ceiving less financial help than they did five years ago, once inflation is taken into account. A family of three can receive a maximum grant of $506 a month, compared with $356 five years ago,
an apparent increase of 42%. But inflation cuts the actual value
of the $506 grant to $318, a drop of 11%, according to figures
derived from the legislative analysis of the governor's proposed
budget.

To a lesser extent, the same can be said for 670,000 individuals
who are receiving aid because they are aged, blind or disabled. In
real spending power, the maximum payments for elderly or disabled have been trimmed by 4.5% since 1978. For the working
poor who are eligible for some assistance, welfare rules are now
such that many would be financially better off if they quit their
jobs and turned to welfare for their complete support, according
to the same legislative analysis. Any family of three with an outside income of more than $600 a month beyond its welfare grant
would have more disposable income if the working family member simply stayed home, because the size of the family's welfare
payment would be more than offset by taxes, child care and other
work-related expenses, according to the legislative analyst's report. Several thousand families with an unemployed parent were
simply booted from the welfare program last year because of the
changes in federal and state eligibility requirements.

Gov. George Deukmejian's proposed 1984 state budget would
reduce the state share of welfare costs by another $235 million.
Deukmejian would eliminate a statutory 5.7% cost-of-living increase in family welfare grants for 1984 and award only a 2.1%
increase to the aged, blind and disabled. These steps, say state
officials, would bring California benefits into line with those of
other major states. Not all the changes that have taken place in
welfare and social services can be pinned to Proposition 13 and
its aftershocks.

However, Marilyn Katz, staff attorney at the Western Center
on Law and Poverty, believes that the state would have tried to
pump additional money into programs that lost federal funds in
1981 if state coffers had not been so thoroughly depleted by the
recession and the need to bail out counties deprived of property
tax support. Others, including former state social services direc-

tor Woods, agree that the changes since 1978 are inseparable from the tax revolt launched by Proposition 13.

Statewide statistics compiled by the state Department of Social Services show the decline in the number of county workers available to handle the increasing caseload. By June, 1981, three years after the passage of Proposition 13 and the last year for which statewide statistics are available, the number of county-level employees in welfare and social service agencies had dropped from 35,802 to 34,378—a decline of 4%. And there are clear signs that county governments have been forced to make even more drastic cuts since then.

In Los Angeles, for example, the county Department of Public Social Services employed 11,243 workers in the budget year before the passage of Proposition 13. By this April, there were 9,604 welfare and social service workers—a drop of almost 15%. And the county administrative officer has proposed more cuts for the next budget year, despite rising caseloads in almost every category of service.Over the same period, the state Department of Social Services work force has grown somewhat, from 2,697 in June, 1980, to 2,872 this April—an increase of more than 6%. (Because of changes in the organization of state government, it is difficult to compare department employment levels before the 1980 fiscal year.) However, that increase was not as great as the growth of the state's welfare population, which has jumped more than 15% in the recession years since 1980.

While actual dollar benefits have been reduced, so have many of the services performed for welfare recipients.

Dee Contreras, an employee union representative in San Diego, noted that county social workers used to show welfare families how to manage on their limited budgets and often would refer them to other agencies for help in obtaining jobs, medical care, family planning services and counseling. In Los Angeles County, caseworkers visit clients' homes less frequently and eligibility workers have less time to review the needs of clients and check their qualifications for welfare.

Some statistics are causing alarm among county officials. Reports of child abuse have been rising dramatically over the past several years, in part because of new reporting requirements and a greater awareness of the problem, but also because of growing economic distress among all classes of people, according to Ray Garcia, chief of governmental relations for the county department. In 1978, the county received close to 25,500 child abuse reports; last year, the number was over 36,000—an increase of more than 40%. Yet the number of county children services workers, whose duties include checking out child abuse reports, has fallen by 18% during the same period—from 801 workers and supervisors in 1978 to 658 in 1982.

Programs to help needy adults are also feeling the budgetary squeeze. A state cap has been placed on the amount available to counties for in-home support services, which are intended to keep the elderly and disabled out of more expensive convalescent and boarding homes by providing housekeeping and cooking. In Los Angeles County, the average number of home care hours per recipient has fallen from eight to just over four per week as a result. Until last year, for example, the county could provide help necessary to improve the person's general level of comfort but not vital to survival. Now all such "comfort" care has been eliminated. Los Angeles County officials say they are proud of their record of absorbing cuts in staff and funds with a minimum of disruption. The county has been able, for example, to keep its error rate in determining eligibility for welfare under 4%—the best record of any major urban area in the country, according to Garcia. But as the number of county welfare workers has dropped, the error rate—a statistical estimate of the percentage of recipients who have been given grants for which they are not qualified or larger than they require—is beginning to creep upwards.

Statewide error rates, once among the lowest in the nation, have also risen.In March, federal officials warned the state that its error rate for 1981 had reached 6.8% and that the state might have to return as much as $35 million to the federal welfare program unless it could show that it had made a "good faith effort" to keep its mistakes to 4% or less. Home visits are no longer routinely conducted for each applicant for general relief, a county-funded program that provides financial support to destitute adults who do not qualify for other kinds of welfare. One county general relief worker said that he and his colleagues now simply process claims and have no time to either carefully check eligibility or to determine if other kinds of programs would be helpful to the recipients. "I'm not sure we're meeting clients needs," he said, "with the exception of shuffling paper."

—PJ

HEALTH PROGRAMS

It is the 3 million to 5 million poor Californians who depend on government-subsidized medical care who have suffered the most from health-care reductions triggered by Proposition 13 and subsequent cuts in local, state and federal spending. While Proposition 13 is not solely to blame, the poor now have fewer medical benefits, pay more out-of-pocket expenses, have greater difficulty finding care and face a longer wait when they do find it. Says Robert White, director of health services for Los Angeles County: "There are lots of people not being cared for, but we don't know how many." The cutbacks also mean that the quality of health care for the poor increasingly will lag behind that enjoyed by the better-insured, more-affluent majority.

Among the most important changes:

■ In some counties, public hospitals—traditionally the health facility of last resort for the poor—have been closed, sold or leased to private organizations to conserve scarce property tax revenues. Forty-nine of the state's 58 counties operated 65 hospitals in 1964. As of last January, 26 counties were operating 33 hospitals. The remaining 32 counties lack county hospitals. Nine such hospitals have closed since the passage of Proposition 13, or their operation turned over to private management firms in attempts to cut costs. "The state lost four county hospitals in the past year, in (some) instances the only hospital in that county," said Dr. Peter Abbott of the state Department of Health Services. "When you close a hospital, people don't know where to go. Some become sicker. Some die."

■ Last summer the Legislature sought to trim about $600 million from Medi-Cal, the state and federally funded health-care program for the poor. Lawsuits and delays in putting the cuts into effect will result in fewer savings than expected. But the cuts have eliminated a wide variety of non-emergency medical procedures, surgeries, drugs and other items, required prior authorization for others, and removed about 50,000 people from the program (18,000 in Los Angeles County alone). Crucial in this was the redefinition of a "necessary" non-emergency service. Medi-Cal once paid for any service "reasonable and necessary for the prevention, diagnosis or treatment of disease, illness or injury." But the new definition limits services to those "necessary to protect life or prevent significant disability." As a consequence, a patient with a hernia, for example, may or may not be covered. If the hernia has become strangulated, Medi-Cal will pay to have it repaired. Short of that, however, the program in effect says to the patient, "It won't kill you, so you will have to live with it because we don't have the money to pay for it." Paul Ward, president of the California Hospital Assn., says the result of these new guidelines is that "nobody (doctors and hospitals) is doing anything they don't have to do in order to save life and limb."

■ About 260,000 people known as medically indigent adults are no longer eligible for Medi-Cal, and counties have been forced to assume responsibility for their care. The state continues to help pay the cost, but at a rate 30% below what it had been spending under Medi-Cal. Counties have to make up the difference. In Los Angeles County, the program change has caused about 40,000 people who had been treated at private facilities under Medi-Cal to turn to already-strained county facilities. Thirty-three other counties contracted with the state to administer a program in which it pays private hospitals to care for the medically indigent. But because they are not being reimbursed for all costs, many hospitals are balking at accepting such patients. One such hospital, the medical center in Sacramento administered by the University of California, Davis, has turned away patients in need of complex diagnostic workups, heart surgery and hemophilia treatment, according to Dr. Curt Weidmer, health officer for El Dorado County. Such care can be provided only by a comprehensive medical center, but UC Davis argues that it cannot afford to cover the difference between its costs and the state payments. "We are not going to pick up county liability as a university hospital," said its medical director, Dr. Don Rockwell.

■ The patient load in the remaining county hospitals continues to rise. In Los Angeles County, for example, admissions were up 18% last January compared with a year ago, outpatient visits were up 17% and emergency walk-in visits were up 20%. The increase is attributed largely to the changes in Medi-Cal; people no longer eligible for private treatment paid by Medi-Cal are turning instead to county hospitals. In addition, those still on Medi-Cal continue to make heavy use of county facilities; they account for nearly 50% of the revenue of county hospitals, compared to about 17% of total revenue for private hospitals. Last year, private hospitals reported a 15% decline in Medi-Cal patients.

The pressure that this has put on county hospital budgets is considerable. In Los Angeles County, the hospital system has boosted revenue by hiring 700 people who make sure Medi-Cal pays all it should for patient care—and collect token payments from the patients themselves.The county began charging patients two years ago (sample fees: $20 for each prenatal or well-baby visit and for each ambulatory sick person). Consumer advocates argue that such charges discourage the poor from seeking health care until an illness becomes serious—and more costly to treat. But Douglas Steele, deputy director of public health services, says: "It appears that people are becoming accustomed to the charges and accepting them."

The effort continues to generate new income. Three years ago, for example, the county collected an average $56,970 a month from outpatients at health centers. In February, it collected $435,019. It is partly for these reasons—plus $62.2 million in service and program cuts by the Board of Supervisors in the past two years—that the county's net cost in local tax dollars for health services has not risen since 1978. In fact, the number of county health workers has been reduced by 2,912, or 12%, from pre-Proposition 13 levels, and one of eight county hospitals— plus 28 of the 77 health centers in existence in 1977—have been closed. One more county hospital (Long Beach General) is about to be phased out, but three new comprehensive health centers have opened and a new hospital (Olive View) is about to open.

Still, Proposition 13 alone cannot be blamed for what has happened to health care for the poor. Other state cutbacks, the recession and accompanying federal cuts ordered by the Reagan Administration have played major roles. And because funds from all levels of government go toward providing health services for the poor, it often becomes difficult to judge the separate impact of each cutback.Government regulations sometimes distort the impact. For example, the state is less likely to cut those services, such as family planning, where the federal government matches state funds 100%—but more likely to cut where there is no federal matching money, such as programs for medically indigent adults. Nevertheless, a variety of experts in California see last summer's Medi-Cal cutbacks—at the time the most severe in the program's 16-year history—as an aftershock of Proposition 13.

They argue that without Proposition 13, the state would not have had to use its huge revenue surplus to bail out local governments. The bail-out, in turn, drained state revenue and helped trigger the Medi-Cal cost cutting, these experts say. For the first three years after the passage of Proposition 13, the impact on health care for the poor was light. But since 1981, the erosion has been steady. While the overall state budget for Medi-Cal—by far the largest health program for the poor—has risen consistently each year in raw dollars, the increases often have failed to keep pace with inflation. The same is true for most county health budgets. Add to that the rapidly rising costs of health care—ranging from 15% to 20% annually—and it becomes clear that something had to give.

The coming year looks even more difficult. The proposed state budget would slash another $632 million from state Medi-Cal funds, leaving them 23% below the estimated expenditure for the current year. Not enough time has passed to tell whether the cutbacks will result in increased morbidity and mortality for the poor, although many health experts believe that they will. Nor is it possible to measure the degree to which the quality of life has been adversely affected. "We can measure dollars saved and spent, but we don't have an index for pain and suffering," one state health economist said.

—HN

PARKS

The story of California's urban parks over the last five years is one of decline and deterioration. Weeds grow where flowers once were planted; recreation centers go unmanned; broken equipment is abandoned rather than replaced, and virtually everything from swim classes to softball now costs more, sometimes much more, than in the years before Proposition 13.While there have been some exceptions, this decline has happened to some degree in most California cities, large and small, rich and poor, as local budgets have been progressively squeezed.

Often identified as expendable, parks and recreation departments have been forced to accept budget cuts more severe than most of their sister agencies in city and county governments. According to a statewide survey by The Times, per capita spending for parks has shrunk by 16.9% over the last five years when adjusted for inflation. In many cases, the strain on operating budgets has been increased by an expansion of parkland under control of local governments. Fed by grants from state and federal governments, parks departments have continued to acquire new lands even as their ability to operate old parks has been pushed to the breaking point.

There has been no real public outcry; the parks, after all, are still there. A casual visitor taking his family for a Sunday picnic might notice little more than shaggy lawns and dirty restrooms. It is a price, parks managers say, that most residents seem willing to pay without serious protest.

"All of our operations have been reduced and there's been very little reaction," said Guy Kulstad, director of public works in Humboldt County, whose experience illustrates how far government can be forced to go to cut spending. "I keep wondering how bad things have to get before people really start to feel it and say, 'Whoa, enough is enough.' " In the late 1970s, Humboldt employed 21 workers to cut lawns, repair restrooms and maintain the county's 18 parks. That work force now numbers six. At first, the county's response was similar to many others across the state: scheduled ground care was cut; campground development was terminated; vandalized restrooms were often closed rather than repaired. Still, it was not enough. Humboldt's leaders eventually were forced to cut maintenance at some parks to virtually zero, or transfer several units to other agencies more capable of caring for them. The county chose the latter, and has given away two parks, one to the National Park Service and another to a community service district. It has also begun negotiations with the state and the federal Bureau of Land Management to take over additional units. Originally there was reluctance about the transfers because local residents feared loss of control, Kulstad says, but the fears dissipated after users were persuaded that there would be little change in access or activities in the parks. The transfers have saved the county $30,000 to $40,000 in annual maintenance costs, Kulstad estimates, a substantial portion of the county's $205,000 yearly park budget.

Humboldt's abandonment approach is rare, but many park districts have been forced to close recreational facilities or reduce their hours. These facilities, such as gyms, swimming pools, small theaters and hobby workshops, often provide the center of activity for children and senior citizens. Statewide, about 41% of park districts in communities surveyed by The Times have either eliminated facilities or reduced hours since 1977-78. The losses have not been spread evenly; large cities have been hit more severely. The City of Los Angeles, for example, closed 24 small centers in 1981 and all remain closed. In addition, funds for the remaining 154 centers have been reduced. At the 10 largest centers, weekly operating hours have been cut from an average of 82 to 50.

Inevitably these cutbacks have had the greatest impact on less affluent users of the park system who often cannot afford formal programs for which fees are charged. "There was a great philosophical debate about the cuts," said James Hadaway, Los Angeles' general manager of Recreation and Parks. "We first proposed that the cuts be more severe in wealthier areas because we knew those neighborhoods could raise private money to restore them. We also knew that poorer neighborhoods couldn't." But finally, Hadaway says, the Recreation and Parks Commission decided to administer the cuts evenly across all neighborhoods. "I wouldn't say we got a violent reaction (from the wealthier neighborhoods) but they pointed out that their tax dollars already subsidized the poor areas. They said, 'You're asking us to pay again, and we want to think about that.' " As the department predicted, the result has been an uneven recreational program throughout the city. In Northridge, a middle-class neighborhood in the San Fernando Valley, park supporters have raised about $100,000 in private funds to restore programs. At Harvard Recreational Center in the poor South-Central district, only about $2,500 has been raised. Along the county's beaches, cutbacks in the number of lifeguards could have an effect on safety. Lifeguard shacks once manned by two have been reduced to one. "These are stations where a high number of rescues take place," said Dean Smith, administrator for Los Angeles County's beaches. "In the past one lifeguard was in the water most of the time and the second guard was there to watch for other problems. Now, that margin of insurance has been lost."

In smaller cities and suburban communities, cuts in recreational services have been less severe. In wealthy San Marino, leaders closed the only park in the city, Lacey Park, on weekends and holidays, thus avoiding the expense of cleanup after the crush of non-resident visitors on those days. Daily use is unaffected. Typically, towns and counties have cut maintenance substantially, but have managed to avoid large reductions in programs. In part, this stems from higher fees for almost all park programs.

Since Proposition 13, many recreational programs have been put on a self-sustaining basis. In the Bay Area city of Hayward, for example, fees represented 8.8% of the total park and recreation budget in 1978; this year they will represent about 20%. Swimming classes at Hayward that cost $4.50 for a two-week course in 1978 now cost $15; art classes have gone from an average $10 per session to $21; a season of softball from $170 per team to $232. Even so, Hayward has been forced to make some adjustments. Three of eight swim centers were closed; art and cultural classes were consolidated from four locations to two. "In all, our programs are less available, less convenient and more expensive," said Bud Critzer, general manager of the Hayward Area Recreation and Park District. "But no single program has been lost. We have managed to preserve the variety and the quality."

At San Diego's Balboa Park, Arman Campillo, the city parks and recreation director, says that even with users digging ever more frequently into their pockets to pay for activities, the city is fighting a losing battle trying to maintain the park's smorgasbord of services. Childrens programs, museums and athletic leagues have changed, and the park planting schedule has been cut (the mall is now planted with perennials once a year rather than changing with the seasons.) The once-popular flower shows in the Botanical Building have been scrapped, with the exception of an Easter lily exhibit financed by a private donor. Volleyball, basketball and softball players who once played for free now pay about $150,000 each year. And the directors of Junior Theater, Youth Symphony and the civic dance program for children are no longer paid for by the city. Museums in the park now pay their own utilities, a hefty expense that was largely responsible for the $2.50 admission fee they now charge.

Throughout the state, maintenance suffered, largely because of termination of the federal Comprehensive Employment and Training Act (CETA) program in 1982. In 1978, about 4,000 CETA employees were used by parks departments statewide. When CETA was discontinued, maintenance staffs shrank dramatically. "In 1980 we had 500 CETA workers. We lost them all," said Henry Roman, budget officer for Los Angeles County's park system. As a result, the county abandoned its practice of keeping maintenance staffs at its larger parks and went instead to roving crews responsible for three or four parks each. "Now we just try to do the basics," Roman said. "Broken commodes stay broken a much longer time; graffiti stays on walls. What you see are parks in a more deteriorated condition."

At the state level, the 277 parks operated by the California Park and Recreation Department initially escaped much of the financial squeeze experienced by local governments—their money was not primarily dependent on the property tax cut out by Proposition 13. Still, says department budget chief Gerald Johnson, many former scientific and interpretive programs have been lost. In some of the state's coastal parks, workers formerly struggled each year to stabilize sand dunes that otherwise would move onto parking lots, Johnson noted, but now there is no money to pay the workers. "We just have to let (the dunes) move," he said.

Until last year, however, park acquisition at the state level proceeded at a healthy pace, thanks largely to money sources that were independent of the tax squeeze. In 1980, Californians approved a $130-million bond issue for new parks, and in recent years the department has received an additional $35 million annually from the state's offshore oil revenues for land purchases. While the flow of money from both those sources is now about to end, the park system has grown even as its revenues have been stretched. Since 1978, the department has added about 125,000 acres of new parkland to the system that contains about 1 million acres. To a lesser extent, the same situation has occurred with many local park departments. State and federal grants for the purchase of parkland remained generally available through 1980, and 61% of those park departments responding to The Times survey reported that their systems have expanded since 1978. In Los Angeles, for example, 24 new parks and an extensive list of recreational facilities have been established in the post-Proposition 13 period. At one point, according to Hadaway, the Parks Department was confronted with the pleasant problem of disposing of $25 million in federal grants within three months.

Who has been hurt most by the park cutbacks? Park managers say services probably have declined the most in poor neighborhoods of large cities. In some such neighborhoods, once active recreation programs have been reduced to shadows of their former selves; equipment for sports is unavailable; gymnasiums and workshops are often closed; supervisors unavailable.

However, surveys taken by several park departments have shown that formal recreation programs are most used by middle-class residents, and some park officials argue that cutbacks and fee increases in this area have affected such middle-class users more than the poor. "If you are looking at outdoor basketball, you'll see a lot more people on the courts down in South-Central," said Hadaway. "But if you're looking at swim programs or karate classes, the real heavy use takes place in Northridge or North Hollywood. I think, in the end, you can say that no one has escaped."

—*RAJ, TG*

LIBRARIES

California public libraries have weathered the financial setbacks about as well as books left in the rain. Despite the tatters, they are still good reading.

It is no small victory given their scant political clout: Librarians have always acknowledged that politically they fare poorly against the "life-and-death" arguments presented at budget time by municipal agencies like fire and police departments. As a service that depended almost exclusively on property taxes, libraries have proved particularly vulnerable to cutbacks. But they have reaped at least one significant benefit—a renewed grass-roots support that, while not yet powerful enough to overcome competition from other services, has begun to spread. "We had to become political," said Alameda County librarian Ginnie Cooper. "It's now as important as knowing how to catalogue books."

Alameda County was the only library system in California to temporarily shut down after passage of the tax measure. With one-third of its usual funds available, the system closed its 14 branches for three months until bail-out money from the state arrived. But the community did not take it quietly. Angry residents stormed Board of Supervisors meetings, interrupted proceedings and demanded that the libraries be opened. Now libraries are a high priority for the county. "The libraries have created a surprisingly good lobby," said George M. Hewitt, Alameda County administrative analyst.

In other cities, the story was much the same. San Franciscans made so much noise that city officials withdrew plans to close six of 26 branches, and instead last year hiked the library budget 26% to $12 million, as against one year of inflation measured at 5.1%. In San Diego, city officials tried to close Valencia Park, one of the library system's 30 branches, when a new facility was opened a mile away. Community displeasure was so great that they left it open. The Orange County Library System, whose 25 branches circulate 13 books per capita compared to the state average of 4.9, has strong support from the Board of Supervisors.

Since 1978 four new branches have been constructed, including an $800,000 solar-heated facility in El Toro. Two others are on the drawing board, and the library also has a new $2-million computerized circulation system.

But overall, libraries did suffer some serious wounds. California, second in per-capita public library financing in 1977, dropped to 11th place in 1981, according to the California State Library. "Proposition 13 has put an end to really progressive growth for California libraries," said Peggy Barber, American Library Assn. spokeswoman, saying that until recently the state had always had ample financing to be a leader in such innovative programs as data sharing, centralized cataloguing and a variety of computerized services. "You can play all kinds of games with money, but it's the service figures that tell the story," California State Librarian Gary Strong said. For the 168 public library systems and their 3,110 outlets, California State Library statistics show that between 1978 and 1982:

■ Patrons' access to libraries has been reduced 20%. Annual hours decreased from 50,936 to 40,607.

■ Staffing dropped 10%, from 9,657 to 8,787. The decline means longer lines at the checkout counter, and cutbacks in services such as children's story hours and answering questions. Los Angeles City Library reports that its phone patrons have to wait up to 20 minutes on hold before they are helped with reference requests.

■ Use of volunteers has increased 282%. The 30-branch San Diego Library system, for emxample, has a full-time coordinator to oversee volunteers who provide 2,700 hours of service a month, or the equivalent of 17 full-time employees. The volunteers do everything from shelve books and mend book covers to get out the payroll.

■ Libraries in 1982 circulated 121 million items compared to 126 million in 1978, and answered 31.8 million reference questions as compared to 34 million in 1978, reflecting the cumulative effect of shorter hours with smaller staffs and fewer new materials.

■ Library expenditures increased from $194 million in 1978 to

$243.5 million in 1982, a 25% increase as against a 39% rate of inflation, but the additional money has been insufficient to maintain services at former levels. Per capita purchasing power dropped from $8.79 to $7.25, a 17.5% decrease.

One-third of the state's libraries, including 16 of the 45 largest, which serve 9 million people or 38% of the state's population, report significant decreases in money to buy books, periodicals and reference works. In Alameda County, patrons of the 14 branches have to share 20 copies of Robert Ludlum's spy thriller "The Parsifal Mosaic." The waiting list is more than 200 names long at each of the branches and those who sign up now will get the book in February, 1984. Even before the tax revolt, libraries were fighting to retain the integrity of their collections. The high cost of printed material had hurt book budgets and, to make matters worse, librarians were finding that they had to replace items more often because books printed on recycled paper deteriorated faster. And because of the growing ethnic mix in California, libraries have had to buy material in several languages, adding to expenses.

Inflation worsened already high prices for printed materials, decreasing the quantity of items that libraries were able to buy. Proposition 13 cutbacks added to the strain. For example, the Riverside city and county library spent $235,000 for 47,000 items in 1978, but purchased only 32,000 items with $372,000 in 1982. As a result, gaps are appearing in collections statewide. While libraries in the past could borrow the resources from other libraries, they are finding that other libraries are in the same boat. Librarians say they are doubtful they will ever catch up because certain periodicals, scientific abstracts and other reference material from this period are now out of print. To make matters worse, Proposition 13 cuts and inflation have curtailed computerization. Urban libraries with large collections, which could benefit most from the systems in terms of cost, are finding they cannot afford to buy them.

The Los Angeles City Library system, one of the largest in the country with a central library and 62 branches, still uses manual checkout procedures and card catalogues because the changeover to computers would cost an estimated $10 million. There is little help coming from outside the affected communities. Federal aid to libraries has been almost non-existent. And while there has been a trend nationally in recent years for the states to pick up larger chunks of library funding, California's contribution has remained minimal. The state in 1983 provided $5.4 million to libraries, or about 23 cents per capita, according to the Urban Libraries Council. That compares with Maryland's $3.24 per capita, New York's $2.18 and the national average of 87 cents.

After four years of effort, library supporters last year saw enactment of Senate Bill 358, intended to provide $25 million, or $1.25 per capita, for the state's libraries beginning in June. However, faced with a staggering deficit, the governor has not included the money in the budget and there is little hope that the Legislature will change his mind. Said Michael F. Dillon, lobbyist for the California Library Assn.: "If you look at the votes, everyone wants to be a 'Friend of the Library.' But when it comes down to getting the money, our job becomes more difficult."

Some librarians have turned to a variety of money raising techniques. These have included everything from traditional book sales to such ambitious endeavors as opening a restaurant in the library lobby and establishing endowment funds. Some have been more successful than others:

■ In San Diego, city council members considered charging a $10 fee for library cards to help the budget. However, library patrons hated the idea and told them so, and the plan was dropped.

■ In Huntington Beach the quiche and pastry bar in the central library didn't make money, but officials plan to try again with hot dogs and soft drinks. The library tried to charge for children's story hour and library cards, but the public wouldn't buy it. It was more successful charging for use of meeting rooms, typewriters and copy machines. And a library staffer who goes door-to-door to retrieve unreturned books has cut yearly losses from $30,000 to $2,000.

■ In Berkeley, voters in 1980 overwhelmingly approved Measure E to restore the city library to pre-Proposition 13 money levels by levying a tax on residences and commercial buildings. But miscalculations in taxable square footage resulted in collection of less than $2 million rather than the expected $2.5 million.

Library hours have been cut from 70 to 52 hours a week in the central library, and from 60 to 36 in branches. Staffers have taken a 10% pay cut.

■ Butte County Library, which has a central library and seven branches, cut staff and hours by 50%, and the book budget plummeted from $175,000 to $32,000. To pay for new branches in Chico and Gridley, a group of patrons formed a non-profit corporation and sold bonds. However, another citizen's group took the issue to court, contending that the corporation was actually a government entity and not abiding by interest rate limitations. The court ruled in favor of the library, but the decision is being appealed.

■ Los Angeles County Library, which with 91 branches is the largest in the country, has retained vitality only through use of volunteers, who contributed 44,000 hours in 1982, compared with 7,500 in 1978, says librarian Linda Crismond. Spurred by the success of endowment funds elsewhere, the library has created a similar foundation. The first benefit dinner show (Anthony Quinn in "Zorba the Greek") netted $20,000.

■ In Alameda County, Newark librarian Elizabeth Talbot, who wears braces on her teeth, devised a contest to raise money to stock a new library. Patrons guess which will come first— removal of her orthodontic appliances or opening of the new branch. The library itself is being built as part of a city civic center project financed by sale of property. "Libraries are facing a tooth and nail financial battle," she says. "We're not going to look any gift horses in the mouth."

—CM

PUBLIC WORKS

Five years of public works cost-cutting have left California with a shabby legacy of pitted streets, chronically flooded intersections and dingy public buildings, particularly in older, urban areas such as Los Angeles and Oakland. The cost-cutting has resulted in postponed road repairs in communities across the state, phase-out of landscaping in some, elimination of street sweeping in others, dimming of street lights, cancellation of construction projects and thinning out of work crews.

Proposition 13 did not cause the crunch, but it aggravated the problem, especially for local street and road budgets already squeezed by declining gasoline-tax revenues and inflation. Five years of neglect of public works clearly has not led to disaster. Bridges have not buckled; sewers have not exploded. But the results are visible, and many experts argue that if the current revenue slide persists, and routine maintenance and construction needs continue to be neglected, a crisis in public works may be unavoidable. "If today's level of (street) maintenance continues during the next 10 to 20 years, the results will be catastrophic," a member of the governor's Office of Planning and Research said.

A Times survey showed that local government spending on all street-related needs is down 11.3% since 1978, when adjusted for inflation. The survey showed that spending for street maintenance declined by 6.3% and spending for street construction fell by nearly 16%. Statewide, state controller reports show that between 1978 and 1982, total money available for spending on city and county roads dropped by more than 10% after adjusting for inflation. Revenues were stunted mainly by a 32% decrease in county gasoline-tax proceeds and by an 11% decline in city general-fund revenues, which include property taxes. The tax revolt also had an effect on revenue for flood-control projects, causing a decrease since 1978 of 4% in statewide revenue, adjusted for inflation, and leading officials in some counties to say they lack the money to protect homes and businesses. On the other hand, a combination of federal aid and higher local fees have allowed revenue growth for solid waste and sewer systems to stay well ahead of inflation—solid waste by 15% and sewers by more than 100%, according to a survey conducted by the state Assembly Office of Research.

Built in the 1940s and 1950s, most public works systems in California are young compared to what exists in many parts of the country, and they have aged more slowly because of the state's mild climate. As a result, officials say that, despite the neglect that has occurred in some areas, much of the state's public works is in satisfactory shape. Polled by the Assembly's Office of Research, a majority of the public works officials who responded said California's streets, sewers, flood-control equipment and solid-waste facilities are in "average" or "good" condition.

When interviewed by The Times, however, many of those same officials also said the durability of public works is a byproduct of an era when local governments could raise more money to spend on capital improvements, and the officials warn that when the time comes to rebuild, they may not have the money to do a good job.

They point out that Proposition 13 has deprived them of one of the most widely used methods of financing capital improvements. Proposition 13 ruled out continued dependence on general-obligation bonds. The issuance of those bonds requires the unlimited authority to raise property-tax revenues to guarantee principal and interest payments to bond purchasers. Before Proposition 13, local agencies relied heavily on the bonds to finance new construction. For example, the Los Angeles County Flood Control District built its entire storm-drain system with $930 million in bonds issued between 1950 and 1978. In the year before Proposition 13, schools and local governments in California issued $444 million worth of general-obligation bonds, an amount equal to nearly 20% of all local spending that year on construction projects. By 1982, the amount of bonds issued had fallen to $117 million, or less than 4% of the amount then being spent on construction projects.

Diminishing property-tax revenues also led officials to empty one public works pot to fill another. By 1982, officials in Los Angeles had diverted the city's entire $7 million public-improvement fund to street maintenance. The transfer left the city without the money to replace or repair 12 branch libraries which do not meet structural standards established under the city's Earthquake Hazard Reduction Ordinance. "The passage of Proposition 13 eliminated the primary source of municipal facilities funding," wrote Keith B. Comrie, the city administrative officer, in a 1983 report on the city's five-year capital program.

The Times survey points to significant reductions since 1978 in the services and projects traditionally performed by local public works departments. Nearly 70% of the cities and counties responding to the survey have reduced or eliminated services, including street sweeping, groundskeeping and building upkeep, that were performed before 1978 by public works departments. And more than 60% of the local governments responding have deferred major maintenance or rehabilitation projects since 1978. The reductions have occurred despite the efforts of cities and counties to regain lost public works revenue through an array of fees, service charges and special assessments. The Times survey showed that 63% of the cities and counties that responded imposed new fees after 1978, and 74% raised fees that were in existence before 1978.

The effects of service reductions have been felt in a variety of ways. In Northern California, public works officials in Colusa, Humboldt and Siskiyou counties during the last two years have let 50 miles of paved roads revert to gravel because they did not have the money to maintain asphalt surfaces. There are about 3,000 miles of county roads in those counties.

In Los Angeles, the street maintenance work force has been reduced from 2,569 people in 1978 to 1,462 in 1982. Public works officials in Los Angeles estimate that 8,500 of the city's 660,000 parkway trees have died since 1978 and say that most of them perished because the city could no longer afford regular care for parkway landscaping.

Oakland has been hit especially hard. Since 1978, the city's public works budget has shrunk by 46% in real dollars. The department's 600-member work force has been reduced to 380. James McCarty, the city's director of public works, said his department no longer can afford to paint center stripes on residential streets. McCarty said that even though many city streets are deteriorating rapidly, his department can afford to resurface city streets at the rate of only once per 200 years. In San Jose last winter, maintenance workers placed buckets in the lobby of City Hall because the city's Public Works Department did not have the money to fix a leaky roof.

Less money for public works also may have contributed to acute personal hardships. Two years ago, 10-year-old Gina Lynn Vacca was struck by a car while roller-skating on a darkened San Diego street. Street lights near her house had been turned off as a cost-cutting measure by the county's Public Works Department. Lawyers for the girl, who suffered brain damage from the accident, contend that the absence of street lighting helped cause the accident and sued the county for $1.5 million in damages. The case has not been resolved. Last winter, Christine Rising and her son were among about 15 families in Larabee, along the Eel River in Humboldt County, who were marooned by landslides for two weeks because the county's Public Works Department no longer had the manpower and equipment to respond to multiple emergencies. Guy Kulstad, the county's public works director, said Larabee was one of several rural communities cut off for days at a time during the last year.

Proposition 13 also took a large bite out of revenue for flood-control projects in the state. In fiscal 1978, $105 million in property taxes accounted for 70% of total flood-control revenue. By 1981—the latest year for which figures are available—property-tax revenues had fallen to $46 million and accounted for only 23% of total flood-control revenues. Federal funds covered some of that loss. It increased by 89% between 1978 and 1982. Even so, total revenues for flood control declined by 4% during that period.

Officials in Santa Barbara and Ventura counties said recently that they lacked the funds to build flood-control channels in several areas where flooding has damaged buildings and driven people from their homes. Gerald Nowak, director of flood control and water resources for Ventura County, said "lives can be lost and structures demolished" because of what he said was inadequate flood-control protection. "The level of protection does not meet federal requirements in a good part of the county," Nowak said. Revenues for flood control in Ventura County fell by 15% in dollars adjusted for inflation between 1978 and 1981, the latest year for which the figures are available.

The Los Angeles County Flood Control District has been able to offset its property tax loss by raising more than $50 million through voter-approved "benefit assessments" since 1978. In 1981, the district accounted for 90% of the revenue raised statewide through benefit assessments. Despite the assessments, the district has cut its work force by 30%, from 1,644 people in 1978 to 1,148 this year. It also has reduced its capital projects by about half of the annual amount undertaken before Proposition 13.

Even before Proposition 13, transportation experts were warning that the state's roads were approaching an age when a massive face lift would be required. Even when the ability to raise property taxes existed, the experts questioned whether cities and counties would be able to pay for a wholesale rehabilitation of streets and roads. In 1978, California ranked 50th among the states in the amount of money that cities and counties spent on road maintenance and improvement. The state's 7-cents-per-gallon gasoline tax, the largest single source of revenue—27%— for local road programs, was lower than the gas taxes of all but three states. As the fuel conservation movement took hold in the mid-1970s and people began to buy less gas, proceeds from the gas tax actually declined. Between 1978 and 1982, the gas-tax contribution to city and county road revenue dropped by 26%.

For the six years before Proposition 13, local general-fund money, the second major source of street revenue for cities, grew by about 24%. But during the five years since Proposition 13, general-fund revenues declined by 11% when adjusted for inflation. Even before Proposition 13, however, the growth rate of local street revenues was running behind the inflation rate of street maintenance and construction costs. Those costs, according to the state transportation commission, increased by 250% between 1970 and 1980, as a result of the ballooning price of petroleum-based asphalt products. In the last five years alone, the cost of resurfacing a mile of roadway has risen from $22,000 to $45,000.

With less money to complete a variety of tasks, public works directors began emphasizing superficial repairs—patching and sealing—over the recognized need for a thorough resurfacing of many of the state's roads. Today, many cities and counties report that after meeting critical maintenance needs, they have little money left for capital improvements. In Los Angeles, 20% of capital improvement funds for streets was diverted to street maintenance during the last five years. Between 1975 and 1980, funds for capital improvements of city streets declined by 57% in dollars adjusted for inflation.

In some rural areas of the state, public works directors report that new construction has come to a standstill. In Colusa County north of Sacramento, Dan Klar, the public works director, said his county has done "no (road) construction or reconstruction in the last four years. We are close to $1 million a year behind in maintaining our roads."

This year, there will be more money available for local public works thanks to the state's recently approved gas-tax increase. The 2-cents-a-gallon increase will make about $100 million in new revenue available to local governments. But most public works officials say the infusion of money will not be enough to overcome the backlog of construction and maintenance needs that have accumulated over the last decade. And many officials say their only recourse is to try to persuade the public that new taxes are necessary. It is likely be an uphill fight even now, after a disastrous winter that caused more than $85 million in damage and created hazards and hardships for residents throughout the state.

"I have spent almost my whole four years trying to build a con-stituency for public works, and I am still trying," said Maureen Kindel, president of the Los Angeles City Board of Public Works. James McCarty, the director of Oakland's embattled Public Works Department, is particularly pessimistic. "There is no con-stituency for hard public works infrastructure," McCarty said. "There are no friends of the sewer or society for the preservation of streets."—*FC*

PUBLIC TRANSIT

Proposition 13 has had an uneven effect on California's public transit systems. It put a big dent in the operating budgets of sys-tems that relied heavily on property tax revenue, such as San Diego's. But it left virtually no mark on systems like the Southern California Rapid Transit District, where a variety of other revenues—unaffected by Proposition 13—keep the buses running. And even for those systems that suffered, the weak economy, inflation, and falling state and federal revenues often caused as much grief as Proposition 13.

At first glance, it is hard to see the damage. Since 1978—the Proposition 13 year—total revenues for the state's transit agencies have risen from $807 million to $915 million, in inflation-adjusted figures. But the source of those dollars has shifted dramatically, in part because of Proposition 13, and the dollars are proving harder to get. In the end, this may be Proposition 13's most important impact on public transit: nudging a number of transit systems into greater reliance on non-property tax revenue sources that turn out to be elusive or unreliable. Here are the key elements that have transit officials worried about the future:

■ Property taxes provided about 19% of all revenue for transit districts in the years just before Proposition 13; that figure had dropped to about 7% by 1980 and continues to decline, although exact numbers are not available statewide. At the same time, the number of transit systems receiving property tax or other local government funds has dropped from 50 to 25.

■ Other taxes, such as sales levies, have taken up some of the slack, but transit districts must compete with other agencies for those dollars. State sales tax money that is funneled to transit systems, for example, now accounts for about 29% of transit's revenues, down about 2%.

■ Other state funds for transit districts are in jeopardy. For fiscal 1984, for example, the state transit assistance program contains $103 million. But with the general fund short of cash, Gov. George Deukmejian has proposed cutting the program to $75 million and some other state officials want to limit it to $43 million. About 90 transit agencies and cities use the money for various purposes, including operations and construction projects. Some also goes to the state's commuter rail program.

■ The loss of property tax revenue placed new importance on federal transit subsidies, which provided 19% of California transit system income last year. But these subsidies are being reduced, and the Reagan Administration wants to wipe them out by 1985. (Large transit systems receive most of these subsidies; they pay 16% of the Orange County Transit District's operating costs, and 13% at the RTD, for example.)

■ Five years ago, the fares paid by passengers provided about 24% of transit income. Since then, the percentage has risen to 26% as fares have been increased to help make up for the decline in other income, including property tax revenue.

All this is happening at a time when the transit business is booming in California. More public transit systems are operating today than before Proposition 13—230 in all, ranging from an eight-passenger senior citizens van in tiny Alpine County in the northern Sierra to the RTD, the nation's third-largest urban transit system. Ridership in the years since Proposition 13, as measured by the state's 11 largest transit systems, has risen dramatically, from 675 million in 1978 to 935 million in 1982. Although this is the the latest estimate available, transit experts say patronage has been going up steadily since then in California and throughout the Sun Belt states.

But this is small comfort to those systems experiencing financial difficulty. One agency—the Marin County Transit District—has thrown in the towel. It is expected to relinquish its remaining revenues to another operator, keeping only a tiny bus service. Other systems have cut costs by running with fewer drivers, mechanics or other employees. Service at night and on weekends has been reduced or eliminated, and some little-used weekday routes have been scrubbed. Many have asked passengers to pay more. Among the state's 11 largest transit systems, fares have more than doubled in most cases, hitting a basic 80 cents or more. Federal subsidies still provide most of the money to buy buses and finance new maintenance buildings and bus stations. But officials predict trouble there too, with equipment prices soaring, Washington tightening its belt and fewer local dollars available to match federal subsidies.

So far, the RTD, based in Los Angeles, has been affected only peripherally by Proposition 13, principally because it never received property taxes. Even so, it is starting to feel a financial squeeze. Because the district has been able to subsidize its basic 50-cent fares—it gets money from the half-cent sales tax increase that took effect last July—the RTD has enjoyed a huge ridership jump. It stands now at 1.5 million patrons a day, up 400,000 daily in 12 months. The district has kept staff and schedules intact. But that may be only temporary. The sales tax subsidies, unique because they were approved for only three years, account for more than 35% of operating revenues. In mid-1985, when the tax distribution formula changes, the RTD's return will drop from $169 million to less than $100 million. Federal operating subsidies for the RTD—$48 million this year—are expected to be phased out in two years. This could mean drastic service cutbacks and skyrocketing fares, probably more than double what a bus ride costs today.

Because of Proposition 13, the RTD also had to delay for a year a program to drop fares to 50 cents, a delay that cost the RTD—temporarily, at least—$125 million and that cost the nearly 1.5 million daily riders about 35 cents a ride, perhapsas much as an extra $60 million or so. The delay came about because Proposition A, a Los Angeles County measure increasing the sales tax a half-cent to subsidize bus fares and build a rapid transit system, ran afoul of the proposition's requirement that it needed a two-thirds majority vote to take effect. Voters approved it in November, 1980, by a 54% majority. The county Transportation Commission asked the state Supreme Court in March, 1981, to decide Proposition A's legality. Thirteen months later the court upheld the commission's contention that the measure was exempt from the two-thirds requirement. The tax finally took effect in 1982 and fares were dropped to 50 cents soon after.

Here is how some other systems have fared:

■ In San Diego, the publicly owned San Diego Transit Corp. operates nearly 425 buses. Before Proposition 13, the system received nearly $3 million a year in property tax revenue from the city. That subsidy was cut to $444,000. The system hired part-time drivers for the first time to save money, and boosted fares from 35 cents to 80 cents. But it ended up losing riders because of the higher fares and route cutbacks. "We're still in the shadow of Proposition 13," a system official says. "We'd have $6 million more a year, instead of zero, and fares would be at the 1981 level—60 cents. Now we're looking at severe federal fund cutbacks. . . ."

■ The Orange County Transit District had built up a $24-million cash backlog, money intended for an eventual rail system. It used $2 million of the backlog to balance its budget after Proposition 13, which cut its share of property tax revenues from $3.7 million to $1.9 million in one year. Now the property tax return is almost back up to the pre-Proposition 13 level because of Orange

County's construction boom and assessed valuation increases permitted by the tax initiative. But the district was also hurt by inflation and declining federal subsidies, which accounted for 48% of operating revenue five years ago but only 15% today. To cut costs, the district has dropped 30 drivers and trimmed about 5% of its service. Fares, which held steady at 25 cents for many years, have gone to 75 cents in peak hours.

■ The Alameda-Contra Costa Transit District in the San Francisco Bay Area faced a sudden shrinkage of its property tax revenues—from $19.1 million to $5.8 million—after Proposition 13 passed. But it was saved from financial calamity by an infusion of new sales tax revenue—earmarked for it and other local transit districts by the Legislature one year before Proposition 13 passed. Even so, the Oakland-based system was forced to raise fares from 25 cents to 60 cents over several steps, drop 26 buses from its 800-plus bus fleet, operate with 50 fewer drivers, and trim its telephone information staff from 34 to 27. At the same time, daily riders have increased 28%, from 167,000 to 215,000.

■ The Bay Area Rapid Transit system, which operates the subway trains in San Francisco and adjoining cities, reacted to Proposition 13 by trimming 150 people from the payroll in such areas as marketing, affirmative action, planning and management. Fifteen of the 60 top management positions were eliminated. Now, with its property tax revenue gone, BART is getting along on its share of the Bay Area sales tax. Said Keith Bernard, general manager: "Proposition 13 was a good catalyst. (It produced) an attitude that has held to this day—to keep things lean." San Francisco itself made a policy decision, ranking the municipal railway's 1,082 buses, streetcars, trackless trolleys and cable cars behind only police and fire in importance to the city's well-being. This year the city is putting $68 million from its general fund into the system, about 43% of Muni's revenues. A city official pointed out that San Francisco's goal has been "to keep Muni whole." With 60 city departments, he explained, it has become clear that "some . . . are more important than others."

■ Long Beach Public Transit, which ranks among the state's dozen largest publicly owned systems, also was a victim, because the initiative stopped the system from seeking a higher proportion of local property taxes which would have quadrupled their income. The system lost about $227,000 a year in property tax, about 2% of total revenues. Fares went from 25 cents, to 35 cents and then to 50 cents—the fare subsidized by Los Angeles County's Proposition A sales tax increase last year. Some late-night trips were dropped to reduce expenses. "People called, they pleaded to restore the night services," a Long Beach Transit official recalls. "If there had been no Proposition 13, we'd have $1 million more to expand. Overall (yes) we're worse off. . . . "

——RH

4

Exporting the Revolt

In Sacramento and around the nation, politicians recognized the popular rush to the California tax-cutting measures as an important change in public attitude toward budget decisions. Public opinion polls taken just before newspaper publication suggest that tax revolt fervor may be softening a bit, although it still remains strong. What seems most clear-cut from interviews across the state and across the nation is that voters will be asked to face the same issues as those raised by the California tax revolt again and again.

California's most successful export in 1978 may have been the tax revolt. Responding swiftly to the signals they read in the state's vote on Proposition 13 in June of that year, politicians and tax-limitation groups in 17 states placed tax-cap measures on the ballots within six months; all but five were approved.

Ultimately, 25 states enacted new restrictions tieing government spending to economic growth—measures that John Shannon, assistant director of the Advisory Commission on Intergovernmental Relations, a Washington study group, likens to "a speed governor on the car." They ranged from South Dakota's requirement that a two-thirds legislative majority approve any tax increase to an Arizona constitutional amendment limiting government spending to 7% of the total personal income in the state. Although most of these tax and spending limitations were based in theory, if not in form, on Proposition 13, only one state enacted a measure comparable in severity to California's: Massachusetts, which had been perceived as having such a costly government that residents and businessmen dubbed it "Taxachusetts."

A high tax burden was not prerequisite for a tax cap; voters' fear of tax increases was sometimes enough. Alabama, with the lowest per capita tax burden in the union, restricted tax increases almost as swiftly as did Massachusetts, which in 1979 was imposing a property tax on its homeowners at nearly twice the national average. Some of these measures were more carefully crafted than others. Michigan's so-called Headlee Amendment, passed by voters in late 1978, limited state expenditures to the share of total personal income they represented in 1978-1979. Much later, that figure was determined to be about 10%—a historical peak for that economically besieged state, and a ceiling so lofty that the legislature would actually have to raise spending by $2 billion this year, or 30%, to meet it. The measure did, however, fix the share of state revenues to be funneled back to localities as state aid at 41.6%. With Michigan's social welfare costs rising geometrically because of its devastated industrial economy, "that has proved to be a major problem" for the state, said Douglas Roberts, deputy state budget director.

As in many other states, Michigan's 15 public higher education institutions have had to raise tuition and other fees to cover their losses; in the wake of tuition increases of more than 20% last fall, the University of Michigan is now charging the second-highest tuition for state residents in the nation (after the University of Vermont). The growth of government spending in almost every state, including those without explicit limitations, has slowed markedly from 1978. According to a study by the Advisory Commission on Intergovernmental Relations, state and local spending per capita rose at an average annual rate of 4.4% from 1957 to 1978, the year of Proposition 13; in the following three years, the average increase dropped to 0.5%. In only three states did spending increase faster after 1978 than before: Alaska, Oklahoma and Wyoming, all of which spent meagerly before 1978 but, particularly after 1973, developed large oil-industry tax revenues.

In most states tax cuts and restrictions were aimed primarily at the property tax, traditionally the revenue tool of first resort for local government, and as such the most visible and onerous tax paid by homeowners, a politically influential class. In most cases, governments took back at least some of the tax savings in new ways. Most states replaced part of the lost property-tax revenue with an array of new sales and excise taxes typically regressive in nature—that is, falling proportionately harder on households with lesser incomes. California enacted a 1-cent standby sales tax in February, to be implemented if it appears the state will end the next fiscal year with a deficit.

In 1981 and 1982, 31 states enacted increases in their gas and motor fuel taxes (five states enacted such increases twice). In the same period, 19 states raised general sales taxes, and 25 imposed or increased so-called "sin" taxes, or levies on alcohol and tobacco. Eleven states even raised income taxes; New Jersey imposed one for the first time in its history, but earmarked the proceeds for local government. Seeking to replace some property tax revenue with sales and income tax money has had an important political effect; it shifted the source of local government money from the local level to the state. "That forced the state to rethink its relationship with local governments," said Helen E. Ladd of the Kennedy School of Government at Harvard University. In 1981, then-Gov. Edward King reluctantly turned over about $265 million in new state aid to Massachusetts cities and towns to cushion the blow, much as California devoted $4.4 billion of its 1979 budget surplus to local aid.

The focus of budget cuts across the country also speaks volumes about America's current political priorities. Virtually without exception, police and fire services were protected from heavy spending cuts, as they were in California. To an extent, this came at the expense of such capital items as public works, which are traditionally financed by long-term municipal borrowing and are not often perceived by the public as immediate necessities. At the far extreme, school systems, with their traditionally large shares of local budgets and public payrolls compounded by declining enrollments that diluted their political support, generally suffered disproportionately deep cuts.

Some observers argue that much of the tax-cut fervor aimed at local expenditures was the result of the public's misdirected ire at the growth of state spending, particularly "public hostility to social welfare programs"—an attitude conceivably nourished by the sharp growth in scope and expense of such programs starting in the late 1960s, said W. Norton Grubb of the University of Texas. Daniel K. Whitehurst, mayor of Fresno and a member of the advisory board to the National League of Cities, suggests that much of the voting public, particularly the middle class, believes that most government services, from bus systems to schools, are irrelevant to their lives. "The point is that people are generally going to vote their self-interest, and now they feel they can cut government services without affecting their self-interest directly."

Perhaps the state facing the most severe test of this notion is Massachusetts, where Proposition 2½ (named after its mandates that property taxes be limited to 2½ % of a community's assessed valuation and that increases be restricted to 2½ % annually after that) forced 182 Massachusetts cities and towns to cut their budgets by a combined $357.3 million in 1981 alone, with further cuts mandated for most in 1982 and 1983. In the first year, according to a study by the Massachusetts Municipal Assn., the cuts forced layoffs of 17,263 municipal employees across the state, even though a special allocation of state aid reduced the expected budget cuts that year by half. Another 3,000 to 5,000 lost state jobs. The required reductions would otherwise have been impossibly deep for some communities. Chelsea, a working-class city shoehorned along the shore of Boston Harbor, would have had to cut its property-tax levy to $4.4 million from $14.5 million—a slice averted, temporarily, by a phasing in of the law and by the state aid.

Under Proposition 2½, not surprisingly, schools were singled out for particularly harsh treatment. The law revoked the state's century-old tradition of fiscal autonomy for the educational system, under which school boards had been permitted to set their own budgets and order up the appropriate tax levy from municipal tax collectors. "The mayor has the authority of a czar now," said Quincy School Superintendent Lawrence Creedon. In his working-class city of nearly 90,000, Creedon said, the schools have absorbed virtually the entire city revenue cut of $10 million over the last two years—or 33% of the pre-2½ school budget—and must maintain a no-growth budget for the coming year About 750 full-time school employees have been laid off, including more than 350 of the system's 1,054 teachers and administrators. A dropout prevention program that reduced dropout rates to 3% from 9% over seven years was eliminated, allowing the rate to rise back to 9% two years later, Creedon said. Of the system's 21 elementary schools, 12 have been closed, and Creedon attributes seven or eight of those closings to losses induced by Proposition 2½.

Implementing Proposition 2½ also exposed some of its fundamental weaknesses as a piece of legislation. "They wrote the damn bill so fast and in such a haphazard way that they didn't even look at Proposition 13, which dealt with some issues much more intelligently," said Lawrence Susskind, director of the Proposition 2½ Monitoring Project, a study program based at Massachusetts Institute of Technology. The Massachusetts measure failed, for instance, to exempt money for repayment of municipal debt from the 2½% limit. Thus, with bondholders deprived of any guarantee that their bonds would be good, the public bond ratings of hundreds of communities were almost instantly suspended, meaning that most were unable to float new bonds to finance buildings or public works. In contrast to California, where Proposition 13 allows municipalities to finance existing bonds (although not new ones) without regard to the tax cap, the repayment of billions of dollars in local bond issues in Massachusetts was cast in doubt. The state legislature hastily fashioned a rescue program allowing any town or city in risk of default to draw an advance on its future state aid to pay its debts.

Nevertheless, even communities that were successfully grappling with Proposition 2½'s cuts were shut out of the bond market. "We went down to Moody's (one of two major bond-rating companies) and explained what we were planning," says James Sullivan, until recently the city manager of Cambridge, which was planning cuts in its department budgets of 25% in the first year of Proposition 2½. "While I think they probably appreciated what we were doing, they still saw the source of revenue support (to repay bonds) being taken away." Cambridge's bond rating has been restored, but at a lower level than before Proposition 2½, meaning that borrowing costs will be higher.

Many states have actually increased taxes in 1981 and 1982, but the Advisory Commission on Intergovernmental Relations cautions against concluding that the tax revolt is over. The round of property tax increases of the last two years were generally necessary to overcome big deficits resulting in part from the recession. "There's no evidence that taxpayers are going to buy tax increases for government expansion," Shannon said. "It's acceptable for government maintenance—if you can show you're hemorrhaging and there's blood on the floor."

—MAH

THE CHANGE IN SACRAMENTO

In 1977, Democratic Assemblyman John Vasconcellos of San Jose described himself in his official biography as being primarily concerned with "cultural assumptions about human nature and potential," among other things. Today, Vasconcellos, chairman of the Assembly Ways and Means Committee, is concerned chiefly with balancing the state budget. Such is nature of political change in Sacramento triggered by the passage of Proposition 13 five years ago.

While it did not rob liberal Democrats such as Vasconcellos of their visions or stifle their political careers, it did, as he plainly put it, "make us more cautious . . . more down-to-earth." The six syllables of the phrase "Proposition 13" have become the foundation of a new language for political debate in state politics.

"To me, Proposition 13 was a revolt against the prevailing government philosophy and style—an anti-establishment action," said Assembly Republican Leader Robert W. Naylor of Menlo Park, who originally opposed Proposition 13 but who since has become a vigorous convert. "Pretty clearly, conservative Republicans made some gains. But you have to credit the Democratic majority with protecting itself rather skillfully," he added, assessing the political winners and losers of the measure.

At the start of 1978, Democrats controlled both houses of the

Legislature, 26-to-14 in the Senate and 57-to-23 in the Assembly. In the years since, the numbers have fluctuated but the result remains the same. Democrats now have a 25-to-15 majority in the Senate and a 48-to-32 grip on the Assembly. Moreover, Democrats generally regarded as traditional liberals are in the leadership just as firmly—or maybe more so—than their pre-Proposition 13 predecessors.

"But despite what appears to be liberal control of both houses of the Legislature, we have been profoundly affected by the passage of Proposition 13," said Assembly Speaker Willie Brown (D-San Francisco), whose 19 years in the Assembly make him the senior member of the house. "We don't think tax increase anymore as anything except a most unwelcome solution to problems. Before, tax increases were commonplace," said Brown, who added with a touch of exaggeration for effect, "Now, we (liberals) even rationally discuss cuts in spending!"

Equally identifiable was the change in composition of the GOP caucus of the Assembly. The numbers did not grow dramatically, but power abruptly shifted from moderate veterans to newly elected hard-line conservatives in the aftermath of Proposition 13. These Republican legislators, first known as the "Proposition 13 babies" and now nicknamed "the cavemen," are predominately anti-government, anti-tax crusaders. "Before Proposition 13, there were these kinds of people but their voices were rarely heard and they were never written about. But now, they are not only heard but a lot is written about them," said Brown.

Originally, entrenched politicians of both parties shunned Proposition 13 in favor of a legislatively sponsored alternative which appeared on the same ballot. But insurgent conservative GOP candidates around the state embraced the Jarvis-Gann initiative, thereby linking it to this day with the right wing of the GOP. Ironically, one result of Proposition 13 was to shift political and governmental authority from local municipalities and counties to the state, a centralization of power that conservatives typically abhor but one that continues to this day. "Local control has eroded to the point where the state, in many respects, has become the city council and the board of supervisors for communities around California," lamented Republican Gov. George

Deukmejian, who also opposed Proposition 13 but has since become an enthusiastic backer of it.

Something that failed to materialize out of the ballot measure
was the election of its co-author, Paul Gann, to the U.S. Senate.
Gann, advanced as the candidate of Republican kingmakers,
tried to use Proposition 13 as a springboard to Washington but
was trounced in 1980 by Democratic Senator Alan Cranston.
Likewise, former GOP Lt. Gov. Mike Curb found that his backing of Proposition 13 was not enough to land him in the governor's office last year, while Deukmejian was elected despite his
initial opposition to it. Democratic Lt. Gov. Leo T. McCarthy,
who was Speaker of the Assembly during the years immediately
before and after Proposition 13, said the measure "drastically
shook" both political parties. "Democrats who exposed programs that required funding saw their programs reduced or eliminated. And it was the coup de grace for the (former Gov. and
U.S. Chief Justice) Earl Warren-moderate wing of the Republican Party, which had been losing ground through the 1960s and
1970s," McCarthy said.

Proposition 13, of course, was not a single, isolated act but an
explosive chapter of a political phenomenon that can be traced
back at least 17 years. That was when Ronald Reagan first an-
nounced his candidacy for governor of California and called for a
"possible tax moratorium" on homes owned by retired persons
and for a study of the overall tax structure because "it's just possible that we can't afford everything." A few years later, in 1973,
Reagan advanced an initiative to limit the growth of government
spending in California, confessing that he was unable within the
legislative system to "get government down and reduce the percentage of the people's earnings that was being taken in taxes."

Reagan's initiative, Proposition 1, failed. But the idea lived on.
With tax crusader Gann leading the way, voters followed Proposition 13 with the so-called "Spirit of 13" initiative in 1979
which, similar to Reagan's plan, placed a ceiling on the growth of
government spending.Gov. Edmund G. Brown Jr., Reagan's
Democratic successor, also was skeptical of government and its
direction from the time he took office. Brown coined the phrase
"lower your expectations" in regard to government and was in

the front rank as Democrats around the country tried to redefine the liberalism of past decades. Brown also succeeded in doing what Reagan could not—serve eight years without a signing what he called a "general tax increase," a phrase that excluded a bi-partisan gasoline tax hike that was enacted. But Brown did not benefit from Proposition 13. An opponent of the measure, he heartily embraced it after voters approved it and found himself saddled with the accusation that he had done an opportunistic "flip-flop."

For all the change that Proposition 13 has wrought, will it be lasting? McCarthy guessed the measure would shape political views in California "for at last a generation;" Naylor called it a "long-term check on the budgetary politics-of-addition." Per-haps as much as anyone, Vasconcellos illustrates the point. Strongly liberal and known for his "humanistic" approach on the political process, Vasconcellos said he has not given an inch in his hopes for humanity. But he has given quite a bit when it comes to the role of government. "We've come to know that we can't solve a lot of the problems people have," he reflected. "But govern-ment still can be an educational and moral leader to help people solve their own problems."

—JB

THE OUTLOOK FOR THE TAX REVOLT

Californians who regret the way they voted on Proposition 13 five years ago may have a chance to make their choice again— and again. Although Proposition 13 settled some public policy issues, such as the distribution of property-tax relief, the mea-sure raised new and agonizing questions about how tax dollars should be raised and spent. And it simply delayed decisions on others. Among those decisions that Californians may soon con-front in the voting booth:

■ Proposition 13 co-sponsors Howard Jarvis and Paul Gann are collecting signatures to qualify for the November, 1984, bal-lot, an initiative that would close "loopholes" in the tax-limiting provisions of Proposition 13.

■ Local governments and school boards may charge in the op-posite direction and ask voters for new revenue-raising powers that will give them more say in local affairs.

■ Community college districts, hard-pressed by budget cuts, are contemplating a move of their own—an initiative that would give them authority to raise property taxes with a simple majority vote of their constituents.

■ A proposal to tax business properties at a higher rate than other properties—to "split" the property tax roll—is also likely to resurface, supporters say, although a split-roll initiative failed to qualify in 1982.

These issues arise as public opinion polls about taxation and spending show that Californians' attitudes are beginning to shift. With the state in financial difficulty, proposals to raise a variety of state taxes have gained more support in the Legislature this year than many had predicted. Legislative staff members point in particular to bills proposing to raise taxes for certain narrowly defined purposes, such as public education. Nevertheless, there is still fervent opposition to any general increase in taxes, and tax analysts see little prospect that the strict limits on property taxes imposed by Proposition 13 will be overturned.

Of the proposals, the new Jarvis-Gann initiative—the so-called Jarvis-Gann II—would have the most far-reaching effect on government. It would close two court-created loopholes in Proposition 13 and would restrict local governments' growing reliance on fees and charges. In so doing, the initiative would foreclose three alternative revenue-raising options that have been used by cities since 1978. The proposed amendment would keep cities from taking advantage of the August, 1982, Farrell vs. San Francisco decision, in which the state Supreme Court said cities can raise taxes without referendum, provided that revenues are not earmarked for special purposes. And it would also bar them from raising taxes under a second case, Carman vs. Alvord, in which the state Supreme Court said public-employee-pension costs could be considered "indebtedness" that could be financed by property tax hikes. The initiative would limit state and local governments' abilities to assess fees and charges for services.

Governments would be allowed to charge fees for service only to cover the direct cost of those services. Two-thirds voter approval would be required to impose new fees, or to raise existing ones by more than increases in the cost of living. Only 13 of California's 430 cities have raised property taxes to pay off pension obligations since Proposition 13, and only between 10 and 20 have used the Farrell decision to raise taxes, the League of California Cities estimated. Yet the Carman loophole offers potential revenues of $800 million a year to California cities, the legislative analyst has estimated.

There is no way to estimate the value of the Farrell decision, which allows cities to raise admissions, utility, parking, business-license, and gross-receipts taxes. But the decision has meant $85 million in business taxes in two years for San Francisco. And this year Los Angeles expects to raise $120 million toward its $1.7-billion budget with a new utility surcharge, and increases in the business-license and hotel-bed taxes. The initiative's limits on fees is the provision that would affect the largest number of cities and counties, although fee revenues account for about 13% of city general revenues and 8% of county general revenues. The limits could pose particular problems for the government "enterprise" operations, such as public utilities, that depend heavily on service charges and are periodically buffeted by skyrocketing energy costs.

The provision would pinch utilities if there were a repeat of the oil-price run-up of 1979 to 1980, when utility oil costs grew 40% but the consumer price index increased only 13.5%. "We take (the initiative drive) very, very seriously," said Kenneth Emanuels, legislative director for the League of California Cities. If the initiative makes it to the ballot, "it will be very difficult for us to explain our side of the question without inflaming a lot of emotion," he said.

Observers say the initiative drive lacks the momentum of the first Jarvis-Gann attempt because property owners do not feel aggrieved by fast-growing taxes and a bulging state surplus, as they did in 1978. But Proposition 13 has a following that will mobilize even to vote on such an abstract issue as the closing of legal loopholes, observers on both sides agree. If the drive does not succeed, the loophole-closing effort may nonetheless bloom again next year as legislation to amend the state Constitution. Such a measure was drafted last year by a committee representing the state Chamber of Commerce, the California Taxpayers Assn. and other business groups, and introduced during this year's legislative session. Sponsors have chosen not to push the bill, pending the outcome of the new Jarvis-Gann initiative drive.

Meanwhile, local government and education officials are stepping up efforts to gain fiscal independence from the state. They say that this effort may take the form of an initiative or a bill to amend the Constitution. In either case, the campaign faces major obstacles, as a preliminary skirmish this year demonstrated.

An effort called Project Independence included the League of California Cities, the County Supervisors Assn. and the California School Boards Assn. Their talks about returning power to the localities were initiated by the California Roundtable, a group of executives of California's biggest firms. But representatives of the Roundtable and the business-backed California Taxpayers Assn. dropped out of discussions after the three government associations proposed a bill that would amend the state Constitution to give counties and schools a fixed share of state and personal-income and sales taxes. The proposal would also have fixed the share of state taxes, such as cigarette taxes, that are shared with local governments.

Before the bill died quietly in committee, it had drawn fire from influential legislators, including Assembly Speaker Willie Brown (D-San Francisco), as well as from business spokesmen. While supporting the goal of greater home rule, both said they oppose giving localities a fixed share of state taxes. "It's like a grown-up son saying, 'I want to be independent from you, dad—give me a permanent share of your income,' " said Jim Kennedy, tax analyst with the state Chamber of Commerce. Gov. George Deukmejian also has convened a task force to study ways of insuring stable revenues for local governments. But Speaker Brown has made clear that he will oppose any solution that involves dedicating a share of state-raised revenues for local use. Indeed, in a recent interview with Times reporters, he said that the state may need to bypass county governments altogether to make sure that the health and welfare programs now administered by counties are carried out according to state law.

Officials of the state's community colleges are considering several ways of raising revenues to help a public program that has been among those hardest hit by the cutbacks of the past five years. An initiative proposed by Chancellor James Young of the Kern Community College District would amend the state Constitution to allow local voters, by a simple majority vote, to raise property taxes for community colleges. The Assn. of California Community Colleges, the colleges' principal lobbying group, is awaiting the results of an opinion poll before deciding whether to support the drive. Meanwhile, the Board of Governors of the California Community Colleges wants community colleges to be able to take advantage of the Farrell decision. They have been pushing for legislation that would allow localities to raise local sales or income taxes or to impose a property tax not based on assessed value to supplement community college revenues.

Proposals to tax business properties at a higher rate than other properties may also make their way to the ballot in the next few years, both opponents and proponents of the idea say.Advocates of the "split roll" argue that business property should be taxed at a higher rate than residential property because commercial property is sold less often than residential. Under Proposition 13, properties are reassessed to their current market value when they are built, sold, or substantially improved. Thus, if residential properties are sold more often than business properties, their assessments are higher and their owners pay higher taxes. Split-roll advocates have argued that the greater turnover of residential properties would cause a shift of the tax burden from business to homeowners. In the five years since Proposition 13, there has been no such shift, because of the way high interest rates and recession have slowed construction and sales of homes. Last year, a split-roll initiative failed when supporters were unable to meet a deadline in presenting signatures to qualify.

Nonetheless, bills designed to split the tax rolls have appeared in the legislative hopper almost every year since 1978, with support from such groups as the public-employee-backed California Tax Reform Assn. And a March public-opinion survey by the Field Institute found that 54% of Californians would favor such a tax shift, if a tax increase became necessary. "It's an issue that we'll have with us maybe forever," said Richard Simpson, a vice president of the California Taxpayers Assn. Many tax analysts and tax officials doubt that there will ever be enough popular support to change the Proposition 13 assessment system, despite the way the system penalizes home buyers.

The proposition provides that homes bought before 1978 are assessed at their 1975 market value, with those taxes increasing by no more than 2% annually. Homes built, bought or improved since passage of the proposition are assessed at market value at the time of the purchase or remodeling. Taxes on these homes then also can rise no more than 2% a year. Alexander Pope, the Los Angeles County assessor, is among those who predict that there will be no change. He said that while recent home buyers are angered by their higher taxes, their feelings change after sev-eral years, as the market values of their homes rises above their assessed values. Pope said that with a little more than one-sixth of residential properties sold each year, the system's opponents will never outnumber those who feel that they benefit from the status quo.

Recent public opinion polls and this year's state budget battle suggest that Californians' anti-tax feelings of 1978 may be soft-ening. A Times Poll in April, for example, showed a drop-off in public approval of Proposition 13. In polls over four years, more than 60% of respondents consistently said that they believed that Proposition 13 would "turn out to be a good thing." In April, this group had dwindled to 42% of those surveyed. Field Insti-tute polls in April and June found that, by a 2-1 margin, Califor-nians favor the compromise 1-cent standby sales tax voted by the Legislature in February. And there is a growing belief that state and local government services have deteriorated since 1978. While the largest share of those surveyed, 48%, saw no change in the overall quality of public services since 1978, 42% said service levels have declined and 6% said services have improved. Field said surveys conducted before 1978 suggested that the number of Californians who were satisfied with service levels had always outnumbered those who are dissatisfied. Yet anti-tax feeling re-mains strong. In the April Field poll, 56% of those surveyed said that, faced with a deficit, the state should cut spending—even if

it meant cutting services—rather than increase taxes. That percentage had grown since August, 1982, when it stood at 46%.
"My reading of the polls is that a lot more people are concerned
about service cuts today than were five years ago," said Jack Citrin, a University of California, Berkeley, political science pro-
fessor who is co-author of a book on the causes of Proposition 13.
"Yet any general tax increase would be strongly resisted." He believes that tax increases are acceptable to the public only to stave
off financial disaster, and for "limited, focused" purposes, such
as improvements to the state's public education system.

The year's legislative session seems to support this view. The
governor and the Legislature agreed on a "trigger" sales tax to
ease the state's financial problems. And the momentum for new
tax increases came principally in education bills. Many tax-poli-
cy analysts believe that in their search for additional revenues,
state leaders will first fill tax loopholes and raise minor state taxes, such as the alcohol and tobacco taxes, as they did this year.
Then they will be forced to turn again to the three principal state
taxes—the state personal income, bank and corporation and
sales taxes, which together account for more than 85% of state
general-fund revenues. Field polls have found for the past four
years that a majority of Californians would support increases in
the alcohol and tobacco ("sin") taxes and oil-severance taxes,
provided taxes had to be raised.

On the local level, analysts expect governments to continue to
raise fees and charges. They say that cities will rely more heavily
on the four taxes that can be raised without a referendum under
the Farrell decision. Whether cities will propose property-tax increases, following the lead of Los Angeles Mayor Tom Bradley,
remains unclear while the Legislature considers how such additional revenues would be distributed. In any case, few analysts
foresee an increase of more than a few percentage points in the
state and local tax burden, which has fallen more than 25% since
1978. "You may see it go up a few points in the next five years,
but not more," said Larry J. Kimbell, director of the UCLA Business Forecasting Project, echoing a popular view. "On tax burden, you have seen a permanent change."

Appendix:
The Los Angeles Times Survey.
Local Government Responses
to Proposition 13

by *KEVIN BACON*

As part of its Proposition 13 study, the Los Angeles Times con-ducted an extensive survey of local governments in California to develop a substantial base of data which would provide a basic context for the extensive reporting efforts that produced the se-ries. The purpose of this chapter is to describe the background, methodology, limitations, and principal findings of the local gov-ernment survey.

Senior editorial staff at the Times expressed a strong desire to develop a firm quantitative information base to underlie the in-terviews and other research that would go into the series. An ad-ditional consideration was the desire to test local government re-sponses to a variety of general assertions about how local governments responded to Proposition 13.

As Times staff began working on this project, they quickly be-came aware of the problems involved with obtaining accurate and current quantitative data about local government finances in California. The best comprehensive source of information on lo-cal finances is the series of annual reports published by the State Controller. Unfortunately, this series lags by 1 to 2 years the cur-rent fiscal year. When the Times began this project (January 1983) the latest data available covered the 1980-81 fiscal year. Data covering 1981-82 was not published until May and June of

1983, well past the deadline for the series.

In addition to these timing problems, there was an absence of published quantitative data about service level changes and changes in non-monetary inputs (staffing, equipment, capital facilities) used to provide public services. While previous studies had addressed these areas, there was no current data available.

Early in the project the Times staff secured the assistance of Kevin Bacon, a management consultant with the international accounting and consulting firm of Price Waterhouse. Bacon, while employed by the California Legislature, had conducted an extensive study of Proposition 13 which was published in 1981 (City and County Finances in the Post-Proposition 13 Era, two volumes, California Legislature, June, 1981). Bacon was retained to assist the Times in designing and analyzing its survey of local government. At The Times, he worked closely with Terry Schwadron, editor on the project, Paul Richter, lead writer on the series, and I. E. "Bud" Lewis, Susan Pinkus, and Mary Klette of the Los Angeles Times Poll to develop and execute the survey described below.

From the start of the project, it was clear that there were definite limitations on the proposed survey. These limitations stemmed from the inherent nature of the newspaper as a communications media. Chief among these was the short time frame allowed for the survey process and the nature of the questions to be addressed. Less than four months time was available from the beginning of the project to the last copy deadline. All aspects of the survey (design, pre-testing, distribution, collection, data entry, and analysis) process had to be completed in a short period. This reduced the time available to respondents to complete the survey to four weeks. In order to encourage a high response rate every effort was made to hold the number and complexity of the questions to a minimum. Finally, the content of the surveys was designed to ask the types of questions Times readers were thought to be most interested in.

A series of meetings were held with Times staff to discuss the types of questions that should be addressed in the survey. In general, these questions addressed the level of expenditures, staffing, selected service levels, and government responses to a standard set of questions about actions taken in response to Proposition 13 of 1978. A key strategic decision affecting study design was the Times' focus of what had happened to specific government services rather than to units of government. Previous studies had focused on units of government such as cities or counties. The Times wished to focus on services such as law enforcement, fire protection, and local schools. This desire led to the decision to develop five separate surveys—one for each of the five local service areas under study.

Given the large number of local government units in California (over 1,000 school districts, 58 counties, 430 cities, and over 5,000 special districts), it was not feasible to conduct in-person interviews to gather the information sought by The Times. Because of the complexity and the need to consult historical data in order to answer many questions, a telephone survey was also ruled out. As a result, a mail survey was determined to be the only feasible means of collecting the desired data. The surveys themselves are contained in Exhibits 1-5, which follow this chapter.

Throughout this chapter, references will be made to inflation adjusted dollar amounts in an attempt to measure the change in real purchasing power available to government. For purposes of this report, we measured inflation by using the Gross National Product Deflator published by the Bureau of Economic Analysis. For the period from 1977-78 to 1981-82, the total amount of inflation measured by this index was 38.6%. We chose this index because it is the most conservative measure of inflation over the period studied. We sought a conservative measure of inflation so that any results implying a decline in government purchasing power found in the study would be unambiguous.

The reader should bear in mind, however, that other measures showed a much larger amount of inflation over the study period. The California Consumer Price Index (all urban consumers), as published by the California Department of Industrial Relations, showed a total amount of inflation of 53.5% over the study period. Use of this index would have shown much larger declines in government purchasing power over the study period. There is a good deal of debate over how well the CPI measures the true rate of inflation, particularly because of its treatment of housing costs. Other measures of inflation, such as the GNP Deflator for State and Local Government, were also considered but were rejected along with the CPI because of a desire to avoid being caught up in a discussion of the applicability of the measure of inflation to overall government spending for the services studied.

The sample selection for each of the five surveys involved the use of a computer program to select a random sample of jurisdictions. The sampling universe varied based on the number of jurisdictions that provided the appropriate service for each of five key services—law enforcement, fire protection, schools, streets and roads, parks and recreation. The probability of any particular unit of government receiving a survey (except counties, all 58 of which were mailed a survey) varied with its share of total local government spending on each service area as reported by the state controller. Hence, a large jurisdiction had a higher probability of being selected than a smaller one because it spent more money and served more people.

The questionnaires were mailed to selected jurisdictions and respondents were asked to return them within three weeks. Follow-up telephone calls were made. Nevertheless, it appears that smaller jurisdictions were less likely to return our survey than larger jurisdictions. As a result, while our survey results fairly depict the responses to Proposition 13 of the jurisdictions that serve the bulk of the state's population and spend the bulk of its funds, the reader should exercise caution when applying the results to the numerous very small jurisdictions in the state. While very numerous, these agencies serve a small proportion of the state's population and spend a small share of local dollars.

The results of the five surveys are discussed in the sections that follow. Each section reviews the composition of the sample, expenditure trends, staffing trends, service level indicators, use of special tax elections, and general responses to fiscal constraints.

The survey covered the period from 1977-78 (the last fiscal year before Proposition 13) to 1981-82. During this period the state government provided extensive fiscal assistance ("bail-out") to local jurisdictions. This assistance totalled $4.4 billion in 1978-79 compared with a $6.5 billion cut in property taxes due to Proposition 13. Bail-out aid grew to $5.9 billion in

1981-82. This aid helped prevent the drastic reductions in service predicted by opponents of Proposition 13 during the 1978 campaign.

In general, the survey results discussed below do not show any drastic reductions in public services in the areas studied. While individual jurisdictions that relied heavily on property taxes before Proposition 13 may have implemented significant reductions in service, the overall trend in our study of jurisdictions was a slow erosion or retrenchment, rather than wholesale reductions in service level or quality. Public safety services (fire and police) have generally been able to keep pace with inflation during the study period, though they have not been able to maintain real per capita spending or staffing at pre-Proposition 13 levels in the face of population growth. Schools have seen a decline in real spending per pupil and in the purchasing power of teacher's salaries. Declining enrollments, however, may have been as important a factor in school financing problems as was Proposition 13. Street and road programs and park programs were the ones most dramatically affected by fiscal constraint. Real spending and staffing were both down by significant amounts. However, the public may not have seen many of these reductions clearly since few physical facilities (parks or roads) were closed as a result. Indeed, while road system mileage changed little, park acreage rose by nearly 10 percent. It may take some time for the effects of reduced maintenance of streets and parks to become visible to the public.

The survey studied fiscal years from 1977-78 to 1981-82. The state government was forced to make significant reductions in bail-out relief to local governments during 1982-83 and 1983-84. This reflected the severe impact of the recent recession on state revenues. Local government revenues (primarily sales and property taxes) were also impacted by the recession. As a result, many of the persons contacted during the study felt that there would be more dramatic service level changes in 1982-83 and 1983-84 than during the study period. It remains for further research to investigate this possibility.

I. LAW ENFORCEMENT SURVEY

A. The Sample

The law enforcement services survey was mailed to 208 jurisdictions, including all 58 counties and 150 of the state's 430 cities. Cities and counties provide the overwhelming bulk of all local law enforcement services in California. The survey itself is reproduced as Exhibit 1. We received usable replies from 114 jurisdictions, a 54.8% response rate. Of these replies, 7 (6.1%) were cities that contracted with their county governments to provide police protection. The remaining 107 agencies provided service directly.

These 114 replies displayed the following characteristics in terms of the type of jurisdiction and the population size:

The Law Enforcement Survey

Type of jurisdiction	Number of replies	Percent	Population served
Cities	87	76.3%	9.0
Counties	27	23.7%	5.4
	114	**100.0%**	**14.4** million

Population group	Number of replies	Percent
0- 10,000	11	9.6%
10,000- 50,000	46	40.3%
50,001-100,000	30	26.3%
100,001-300,000	20	17.5%
300,001-500,000	2	1.8%
500,000+	5	4.5%
	114	**100.0%**

The population served by each jurisdiction in the survey represented the 1982 population of each city or the 1982 unincorporated area population of each county (adjusted for the population in contracting cities) responding to the questionnaire. The five largest jurisdictions in our sample (LA City, LA County, Sacramento County, San Diego County, and the City of San Jose) served a combined population of 6.7 million persons in 1982.

Their actions affected over 27% of the total population in the state.

B. Operating Expenditures

From our sample, we received complete information about total operating expenditures for the period 1977-78 to 1981-82 from 104 agencies. Total operating costs included county costs for operating jails since these are operated by county sheriffs. Court costs and probation costs were not included in these figures. The following table summarizes the survey data on operating expenditures:

Total Operating Expenditures
Dollars in thousands except per capita amounts

Number of jurisdictions:	**104**
Population served in 1981-82:	
Cities (81)	**8.9** million
Counties (23)	**5.2** million
Total expenditures:	
1977-78	$1,038,691
1981-82	1,686,215
Percent change	**+62.4%**
Constant dollar 1981-82	
Expenditures	$1,216,605
Percent change since 1977-78	**+17.1%**
Constant dollar expenditures per capita:	
1977-78	$79.33
1981-82	86.41
Percent change	**+8.9%**

As the table above indicates, law enforcement expenditures increased 17.1% on an inflation adjusted basis between 1977-78 and 1981-82. On a per capita basis, expenditures increased 8.9% in our sample. Among the 104 responding agencies, fully 75% reported increasing their inflation adjusted per capita expenditures over this period. Only 21.2% of our respondents reported reductions in per capita expenditures. Counties were more likely to report reductions (30.5%) than were cities (18.5%). All five of the largest jurisdictions in our sample reported increasing the amount of inflation adjusted expenditures per capita. Amongst these 5 largest jurisdictions, the 3 counties (Los Angeles, San Diego, Sacramento) showed significantly larger increases in per capita expenditures than did the two cities (Los Angeles and San Jose).

C. Components of Total Operating Expenditures

Sixty-seven jurisdictions provided complete information about the various components that made up total operating expenditures. These 67 jurisdictions served a total population of 9.2 million in 1981-82. The three components of spending data requested were salaries and benefits, employer pension costs, and all other operating expenditures. The following table displays the composition of spending in 1977-78 and 1981-82 and how it changed. All figures are in current dollars.

Composition of Law Enforcement Expenditures
Dollars in thousands

Number of jurisdictions   **67**
Population served in 1981-82   **9.2** million

Components	1977-78	%	1981-82	%	77-78 to 81-82 % Change
Salaries & benefits	$475,600	68.0%	$ 694,204	63.8%	46.0%
Employer pension costs	148,021	21.2%	272,172	25.0%	83.9%
All other operating costs	75,939	10.8%	121,411	11.2%	59.9%
Total operating expenditures	**$699,560**	**100.0%**	$1,087,787	**100.0%**	**55.5%**

The most striking finding in the table is the rapid growth in employer pension costs over the study period. While overall spending grew by 55.5%, employer pension costs grew by 83.9%. Pension costs grew from a 21.2% share of total operating spending in 1977-78 to a 25.0% share in 1981-82. The share devoted to salary and benefits dropped in response to this shift. The City of Los Angeles saw pension costs grow 88.5% over this period while it was reducing the total number of officers by 6.9%. This increase reflected the costs to the City of financing the unfunded liability in their pension system due to some very liberal cost of living increase provisions for "safety" members. While these provisions have since been repealed, the City will be required to spend substantial sums in the future to meet past pension obligations.

Due to the large size of the City of Los Angeles, we removed it from this sample to see if the trends in the table still held for the remaining jurisdictions. With Los Angeles removed, the remaining 66 jurisdictions showed total expenditure growth of 61.5% while employer pension costs grew by 76.6%. Once again this growth resulted in an increased share of spending being devoted to pension costs and an offsetting reduction in the share devoted to salaries and other benefits. This pattern held true in every population size group in our sample with the exception of the two agencies in the 300,001 to 500,000 population group. Their pension costs grew slightly slower than total law enforcement expenditures.

D. Capital Spending
Our survey only provided limited data on capital expenditures. We obtained data from 95 law enforcement agencies on capital outlays. Total capital expenditures rose from $12.0 million in 1977-78 to $33.5 million in 1981-82, a 275% increase when measured in current dollars. Capital spending represented slightly less than 2% of total spending reported in this survey.

E. Staffing Changes
1) Sworn Officers
Due to the inherent difficulties of measuring the output of law enforcement agencies ("public safety"), much attention is focused on measuring inputs as a way to determine the adequacy of local governments' attention to public protection. Of 106 agencies reporting on the number of sworn peace officers, 73.6% reported increasing the number of officers between 1977-78 and

1981-82. Only 19.8% reported reducing the number of sworn officers while 6.6% reported the number unchanged.

In our sample, counties were more likely to report reduced staffing (33.6%) than were cities. Larger jurisdictions were also more likely to report reductions than were smaller ones. Of 26 jurisdictions in our sample serving more than 100,000 people, 9 (34.6%) reported having fewer sworn officers in 1981-82 than in 1977-78. Of 80 smaller jurisdictions, only 12 (15%) reported fewer officers in 1981-82.

Among our 106 responding jurisdictions, 21 reported fewer officers, showing a cumulative net reduction of 656 FTE positions. The largest reduction occurred in the City of Los Angeles where 511 positions were eliminated, a cut of 6.9%. The largest percentage reduction occurred in Sierra County where 6 of 16 positions were eliminated, a cut of 37.5%. The remaining 85 jurisdictions reported no change or a net increase. These 85 jurisdictions reported adding 1428 FTE sworn officers. The net increase in the entire sample was 772 positions. The table below summarizes these findings.

Number of Sworn Peace Officers

Number of jurisdictions	**106**
Population Served in 1981-82:	
Cities (80)	**8.6** million
Counties (26)	**5.4** million
Total sworn staff:	
1977-78	26,115
1981-82	26,887
Percent change	**+3.0%**
Staff per 10,000 residents:	
1977-78	20.0
1981-82	19.2
Percent change	**-4.0%**

As the table illustrates, while the number of sworn officers increased, the ratio of officers to total population declined between 1977-78 and 1981-82. This finding is particularly interesting in light of the earlier data on real expenditures for law enforcement.

That data showed real per capita expenditures up 8.9%. This large real increase in per capita expenditures was not translated into more officers per capita. One explanation for this trend may be found in the data on the composition of spending. The rapid increase in employer pension costs, particularly costs related to unfunded prior pension liabilities, consumes a larger share of law enforcement budgets but may not provide any additional man-power on the streets. It is also possible that the growth that did occur in salary costs was utilized to improve salaries of the existing force rather than to expand the number of officers in proportion with the growth in total expenditures.

We also collected data on the number of calls from the public received by police. In our sample, there was an increase of 13.8% in calls from the public which exceeded the 8.2% growth in population in our sample. Given the 3.0% increase in sworn staff, it appears that the existing staff has been "worked harder" since 1977-78. An unknown portion of these calls, however, were ones for which an officer was no longer dispatched. In our sample, 47.5% of the departments reported that they had changed dispatch policies and no longer sent officers to certain types of calls. Of the 25 largest jurisdictions, 18 (72%) indicated they had made such a change.

In our sample, 50.9% of the agencies reported a lower ratio of officers per 10,000 population in 1981-82 than in 1977-78. Only 42.5% reported an improved ratio. Counties (57.7%) were more likely to report reduced ratios than were cities (48.8%). Large jurisdictions serving 100,000 residents or more were more likely to report declines (61.5%) than were smaller ones (47.5%).

2) Layoffs

In most cases, where reductions were necessary, they were made through attrition rather than layoffs. In our sample, 21 jurisdictions reduced the number of sworn officers by a total of 656 positions. Only 12 of these jurisdictions actually instituted lay-offs. The total number of officers laid off totalled 35, 5.3% of the 656 positions eliminated.

3) Civilian Employees

We received complete data on the number of civilian employees of law enforcement agencies from 92 departments. These agencies served 13.4 million persons in 1981-82. Among these 92 agencies total civilian staff rose from 9,690 to 10,560, and 8.9% increase between 1977-78 and 1981-82. Only 12.0% of the respondents reported a lower number of civilian employees in 1981-82 while 77.2% reported a larger number. Proportionately, fewer agencies reduced civilian employees than reduced sworn staff. The overall pattern of growth held true for both jurisdiction types and all size groups.

F. Response Time
Seventy-four (74) law enforcement agencies, serving 11.4 million persons in 1981-82, provided data on their average response time to calls for assistance. Of these 74 agencies, 44.6% reported no change in response time, 28.4% reported faster response time, and 27.0% reported slower response time. Counties and larger jurisdictions (serving more than 100,000 persons) were more likely to report improved response time than were cities or smaller jurisdictions.

Between 1977-78 and 1981-82, the weighted average response time in our sample showed a very slight improvement, moving from 4.46 minutes to 4.36 minutes (times were weighted by population served). The median response time increased slightly from 3.45 minutes to 3.50 minutes. Among the 5 largest jurisdictions in our sample, only the County of San Diego reported a slower response time, slipping from 8.3 to 8.9 minutes. The slowest response times were reported by rural county sheriff's departments where small departments must serve large geographic areas.

G. Arrests
Ninety-four agencies, serving 13.5 million persons in 1981-82, reported data on the total number of arrests made by their officers. While the total number of officers in this group increased by 2.9%, they reported making 8.2% more arrests in 1981-82 than in 1977-78. This pattern held true across jurisdictional types with over 71% of all agencies reporting more arrests per officer in 1981-82 than in 1977-78. Interestingly however, 3 of the 5 largest

jurisdictions (LA City, LA County, and Sacramento County) reported slight declines in arrests per officer over the study period. Interviews in Los Angeles City Police Department indicated that the department had redirected officer time away from "nuisance type" misdemeanors toward more serious crimes. According to LA police sources, this resulted in better control of more serious crimes.

H. Clearance Rate

This clearance rate measures the percentage of cases which are conclusively resolved (generally, arrest or determination that a crime did not occur) from the point of view of the police. We asked for data about the clearance rate for "Part I" offices, the most serious types of felonies. Seventy-nine agencies, serving 12.2 million persons provided data on their clearance rate for Part I offenses. In our sample, 48.1% reported an improved clearance rate, 10.1% reported an unchanged rate, and 41.8% reported a reduced clearance rate. This mixed pattern held true across both types of jurisdiction and all population size groups.

I. Equipment Life

Ninety-four departments provided data on the average number of miles a patrol car is driven before it is replaced. In our sample, 55.3% of the departments reported no change in the number of miles a vehicle was driven before replacement, while 34.0% reported an increase. The weighted average number of vehicle miles before replacement took a large jump from 69,000 to 84,000 miles (+21.7%) due to the fact that both Los Angeles County and the City of Los Angeles significantly increased vehicle mileage before replacement. LA City increased its average mileage by 66%, jumping it from 60,000 to 100,000 miles over the study period. This figure was only surpassed in several very small rural counties where even before Proposition 13 mileage had to surpass the 100,000 mark before replacement occurred.

J. Special Tax Elections

Of 102 agencies responding, 13 (12.7%) indicated that a special tax election was held to raise revenues for law enforcement.

Such elections were authorized by Proposition 13. Non-property taxes can be levied provided a 2/3 popular vote was obtained. Of the 13 elections held, only 3 were successful (23.0%). These elections occurred in the cities of Eureka and Hillsborough and the unincorporated area of San Mateo County. In the two large cities that held such elections, Los Angeles and Oakland, these measures were defeated decisively with 58% and 55% of the voters, respectively, voting against these taxes.

K. General Responses to Fiscal Constraints

The table on the following page presents data on responses of our sample agencies to a list of 11 general types of actions commonly thought to have been taken in response to fiscal constraints since Proposition 13. One hundred and three agencies provided replies to these questions.,

As the table points out, larger jurisdictions were more likely to institute any of these 11 actions than was the sample as a whole. The average law enforcement agency in our sample instituted 4 of these 11 measures. Los Angeles City took 9 of the 11 actions. The City of Eureka took the most actions on the list, reporting 10 of the 11 items on the list were implemented by this hard hit Northern California community. The two most commonly adopted actions involved raising revenue through new or increased fees for service. The two least acted upon options were closing a facility that was not being replaced and reducing the number of days per week any service was available to the public.

In the light of the rapid growth of pension costs, it is interesting to note that only 15.5% of the sample reported taking actions designed to control future pension costs. However, both the City of Los Angeles and Los Angeles County, the two largest police agencies in the state, reported taking such actions.

II. FIRE PROTECTION SURVEY

A. The Sample

The fire protection survey was mailed to 358 jurisdictions including all 58 counties, 150 of the state's 430 cities, and 150 of the approximately 600 special districts that provide fire protection service. The survey is reproduced as Exhibit 2. We received 202

General Responses to Fiscal Constraints
Since 1977-78

Number of jurisdictions	103
Population served in 1981-82:	
Cities (76)	8.5 million
Counties (27)	5.4 million

Action taken	Percent respondents answering yes	
	Overall sample	Jurisdictions over 100,000
1. Reduced future employee pension benefits	**15.5%**	29.6%
2. Instituted new fees or charges	**65.0%**	77.7%
3. Increased existing fees or charges	**87.3%**	92.3%
4. Permanently closed a facility that was not being replaced	**8.8%**	18.5%
5. Reduced the ratio of administrative or support staff to staff providing direct service	**46.5%**	61.5%
6. Began or increased contracting with the private sector	**19.0%**	30.7%
7. Reduced the number of days per week any of its services are available	**14.9%**	15.4%
8. Reduced the number of hours per day when staff handles public inquiries	**22.3%**	26.9%
9. Reduced janitorial services	**37.6%**	42.3%
10. Deferred major maintenance project	**48.5%**	63.0%
11. Used volunteers to replace paid employees	**44.0%**	53.8%

usable replies, a 56.4% response rate to the survey. Of these replies, 41 (20.39%) indicated that their jurisdiction either contracted with another agency for the provision of fire protection or
was not required to provide such service (counties or cities
served by an independent special district). The remaining 161
jurisdictions served over 15.2 million people in 1981-82, which
was over 63% of the total state population.

These 161 jurisdictions that provided services directly displayed the following characteristics, in terms of type of jurisdiction, population size, and staffing pattern:

The Fire Protection Survey

Type of jurisdiction	Number of replies	Percent
Cities	81	**50.3%**
Counties	8	**5.0%**
Special district	72	**44.7%**
	161	100.0%

Population size	Number of replies	Percent
0- 10,000	33	**20.5%**
10,001- 50,000	67	**41.6%**
50,001-100,000	37	**23.0%**
100,001-300,000	16	**9.8%**
300,001-500,000	3	**1.9%**
500,000+	5	3.2%
	161	100.0%

Staffing pattern	Number of replies	Percent
All volunteers	4	**2.5%**
Volunteers and paid staff	79	**49.1%**
All paid staff	78	**48.4%**
	161	100.0%

In examining the results presented below, the reader should
bear in mind that the five largest departments in our sample
served 7.3 million people in 1981-82 (LA City, LA County, San
Jose, Orange County, San Francisco). Their decisions affect over
30% of the population in the state. At the other end of the spec-

trum, it is clear that our sample did not provide much data about the large number of very small, largely rural volunteer fire departments. While they do not serve a large portion of the population, they are often the most significant local government agency in rural areas.

B. Operating Expenditures

Expenditure data is perhaps the simplest measure of the resources available to a public sector service agency. From our sample we received information about total operating expenditures for the period from 1977-78 to 1981-82 from 165 agencies. This total included agencies that contracted with another jurisdiction and reported expenditure data. The following table summarizes the survey data on operating expenditures:

Total Operating Expenditures
Dollars in thousands except per capita

Number of jurisdictions	**165**
Population served in 1981-82:	**15.9** million

Total expenditures	
1977-78	$618,800
1981-82	$912,500
Percent change	**+47.5%**

Constant dollar 1981-82	
Expenditures	$658,400
Percent change since 1977-78	**+6.4%**

Constant dollar expenditures per capita	
1977-78	$42.04
1981-82	$41.18
Percent change	**-2.0%**

As the above table illustrates, total fire protection expenditures increased 6.4% on an inflation adjusted basis over the 1977-78 to 1981-82 period. On a per capita basis, total expenditures fell by 2.0% in our sample jurisdictions. This decline, however, was not uniformly present in the sample. The five largest jurisdictions reported an aggregate 1.4% increase in per capita inflation adjusted spending. The 30 smallest departments (population under 10,000) experienced a 10% decline in inflation spending per capita (a 2.9% real spending decline before adjusting for population growth). Overall, 56.5% of 165 agencies responding reported a decline in inflation adjusted per capita expenditures per capita. Special districts (76.7%) and small agencies serving under 10,000 residents (66.7%) were most likely to show a decline in inflation adjusted spending per capita. Four of the five largest fire departments showed an increase in inflation adjusted expenditures. Only the Los Angeles County Fire Protection District showed a decline (-11.6%) among the largest departments.

C. Components of Total Operating Expenditure

One hundred twenty fire departments provided complete information about the various components that made up total fire department operating spending. While 165 districts reported total spending, only these 120 were able to supply a complete breakdown for all survey years. The three components we requested information on were salaries and benefits, employer pension costs, and all other operating costs. The following table displays the composition of spending in 1977-78 and 1981-82 and how it changed. All figures are in current dollars.

Composition of Fire Department Expenditures
Current dollars in thousands

Number of jurisdictions			**120**		
Population in 1981-82			**13.8** million		

Component	1977-78	%	1981-82	%	77-78 to 81-82 % change
Salaries & Benefits	$375,976	67.0%	$545,861	65.6%	**+45.1%**
Employer Pension Costs	114,841	20.5%	208,517	25.1%	**+81.6%**
All Other Operating Costs	70,731	12.5%	77,238	9.3%	**+9.2%**
Total Operating Expenditures	$561,548	100.0%	$831,616	100.0%	**+48.1%**

The most dramatic finding in the table is the extremely rapid growth in employer pension costs over the study period. While overall spending grew 48.1%, employer pension costs grew 81.6%. As the table indicates, most of this growth occurred at the expense of spending for non-personnel operating costs. Had pension costs grown at the average rate of growth, there would have been another $55 million available in 1981-82 for operating costs, for hiring additional employees, or for improving direct salary levels. It can be argued that the general public sees few, if any, direct or visible benefits from these rapid pension costs increases. In many cases, a significant part of these costs represent present costs of past (unfunded) pension obligations.

In every population size group in our sample, the rate of growth of employer pension costs exceeded the rate of growth for total operating expenditures. This trend was most dramatic in the largest fire departments, where pension costs grew 91% while total expenditures grew 50%. Even in the slowest growing group, departments serving populations between 50,001 and 100,000, pension costs grew 60% while total expenditures were growing 39.5%.

D. Capital Spending
Our survey only provided limited data on capital expenditures. We obtained data from 145 fire departments on capital outlays. Total capital spending rose from $21.3 million to $24.1 million (in current dollars) between 1977-78 and 1981-82 (+13.1%). In inflation adjusted terms, real capital outlays fell by 18.4% over the study period.

E. Staffing Changes
Of 152 agencies reporting staff information for the entire study period, slightly more than one-third (37.5%) reported a reduction in the total number of fire department staff. Slightly under one-third (30.9%) reported no change, while the remainder (31.6%) reported an increase in staff. This pattern held true across jurisdiction types and for all population size groups except the very largest and very smallest. Among the largest depart-

ments, 60% reported reduced staffing. The largest declines occurred in the Los Angeles City (-387) and the Los Angeles County (-189) fire departments. Among jurisdictions serving less than 100,000 persons, 61.5% reported no change and only 26.9% reported a decrease in staff.

Total Fire Department Staffing

Number of jurisdictions	**152**
Population in 1981-82	**15.2** million

Total staff	
1977-78	18,665
1981-82	18,445
Percent change	**-1.2%**

Staff per 10,000 residents	
1977-78	13.3
1981-82	12.2
Percent change	**-8.3%**

The rate of decline held true in four of the six population size groups. The only group showing a sizable increase was the group serving populations between 100,001 and 300,000 population where staff grew 2.0%. This category, however, also experienced the fastest population growth of all agencies responding to this question.

This decline in total staff levels in the face of increased real expenditures of 6.4% (see B. above) may be explained in part by the rapid rise in pension costs. As a larger share of the budget was absorbed by pension costs, direct salaries and benefits and operating costs fell as a share of total spending. Particularly in the larger jurisdictions, this resulted in reduction in fire department staffing.

In most cases reductions, where necessary, were made through attrition rather than by layoff. In our sample, 1027 FTE positions were eliminated, 807 new positions created, resulting in a net loss of 220 jobs. Of the 1027 positions eliminated, only 190 (18.5%) required a layoff.

Fire department staffing per 10,000 residents fell by 8.3% over the study period. In our sample, 71.0% of all departments reported a decline in the ratio of staff per 10,000 residents. Only

19.7% reported an improvement in their staffing ratio. This pattern held true for all types of jurisdictions and for all population size groups.

One final staffing item measured was the change in average fire crew manning per pumper truck. Reductions in manning per pumper are sometimes advocated as a means to improve the productivity of fire departments. Others criticize such moves as a dangerous reduction in the ability of a department to quickly suppress a fire. Such moves are nearly always controversial. In our sample, 67.0% of 152 responding agencies left manning levels unchanged. Only 23% of our respondents reduced manning levels; however, such action was taken in 3 of the 5 large fire departments in our survey (Los Angeles City, Orange County, and San Francisco).

F. Response Time

We received replies from 140 fire departments concerning their average response time on fire calls. These 140 agencies served a combined population of 14.2 million persons in 1981-82. Between 1977-78 and 1981-82, the weighted average response time remained unchanged at 3.9 minutes (times were weighted by population served). The modal response time in our sample was unchanged as well, remaining at 4.0 minutes. Response time was unchanged in 74.3% of our sample jurisdictions. Only 13.5% of those responding indicated a slower response time. Among the largest agencies only one, Los Angeles City, reported a slower response time, slipping from 2.0 to 2.1 minutes in 1981-82.

Data for paramedic or first aid response times showed a very similar pattern. With 135 agencies replying, there was no change in the weighted average 4.5 minute response time reported in 1977-78 and 1981-82. Only 17% of all agencies reported a slower response time while 68.9% reported no change.

G. Facilities and Equipment

Our data indicated that in the aggregate there was no reduction in either the number of fire stations or vehicles between 1977-78 and 1981-82. The table on the following page summarizes our findings in this area.

Only 10 jurisdictions (6.5%) reported reducing the number of operating fire stations. The City of Oakland reported a net reduction of four stations and San Francisco three stations. All other reductions involved a single station. The largest reduction in vehicles also occurred in Oakland, where the number of vehicles of all types was reduced from 121 to 90. Overall, 78.1% of all jurisdictions reported a constant or increased number of fire department vehicles. This pattern held true across all types and sizes of jurisdictions.

Fire Equipment and Facilities

	1977-78	1981-82	Percent change
Number of jurisdictions	155	155	—
Population served	14.2 million	15.4 million	**+8.5%**
Fire stations	1,015	1,029	**+1.4%**
Fire vehicles	4,916	5,096	**+3.7%**

H. Special Tax Elections

Proposition 13 allowed local governments to increase non-property taxes (often referred to as "special taxes") if they obtained a two-thirds majority at a local election. Of 162 districts responding, 47 (29.0%) reported holding "special tax" elections for support of fire protection services. There were 23 successes (48.9%) and 24 failures. The largest jurisdiction to approve such a tax increase was the City of Hayward (population 94,900). The largest jurisdiction to hold such an election was the City of Los Angeles, where a tax to support fire services received a 54% majority vote, well short of the required two-thirds majority. Special districts in the sample were much more likely to hold such elections, reporting them in 55.% of the 72 districts in the same. Only 4.9% of the 81 cities in the sample reported such elections.

I. General Responses to Fiscal Constraints

The following table presents data on the responses of our sample fire departments to a list of 11 general types of actions commonly thought to have been taken in the face of fiscal constraints since Proposition 13. One hundred sixty-one different departments replied to this question. These agencies served 15.2 million people in 1981-82.

As the table points out, the larger jurisdictions were more likely to institute one or more of these actions than were small fire departments. Indeed, the Los Angeles County Fire Department reported instituting 8 of the 11 actions on the table, while the Los Angeles City Department instituted 7 of the 11. The average for the whole sample was 2 of 11. The two most commonly adopted actions from the list were to defer major maintenance projects or to institute new fees or charges. The least accepted alternative was to reduce the hours per day that staff dealt with requests from the public.

The small percentage of districts that moved to reduced future pension benefits is perhaps the most striking finding in this area. Only 6.6% of the districts in the sample moved to reduce pension benefits. This takes on added significance in light of our earlier findings concerning the rapid growth of pension costs relative to other expenditure categories. However, the very largest jurisdictions did take action in this area. Both the Los Angeles City and the Los Angeles County fire departments reported taking action to reduce future pension benefits.

III. K-13 SCHOOL SURVEY RESULTS

A. The Sample

The school district survey was mailed to a sample of 150 of the 1,042 grades K through 12 school districts that reported general fund transactions to the State Controller for the 1980-1981 fiscal year. The districts and their general fund expenditures were entered into a computer data base and the sample was selected by a computer program that weighted each district's chance of selection by its proportion of the total expenditures of all districts. County offices of education and Regional Occupational Centers and Programs were excluded from the study.

The questionnaire mailed to the sample districts is displayed in Exhibit 3. It consisted of 115 items which required the respondents to supply figures, check the appropriate reply, or supply a narrative response to two open-ended questions. The numerical data supplied covered three fiscal years 1977-78 (the year before Proposition 13), 1979-80, and 1981-82.

General Responses to Fiscal Constraints Since 1977-78

Number of Jurisdictions   **161**
Population served in 1981-82   **15.2** million

Action taken	Percent respondents answering yes Overall sample	Jurisdictions over 100,000
1. Reduced future employee pension benefits	**6.6%**	26.0%
2. Instituted new fees or charges	**42.8%**	45.8%
3. Increased existing fees or charges	**34.4%**	50.0%
4. Permanently closed a facility that was not being replaced	**6.6%**	25.0%
5. Reduced the ratio of administrative or support staff to staff providing direct service	**28.5%**	43.5%
6. Began or increased contracting with the private sector	**16.5%**	29.2%
7. Reduced the number of days a week any of its services are available	**6.6%**	4.1%
8. Reduced the number of hours per day when staff handles public inquiries	**4.6%**	4.1%
9. Reduced janitorial services	**15.9%**	33.3%
10. Deferred major maintenance project	**44.7%**	69.6%
11. Used volunteers to replace paid employees	**15.0%**	25.0%

Usable replies were received from 96 of the 150 districts in the sample (64%). Districts ranged in size from those having a regular Average Daily Attendance (ADA) of 197 to 517,540 in 1981-82. These 96 districts had a combined regular ADA of 1,712,962 during 1981-82. This total excluded summer school and adult ADA and represented 43.3% of the total statewide ADA reported in elementary and secondary schools in 1981-82. Excluding the

517,540 ADA reported by the Los Angeles Unified School District (LAUSD), the remaining 95 districts in the sample represented 34.8% of all ADA in California outside the LAUSD.

The 96 replies were supplied by districts from 20 of the State's 58 counties. The following tables present a breakdown of the replies in terms of the type and size of the districts responding to the survey.

The School District Survey

Type of district	Number of replies	Percent of Total such districts in state	Regular ADA in 1981-82
Elementary	24	3.6%	**112,319**
High School	17	14.8%	**146,083**
Unified	55	20.7%	**1,454,560**
	96		1,712,962

1981-82 regular ADA	Number of replies	Regular ADA in 1981-82
Less than 500	4	**1,320**
501- 2,000	10	**12,043**
2,001- 5,000	15	**49,198**
5,001-15,000	38	**377,146**
15,001-40,000	25	**558,611**
Greater than 40,000	4	**715,964**
Total	96	1,712,962

Our analysis of the replies received shows that our sample is more heavily weighed toward the larger districts than is the whole population of districts. This reflects two factors—a bias in the sample toward the larger unified school districts that serve 67% of all ADA (while representing only 25% of all districts) and the fact that smaller districts were less likely to return our survey (even after a follow-up letter and phone call). This lower response rate may reflect the fact that smaller districts have less staff available to complete such surveys. As a result, the reader should be cautious in drawing any conclusions concerning small school districts.

B. Enrollment Decline

Perhaps as important a factor as Proposition 13 and the other fiscal changes of the late 1970's was the effect of declining enrollment on California schools. Since the bulk of state aid for local schools is enrollment driven, declining enrollment would have led to some financial problems for school districts regardless of the tax revolt. Regular enrollment (excluding adult and summer school ADA) in our sample declined 8.9% between 1977-78 and 1981-82. Only 24% of the districts in our sample showed stable or growing regular ADA. Summer school ADA fell 89.5% in our sample reflecting the withdrawal of state support for most summer school programs after Proposition 13 passed. Adult program ADA fell 11.8% between 1977-78 and 1981-82. Total ADA of all types in our sample districts fell 13.2% between 1977-78 and 1981-82. The statewide average for this time period was a 9.4% decline in total ADA. As a result, the reader should bear in mind that the sample districts' actions taken after 1977-78 may reflect greater than average enrollment declines than the state as a whole. Some portion of their responses may be due to this larger decline rather than to changes in the overall public school finance system.

C. Expenditure Data

Perhaps the simplest measure of what has happened to K-12 schools since 1977-78 is the amount of general fund expenditures made per regular ADA. While this measure ignores the effects of the many categories education programs (i.e., Special Education, etc.) on spending patterns within and across districts, it does give us a rough idea of the total resources available for education.

From our sample, we received complete data about total general fund expenditures for the period 1977-78 to 1981-82 from 94 districts. The table on the following page summarizes our findings.

General fund expenditures per regular ADA (excluding adult and summer ADA) increased from $1,983 to $2,633 between 1977-78 and 1981-82 measured in current dollars, an increase of 32.8%. When adjusted for inflation, however, there was a decline

General Fund Expenditure Data
Dollars in thousands except per capita

Number of districts	**94**
Regular ADA in 1977-78	**1,868,110**
Regular ADA in 1981-82	**1,701,849**

Total general fund expenditures	
1977-78	$3,705,197
1981-82	$4,481,499
Percent change	**+20.95%**

Expenditures per regular ADA	
1977-78	$1,983
1981-82	$2,633
Percent change	**+32.8%**

Constant dollar expenditures per regular ADA	
1977-78	$1,983
1981-82	$1,900
Percent change	**-4.2%**

of 4.2% reflecting a drop in real expenditures per regular ADA from $1,983 to $1,900 in constant 1977-78 dollars. If we remove the Los Angeles Unified School District (LAUSD), our sample showed a decline in real expenditures per regular ADA from $1,983 to $1,900 in constant 1977-78 dollars. If we remove the Los Angeles Unified School District (LAUSD), our sample showed a decline in real expenditures per regular ADA of -6.2%. This reflects the fact that the large Los Angeles Unified School District (LAUSD) showed virtually no change in inflation adjusted general funding spending per regular ADA (+0.3%) during the study period.

In our sample, 67% of the districts reported declines in real expenditures per regular ADA while the remaining 33% were stable or reported increases. High school districts, districts with under 500 ADA, and those with enrollments between 15,000 and 40,000 were more likely to show declines than the sample as a whole. The districts with the fastest growing enrollments were most likely to reflect a drop in real expenditures per ADA while those experiencing the sharpest decline in ADA were more likely to remain stable or show an increase. This last finding reflects the legislature's action putting a "declining ADA" factor in school finance legislation to slow the reduction in state aid to such districts.

The overall decline of 4.2% in inflation adjusted expenditures per regular ADA reflects a significant decline in the real resources available to education in our sample districts. While current dollar expenditures grew by over $675 million in our sample districts, this growth was not sufficient to keep pace with inflation even though enrollments dropped 8.9%. During interviews, several observers pointed out that the decline may have been more severe than these numbers indicate. They pointed out that the fixed costs of a school district may not change much with declines in enrollment. Reductions in staff usually affect the least senior (and lowest paid) staff first. The number and operating costs of school sites are not reduced proportionately with declines in ADA. As a result of these rigidities, the average real cost per ADA may actually go up during periods of enrollment decline without corresponding improvement in service.

The reader should exercise some caution when trying to generalize these findings to all other school districts. Due to the effects of the school finance equalization legislation mandated by the Serrano v. Priest decision of the California Supreme Court, it is possible that low-spending districts have experienced more rapid growth over this period than the statewide average. This reflects the "squeeze" put on high-spending districts as the state attempts to slow down their spending while it helps power districts reach the state average.

D. Staffing Changes
1) Total Staff

Of the 96 districts responding to our survey, 67 provided complete data about staffing and enrollments for each of the years in the study period. The table on the following page examines the composition of staffing for districts reporting data for all types of ADA (regular, adult, and summer school).

As the table indicates, total staffing fell by 10.5% in our sample districts while total enrollment (regular, adult, and summer)

Total School District Staffing

Number of jurisdictions			67		
Total ADA served:					
1977–78			**1,827,722**		(includes regular
1981–82			**1,592,665**		summer and adult
Percent change			**-12.9%**		ADA)

Type of staff	1977–78	%	1981–82	%	% change
Teachers	76,316	44.2%	70,582	45.7%	**-7.5%**
Instructional					
support	6,960	4.0%	5,974	3.9%	**-14.2%**
Certificated					
administrative	6,152	3.6%	5,917	3.8%	**-3.8%**
Classified, clerical,					
other	83,172	48.2%	71,941	46.6%	**-13.5%**
	172,600	100.0%	154,414	100.0%	-10.5%

fell by 12.9%. In terms of the composition of school district staff, it is clear that districts made efforts to minimize reductions of classroom teachers while making the largest reductions in classified staff (maintenance, clerical, and other support staff). Teachers now make up a slightly larger proportion of total school district staff than before Proposition 13. The group least likely to be cut back was certificated administrative staff. It is also interesting to note that the ratio of total ADA per teacher (student/teacher ratio) actually improved by 5.8% during this period.

The pattern described above was altered when we excluded the Los Angeles Unified School District (LAUSD). In the LAUSD total, ADA dropped 11.2% while total staff dropped 10.0% between 1977-78 and 1981-82. Within the district there was virtually no change in the number of teachers or administrators. Sharp reductions were made in instructional support staff (-21.5%) and classified staff (-16.1%). The table on page A30 represents the sample data after excluding the LAUSD.

As the table indicates, there was more nearly a proportionate reduction in the number of teachers as compared to total ADA, and the cutback in instructional support staff was more nearly equal to the cut in teachers. Once again, administrators were the

Total School District Staffing

Excludes LA Unified School District

Type of staff	1977-78	1981-82	77-78 to 81-82 Percent change
Teachers	47,606	41,863	**-12.1%**
Instructional support	4,533	4,070	**-10.2%**
Certificated administrative	4,120	3,886	**-5.7%**
Classified, clerical, other	37,797	33,894	**-10.3%**
Total	94,056	83,713	**-11.0%**
Total ADA	1,176,913	1,014,810	**-13.7%**
ADA/Teacher ratio	24.72	24.24	**-1.9%**

class of employee least likely to be eliminated. The total staff reduction still lagged behind that of total ADA.

With the exception of the LAUSD, the pattern described above was repeated across district types and size groups within our sample.

2) Layoffs

We asked the districts in our sample if they had made layoffs (as opposed to reductions through attrition) since 1977-78. Eighty-eight districts replied to this question. These 88 districts indicated that they laid off a total of 5,506 certificated employees (teachers, instructional support, and administrators). Such layoffs occurred in 45.6% of the districts responding. This represented 65.2% of the total number of such jobs eliminated over this time period. For classified employees, they reported 7,287 layoffs, 66.4% of the total of such jobs eliminated between 1977-78 and 1981-82. Such layoffs occurred in 58.0% of the districts responding. These percentage of layoffs to total jobs eliminated are much higher than those we found in our other surveys. It may be indicative of low turnover in school district employment and a resulting lack of opportunity to achieve reductions through attrition.

E. Cost of Living Salary Adjustments

We requested data on the average cost of living salary adjustment (COLA) for certified teachers for the years 1978-79 to 1982-83. Eighty districts provided usable replies to this question. The table below summarizes these replies.

Cost of Living Salary Adjustments

Number of districts	**80**
Number of teachers 1981-82	**74,188**
Weighted average cost of living adjustment for 1977-78 to 1982-83	**32.82%**
Range of increases	**16.82% to 46.88%**
LA Unified School District	**31.07%**
Sample without LAUSD	**33.92%**
Measures of inflation 1st quarter 1978 to 1st quarter 1983:	
GNP deflator	**46.6%**
California CPI-Urban	**56.2%**

As the table indicates, the weighted average COLA for teachers in our sample was 32.82%. The sample COLA's were weighted by the number of teachers in each responding district in 1981-82. Using either the most conservative (GNP Deflator) or the most liberal (California CPI-Urban) measure of inflation, it is clear that teacher salaries in our sample did not keep pace with inflation. On the average, they fell 13.8 to 23.4 percentage points behind the increase in the cost of living during the period of 1978-79 to 1982-83. This marks a substantial decline in the real income of teachers during this period. This decline may reflect, however, the relative labor market conditions facing teachers (an oversupply of teachers for a shrinking number of positions) as much as it reflects the fiscal constraints facing school districts after Proposition 13.

In our sample, elementary districts (28.76%) reported the lowest average increase while high school districts (35.15%) the highest. Arrayed by the number of teachers employed, districts

with under 100 teachers granted the largest average increase
(37.07%) while large districts employing over 2,000 teachers
granted the smallest average increase (31.47%). The largest increase (46.88%) was reported by Central Union Elementary
District which is located in Kings County and has approximately
1,500 ADA. The lowest increase (16.81%) was reported by Ocean
View Elementary District which is located in Orange County and
has 10,500 ADA.

F. New or Increased Fees

We asked the districts in our sample to indicate if they had
imposed new fees or increased existing fees in any of five areas.
The table below displays the results we obtained.

New or Increased Fees

Percent respondents answering yes

Fee	Total Sample	Districts over 15,000 ADA	Total number of replies
Pupil transportation	**16.8%**	28.6%	95
Extracurricular activities	**27.4%**	22.2%	95
Community service courses	**44.6%**	48.1%	92
Field trips	**25.3%**	28.5%	95
Community group use of facilities	**80.2%**	82.1%	96

The most popular source of new or increased fees was charges
made for use of school facilities by local community groups while
the least popular was increased charges for school bus services.
There was not a great deal of difference between large school districts (those over 15,000 ADA) and the total sample.

G. Duration and Extent of School Programs

The survey also requested data concerning changes in the average length of the instructional school day and school year, the
employee school year (additional paid days for staff outside of
the academic year), and the number of periods offered in the
high school day. The following table summarizes these questions.

Duration and Extent of School Programs

Length of instructional school day		Shorter	Same	Longer	Number of replies
Grades:	**K—3**	0.0%	91.1%	8.9%	79
	4—6	3.8%	89.9%	6.3%	79
	7—8	7.5%	88.8%	3.7%	80
	9—12	5.5%	89.9%	5.5%	72

Length of instructional school year		Shorter	Same	Longer	Number of replies
Grades:	**K—8**	8.6%	88.9%	2.5%	79
	9—12	9.3%	88.0%	2.7%	72

Length of employee school year		Shorter	Same	Longer	Number of replies
Grades:	**K—8**	14.5%	84.3%	1.2%	79
	9—12	13.9%	84.7%	1.4%	72

Number of periods in high school day 1981-82 compared to 1977-78	Fewer	Same	More	Number of replies
	22.2%	77.8%	0	72

As the table indicates, reductions in the length of the instructional school day and year were not a common policy choice during the study period. A slightly more frequent option was a reduction in the employee school year. Among high school and unified school districts, over one-fifth (22.2%) chose to reduce the number of periods available to high school students each day. One surprising finding was the fact that the patterns described in the table above seemed to hold true for all the various size groupings and relevant district types. There were not any obvious differences in the responses from the various groups as compared to the sample as a whole.

H. Reduction or Elimination of High School Electives

We asked our sample if they had been forced to reduce or eliminate high school electives due to financial constraints since 1977-78. Of 71 districts responding, 69% indicated they had cut electives while 31% had not. Of the 49 districts that answered yes, 8 (16%) indicated that declining ADA was the primary cause of reduced electives while 84% indicated that general fiscal constraints were the most important factor leading to fewer electives.

For the districts that indicated they had cut elective courses, we asked them to list which classes from a list of 13 choices were affected by their actions. The following table summarizes these actions.

High School Electives Reduced or Eliminated

Total replies: **49**

Elective	Percent reducing or eliminating the elective
Mathematics	**32.6%**
Physical Sciences	**40.8%**
Life Sciences	**32.6%**
Music	**67.3%**
Art	**59.1%**
Drama or Speech	**65.3%**
Social Sciences	**44.9%**
Foreign Language	**61.2%**
Home Economics	**55.1%**
Business Education	**42.9%**
Vocational Education	**63.3%**
Physical Education	**44.9%**
Literature/Writing	**26.5%**

In our sample, literature, math, life science, and physical science were the electives least likely to be reduced or eliminated. Music, drama, vocational, and art courses were most likely to be reduced or eliminated. In most cases, districts reduced electives by dropping them only at some high schools in the district rather than by eliminating such courses throughout the district. Such actions might also reflect declining ADA and student demand patterns as well as fiscal constraints.

I. General Responses to Fiscal Constraints

The table on following page presents data on responses of our sample districts to a list of 19 general types of actions commonly thought to have been taken in response to fiscal constraints since Proposition 13.

As the table indicates, elimination or reduction of summer school most state funding for summer school was eliminated, deferring major maintenance, and reducing cleaning and custodial support were the actions most often instituted. Eliminating bus service, using volunteers in place of paid staff, reducing librarian support, and returning administrators to classroom duties were the actions least likely to be adopted. It is interesting to note, however, that these last four items were the only ones not adopted by a majority of the districts in our sample.

It is interesting to note the high percentage of districts that increased elementary (67.1%) or secondary (67.5%) class size. This finding contradicts the slight improvement in the student/teacher ratio discussed earlier. It may reflect the fact that general class sizes were increased while special education class sizes (generally much smaller) absorbed any improvement in the overall student/teacher ratio. This would appear to have a direct impact on the quality of service provided in the classroom. It was suggested to us that the difference between the percentage of large districts that increased class size and the sample as a whole may reflect provisions in collective bargaining agreements that limit class size in the larger districts.

IV. STREETS AND ROADS SURVEY

A. The Sample

The streets and roads survey was mailed to 208 jurisdictions, including all 58 counties and 150 of the State's 430 cities. Special districts were not included since they do not maintain any significant portion of the public streets and roads in California. State and interstate highway system roads maintained by Caltrans were also excluded from the survey. The survey is reproduced as Exhibit 4. We received 129 usable replies, a 62.0% response rate.

General Responses to Fiscal Constraints Since 1977-78

Action taken	Total replies	Districts over 15,000 ADA	Number of replies
		Percent respondents answering yes	
1. Increase elementary class size	**67.1%**	37.5%	79
2. Increase high school class size	**62.5%**	48.0%	72
3. Reduce professional support staff (nurses, counselors, etc.)	**75.8%**	85.1%	95
4. Reduce librarian support	**45.7%**	50.0%	92
5. Reduced or eliminate summer school	**98.9%**	100.0%	94
6. Reduce number of custodians	**82.1%**	70.0%	95
7. Reduced regular cleaning	**83.2%**	92.6%	95
8. Defer major maintenance	**86.2%**	85.0%	94
9. Reduced administrative staff at school sites	**62.1%**	77.7%	95
10. Reduce district level administrators	**79.2%**	60.0%	96
11. Reduce sports program	**53.3%**	63.0%	92
12. Reduce other after-school activities	**53.2%**	25.0%	94
13. Reduce curriculum supports such as field trips	**81.9%**	78.6%	94
14. Reassign administrators to classroom duties	**49.5%**	71.4%	95
15. Reduce per pupil spending on instructional materials	**60.2%**	55.0%	93
16. Eliminate pupil busing	**6.5%**	3.7%	92
17. Reduce pupil busing	**58.1%**	50.0%	93
18. Reduce number of paid instructional aides	**73.9%**	80.8%	92
19. Substitute volunteers for paid staff	**34.8%**	15.8%	92

Of these replies, 4 (3.1%) indicated that they contracted with another agency for the provision of street and road services. The 129 responding agencies served 14.8 million people in 1981-82, which was over 60% of the total state population.

The 129 jurisdictions that responded to our survey displayed the following characteristics, in terms of jurisdiction type and size of population served. The reader should note that county population figures only include the unincorporated area population, hence there is no overlap with the population reported by cities in the sample.

The five largest jurisdictions in our sample (City of Los Angeles, Los Angeles County, Contra Costa County, Sacramento County, and the City of San Jose) served 5.9 million people to 1981-82. This represented 39.8% of our sample population and 24.2% of the total state population.

Response to the Streets and Roads Survey

Type of jurisdiction	Number of replies	Percent
Cities	94	**72.9%**
Counties	35	**27.1%**
	129	100.0%

Population served	No. of replies	Percent
0- 10,000	13	**10.1%**
10,000- 50,000	50	**38.8%**
50,000-100,000	37	**28.7%**
100,001-300,000	20	**15.5%**
300,001-500,000	4	**3.1%**
500,000+	5	**3.8%**
	129	100.0%

B. Expenditure Data

Complete data on total street and road expenditures was provided by 119 cities and counties. The data covered the period from 1977-78 to 1981-82. The table on page 38 summarizes the survey data on operating expenditures.

As the table indicates, street and road expenditures in our sample fell by 10.9%, measured in constant dollars, between 1977-78 and 1981-82. On a per capita basis, the drop was an even

Street and Road Expenditures

Dollars in thousands except per capita

	Number of replies	1982 population
Cities	84	9.0 million
Counties	35	5.5 million
	119	**14.5** million

Total expenditures	
1977-78	$640,945
1981-82	791,575
Percent change	**+23.5%**

Constant dollar 1981-82	
Expenditures	$571,121
Percent change since 1977-78	**-10.9%**

Constant dollar expenditure per capita	
1977-78	$47.30
1981-82	$39.47
Percent change	**-16.5%**

larger 16.5%. There was virtually no change in the total number
of lane miles of streets and roads in our sample during this period
(+0.3% increase). Consequently, the public works department in
our sample were expected to maintain essentially the same road
systems with 10.9% less real resources. It should also be noted
that the adjustment for inflation used in this sample was the
GNP deflator rather than an index related specifically to construction and maintenance costs. Several respondents pointed
out that inflation in this area outstripped the general rate of inflation due to the large weight assigned to petroleum-based
products in road and street indices.

This decline in inflation adjusted spending was not uniform
throughout our sample. In the sample as a whole, 57.1% of the
jurisdictions responded that real (inflation adjusted) spending
declined over the study period while 41.2% reported an increase.
Cities were more likely to report increased real expenditures
(47.6%) than were counties (25.7%). Smaller jurisdictions were
more likely to report increasing real expenditures than were larg-

er jurisdictions. Of 28 jurisdictions serving over 100,000 persons in our sample, only 8 (28%) reported an increase in real expenditures for these purposes. Among the largest jurisdictions in our survey, 4 of 5 reported reduced real expenditures for streets and roads (Los Angeles City -28.3%, Los Angeles County -5.4%, Contra Costa County -22.6%, Sacramento County -11.8%). Only the City of San Jose reported an increase in real expenditures (+34.3%).

One other point worth noting is that we made no attempt to measure the adequacy of street or road spending in either 1977-78 or 1981-82. Several of the jurisdictions that reported large increases in real expenditures did so because the 1977-78 figures reflected very low levels of support for these programs. The 1981-82 figures represented large increases over earlier levels but may still have fallen short of acceptable levels.

C. Components of Total Expenditures

One hundred fifteen street and road departments provided complete data about the various components that made up total expenditures. The three components we examined were maintenance expenses, construction and right-of-way expenses, and all other administrative and engineering costs. The table below displays the composition of spending in 1977-78 and 1981-82 and how it changed.

Composition of Street and Road Expenditures
Current dollars in thousands

Type of jurisdictions		Number of replies		1982 population	
Cities		80		8.8 million	
Counties		35		5.5 million	
		115		**14.3** million	

Component	1977-78	%	1981-82	%	77-78 to 81-82 % change
Maintenance	$296,275	46.5%	$383,054	48.7%	29.3%
Construction	229,425	35.9%	271,917	34.5%	18.5%
Other	111,958	17.6%	132,419	16.8%	18.3%
Total	**$637,658**	**100.0%**	**$787,390**	**100.0%**	**23.5%**

As the table indicates, there was no dramatic shift in emphasis between construction and maintenance spending during the study period. This stability in spending patterns held true across population size groups. Counties as a group reduced construction's share of spending slightly more than did cities, reporting its share dropping from 33.0% of the total in 1977-78 to 29.7% in 1981-82. The share of maintenance expenditures went up by a corresponding amount.

D. Staffing Changes
In our sample, 117 jurisdictions provided complete data about total street and road program staffing and the number of those positions funded through the federal CETA programs. CETA data was requested because a significant number of CETA funded workers were employed in public works' activities. CETA program funding for public sector jobs was essentially eliminated during the period between 1977-78 and 1981-82. We sought to measure what impact this change had on total employment in this area. The following table summarizes our findings.

Street and Road Program Staffing

Type of jurisdictions	Number of replies	1982 population
Cities	84	**8.8** million
Counties	33	**5.4** million
	117	14.2 million

	1977-78	1981-82	% change
Total	14,861	12,360	**-16.8%**
CETA Staff	1,882	90	**-95.2%**
Non-CETA Staff	12,979	12,270	**-5.5%**

Of the 117 agencies reporting, 66.7% reported a reduction in the total number of street and road staff while 16.2% reported no change and 17.1% reported an increase in staff. Cities were more likely to increase staff than were counties. Smaller jurisdictions (under 50,000 population) were also more likely than larger agencies to increase the number of such staff. Among the nine largest jurisdictions in our sample, only one agency (Riverside

County) reported an increase in total staffing. The largest single reduction occurred in the City of Los Angeles where 1,604 positions were eliminated, a 33.1% reduction in staff. It should be noted, however, that 1,112 of these positions lost (69.3%) were CETA funded.

Within our sample, 2,746 positions were cut and 245 new positions added, resulting in a net decrease of 2,501 positions. Of the 2,746 positions cut, 1,792 were CETA funded jobs (65.4%). If we exclude reductions in CETA funded positions, there was a net reduction of 5.5% in the total number of regular positions in these programs.

Reductions in non-CETA funded positions were primarily made through attrition rather than layoffs. In our sample, 1,004 non-CETA positions were eliminated and of these 398 (39.6%) were made by layoffs with the remainder made by attrition.

It is interesting to note that the drop in total employment (-16.8%) exceeded the decline in real spending in our sample (-10.9%). One possible explanation for this may be that funding for CETA positions may not have been included in the street and road expenditure figures reported in our survey. Some jurisdictions accounted for CETA expenditures in a separate budget unit from the one that actually utilized these employees. Such a practice may explain the discrepancy between the two figures noted above.

E. Street and Road System Service

We were unable to directly measure the driving condition of the streets and roads maintained by local governments in California. There is no set of statewide standards or an index which tracks the physical condition of local roads and streets. As a substitute, we chose to measure two outputs of street and road departments, the number of lane miles repaved and the number sealed (a maintenance procedure) in the years covered by the survey. The reader should note that no judgment was made of the adequacy of the level of such activity in either the base year (1977-78) or the last year of the survey (1981-82). All the data below indicates is the change in activity over this period. A number of authorities have argued that street and road maintenance was already inadequate before Proposition 13 primarily due to inadequate gas tax revenue, the prime source of financing for these purposes. It has been argued that Proposition 13's effect on these programs was at best indirect, since property taxes were not the major source of financing for these activities. Proposition 13's effect was to simply make it more difficult for local governments to use property taxes (or other tax revenues) to supplement static or declining gas tax revenues. The table below presents the survey results for these activities.

Street and Road System Mileage and Mileage Subject to Maintenance

87 Cities: 9.1 million population in 1981-82			Percent
	1977-78	1981-82	change
Total lane miles in street system	68,680	71,514	**+4.1%**
Lane miles repaved	1,215	1,224	**+0.7%**
Lane miles sealed	1,915	2,206	**+15.2%**

33 Counties: 5.4 million population in 1981-82			Percent
	1977-78	1981-82	change
Total lane miles in street system	105,909	103,651	**-2.1%**
Lane miles repaved	1,776	1,183	**-33.4%**
Lane miles sealed	4,355	3,557	**-18.3%**

The most striking result in the table is the relatively large decline in mileage repaved or sealed by counties in contrast to the results reported by cities. This result is somewhat puzzling because the total expenditures reported by cities and counties showed roughly the same change (-10.9% in real dollars) over the same period. We were unable to find an explanation for this discrepancy.

The large change in the total mileage in city street systems (+4.1%) arises from two sources: acquisition of county roads when land is annexed to a city and new construction. Much new construction is financed directly by developers who are required to build streets and deed them over to local government. In our sample, 86.3% of all agencies reported that developers are routinely required to construct streets and roads (or donate money in lieu of construction) and dedicate them to the local government. The decline in county mileage reflects both annexations and formal abandonment of some roads in rural areas (e.g., rural San Bernardino County).

F. Special Tax Elections

Of 123 jurisdictions responding, only 12 (9.8%) reported holding "special tax" elections under the provision of Proposition 13 that allows local tax increases with two-thirds voter approval. Of these 12 elections, only two were successful (City of Hillsborough and San Luis Obispo County). The largest jurisdiction to hold a special tax election for road purposes was San Diego County, where such a measure received only a 38% yes vote.

G. General Responses To Fiscal Constraints

The table on page 44 presents data on the responses of our sample street and road departments to a list of 11 general types of actions commonly thought to have been taken in response to fiscal constraints since Proposition 13. One hundred twenty-one different departments responded to this question.

As the table illustrates, the most frequently adopted actions were to increase existing fees (74.8%) followed by instituting new fees (62.8%) or deferring major facility maintenance (61.5%). The least likely to be adopted actions were reducing future employee pension benefits (9.8%) and permanently closing a service facility (10.5%).

The average jurisdiction in our sample reported instituting four of these 11 measures. One city, Newark, reported taking action in all 11 areas. Among the largest jurisdictions, the County of Los Angeles reported taking 9 of 11 actions while the City of Los Angeles reported 4 of the 11.

V. PARK AND RECREATION SURVEY

A. The Sample

The park and recreation survey was mailed to 344 jurisdictions, including all 58 counties, 150 of the state's 430 cities, and 136 of the 279 special districts that provide recreation and park

General Responses to Fiscal Constraints Since 1977-78

Number of jurisdictions	121
Population served in 1981-82:	
Cities (86)	**9.1** million
Counties (35)	**5.4** millions

	Percent respondents answering yes	
Action taken	Overall sample	Jurisdictions over 100,00
1. Reduced future employee pension benefits	**9.8%**	21.4%
2. Instituted new fees or charges	**62.8%**	65.5%
3. Increased existing fees or charges	**74.8%**	72.4%
4. Permanently closed a facility that was not being replaced	**10.5%**	27.6%
5. Reduced the ratio of administrative or support staff to staff providing direct service	**47.9%**	63.0%
6. Began or increased contracting with the private sector	**35.5%**	37.9%
7. Reduced the number of days per week any of its services are available	**19.4%**	24.1%
8. Reduced the number of hours per day when staff handles public inquiries	**14.8%**	28.6%
9. Reduced janitorial services	**48.4%**	53.6%
10. Deferred major maintenance project	**61.5%**	67.9%
11. Used volunteers to replace paid employees	**25.2%**	20.7%

services. The survey is reproduced as Exhibit 5. We received 183 usable replies, a 53.2% response rate to the survey. Of these replies, 7 (3.8%) indicated that they did not provide park or recreation services (5 were counties and 2 were cities served by an independent special district).

The 183 jurisdictions that provided park and recreation services displayed the following characteristics in terms of type of jurisdiction and population size:

Characteristics of the 183 Jurisdictions

Type of jurisdiction	Number of replies	1982 Population served
Cities	95	**9.4** million
Counties	29	**16.6** million
Special districts	59	**5.1** million
	183	

Population size	Number of replies	Percent
0- 10,000	23	**12.6%**
10,000- 50,000	78	**42.6%**
50,000-100,000	41	**22.4%**
100,001-300,000	22	**12.0%**
300,001-500,000	8	**4.4%**
500,000+	11	**6.0%**
	183	100.0%

The population figures reported by the respondents reflect a significant amount of overlap. County park programs and some special districts often serve as regional park resources that serve populations also served by city parks or smaller special districts. No effort was made to correct for this overlap in our survey. It should also be noted that the population figures supplied by special districts are estimates, since there is usually no census data available similar to that provided for cities and counties.

B. Operating Expenditures

Data on total park and recreation operating expenditures was collected from 167 park agencies. The data covered the period from 1977-78 to 1981-82. The table on the following page summarizes the survey data on operating expenditures.

As the table indicates, park and recreation operating expenditures in our sample fell by 11.6% between 1977-78 and 1981-82

Total Operating Expenditure Data

Dollars in thousands, except per capita

Number of jurisdictions   **167**

Population served in 1981-82:
    Cities (93)   **9.2** million
    Counties (25)   **16.0** million
    Special districts (49)   **4.9** million

	Total sample	Without LA city
Total expenditures		
1977-78	$316,059	$239,292
Percent change	**+22.4%**	**+35.1%**
Constant dollar 1981-82 expenditures	$279,224	233,260
Percent change since		
1977-78	**-11.6%**	**-2.5%**

Percent change in constant dollars
  Expenditures per capita 1977-78 to 1981-82
  (Estimated based on average statewide population growth of 7.96%)
         -18.2%   **-9.7%**

when measured in constant dollars. Due to the overlap of the population served by our respondents, we were unable to directly measure per capita expenditures. The figure reported above was indirectly estimated by adjusting the constant dollar expenditure figure for 1981-82 to reflect the statewide population growth rate of 7.96% between 1977-78 and 1981-82. Assuming that the total unduplicated population in our sample grew at the same rate as the state as a whole, we estimate that real per capita expenditures for parks fell 18.2% over the study period.

The table also displays the results from our sample if the City of Los Angeles is removed. Los Angeles City had the largest single park budget of any jurisdiction in our sample both in 1977-78 ($76.7 million) and in 1981-82 ($63.7 million). Excluding the City of Los Angeles, the decline in inflation adjusted expenditures and expenditures per capita is less severe, showing declines of -2.5% and -9.7%, respectively.

This pattern of decline in total inflation adjusted expenditures

and expenditures per capita held true across all types of jurisdiction and all population size groups except those serving between
300,000 and 500,000 population. Overall, 73.2% of our sample jurisdictions reported a decline in inflation adjusted expenditures
per capita while only 26.8% showed an increase. The only sub-
group that deviated from this pattern was the 300,000 to 500,000
population size group. There, 4 of 8 respondents indicated a
growth rate of 10% or more in real per capita expenditures for
parks. The four agencies were the park departments in Monterey, San Joaquin, Santa Barbara, and Sonoma counties. Of the 10
largest jurisdictions reporting, 8 of 10 reported a decline in real
per capita expenditures. The largest decline, 45.1%, was reported by the City of Los Angeles. The Los Angeles County park program reported an 18.1% decline.

C. Components of Total Operating Expenditures

One hundred four park departments (or districts) provided
complete data about the various components that made up total
park department operating expenditures. The three components
we requested information on were salaries and non-pension benefits, employer pension contributions, and all other operating
costs. The table on the following page displays the composition of
spending in 1977-78 and 1981-82 and how it changed. All figures
are in current dollars.

The most striking finding from this data is that direct salary
and non-pension benefit costs grew at a slower rate than did
pension or other operating costs. Measured with or without the
City of Los Angeles, our sample devoted a larger share to non-
personnel costs after Proposition 13 than before. This suggests
that park departments may have given higher priority to providing and maintaining facilities than to providing staff for recreation services to the public. The large differences between the figures including and excluding the City of Los Angeles reflect the
severe cuts in park programs made in that city (-17.0% in current dollars). It is interesting to note that in Los Angeles pension
costs declined the least (-2.5%),while other operating costs
(-30.8%) and salaries (-14.4%) declined at a much more rapid
rate.

Composition of Park Department Expenditures
Dollars in thousands

Number of Jurisdictions **104**

Population in 1981-82:
Cities (53)	**6.8** million
Counties (15)	**2.4** million
Special Districts (36)	**2.5** million

Components	1977-78	%	1981-82	%	77-78 to 81-82 % change
Salaries & benefits	$120,072	**62.7%**	$134,481	**61.1%**	**+12.0%**
Employer pension costs	16,306	**8.6%**	19,332	**8.8%**	**+18.5%**
All other operating costs	59,929	**28.7%**	66,782	**30.1%**	**+21.6%**
Total operating costs	$191,307	100.0%	$220,595	100.0%	15.3%

Excluding Los Angeles City

Component	1977-78 % of total	1981-82 % of total	77-78 to 81-82 % change in spending
Salaries	60%	57%	32%
Pension	8%	8%	36%
All Other	32%	35%	46%
Total	100%	100%	37%

The shift toward devoting a greater share of operating expenditures to non-personnel related costs noted above held true across jurisdiction types and across the population groups (in excess of 500,000). There,the large impact of the City of Los Angeles reversed the general trend.

D. Capital Spending
Our survey only provided limited data on capital expenditures. We obtained complete data from 148 park departments (or districts) on capital outlays. Total capital spending fell from $121.4 million in 1977-78 to $115.2 million in 1981-82, a decline of 5.1%

in current dollars. In inflation adjusted terms, real capital outlays fell by 31.5% over the study period.

E. Staffing Changes

In our sample, 131 jurisdictions provided complete information on park program staffing and the number of park jobs filled
by workers funded through the federal Comprehensive Employment and Training Act (CETA). We requested data on the number of CETA funded positions since park programs were a major
employer of CETA workers. This program has essentially been
terminated by action at the federal level since 1978. We hypothe-
sized that this change in federal funding for CETA would have a
major impact on staffing for park and recreation programs. Our
data confirmed that view.

Of 131 agencies reporting, 83.2% reported a decline in the total
number of park and recreation staff while only 14.5% reported
an increase in staff and 2.3% remained constant. This pattern
held true across types of jurisdiction and population size groups.
In the largest jurisdictions in this sample, 9 of 10 reduced staff.
Only one agency, Orange County, showed a small increase in park
and recreation staff. The largest, absolute declines in total staff
occurred in the City of Los Angeles (-2389) and the County of
Los Angeles (-1041). The following table summarizes our data:

Park and Recreation Program Staffing

Number of Jurisdictions	**131**		

Population served in 1981-82:

Cities (72)	**8.0** million		
Counties (20)	**15.4** million		
Special districts (39)	**3.9** million		

Type of staff	1977-78	1981-82	Percent change
Administrative	1,499	1,203	**-19.7%**
Maintenance	8,928	5,556	**-37.8%**
Recreation program	4,884	3,670	**-24.9%**
Total	15,311	10,429	-31.9%

Of the 4,883 positions eliminated in our 131 sample jurisdictions, 2,815 (57.6%) were CETA funded positions. The majority of these appeared to be employed in maintenance positions. Of the net reduction of 4,883 positions in our sample jurisdictions, 3,430 (70.2%) positions were due to reductions instituted by the City of Los Angeles or the County of Los Angeles park departments. Excluding those two jurisdictions, the remaining 129 jurisdictions reported an average reduction in total park staff of 17.9%.

Among the 131 sample jurisdictions, 67.7% reported a reduction in the number of park staff while 23.3% reported an increase and 9% remained unchanged. This pattern held true across jurisdiction types. Larger jurisdictions, particularly those serving populations of 500,000 or more were more ikely to reduce staff than were smaller agencies. Eight of the 10 largest jurisdictions in our sample reported cuts of 10% or more in total park department staff. The two groups most likely to increase staff were those serving populations under 10,000 and those serving populations between 50,000 and 100,000.

In most cases, reductions in non-CETA staff were made through attrition rather than by layoffs. In our sample, 5,114 jobs were eliminated, 231 new positions were created, resulting in a net loss of 4,883 positions. Of these 5,114 positions lost, 2,068 were non-CETA funded positions. Total non-CETA layoffs amounted to 524 or 25.3% of the non-CETA staff reduction.

Perhaps the most puzzling finding in our park and recreation survey was the discrepancy between the average reduction in total staff (-31.9%) and the average drop in real expenditures (-18.2%). Even when the two large Los Angeles area jurisdictions are excluded, there still is a discrepancy. One explanation suggested is that many park departments did not report CETA funding in the expenditures they reported in the survey. Many cities and counties accounted for CETA expenditures in a separate budget unit from the one that actually utilized these employees. Such an accounting practice may explain the large discrepancy between the two figures noted above.

F. Park Facilities

One hundred seventy (170) park agencies provided information about the total amount of developed park land in their system in 1977-78 and 1981-82. The total developed acreage in our sample rose from 211,976 to 233,100, an increase of slightly less than 10%. In our sample, 61.8% of all jurisdictions reported increasing the number of acres of developed park land, 30.0% reported the same amount of developed park land, and only 8.2% reported a reduction in park acreage. Only 1 of the 37 largest jurisdictions in the sample reported reducing the amount of park land while 27 of 37 (73.0%) reported increases. Smaller jurisdictions were slightly more likely than the sample as a whole to report reductions. Cities as a group were also less likely to report reductions (4.3%) than were counties (10.7%) or special districts (13.7%).

The number of park sites in the sample showed a similar pattern of increase. The total number of park sites rose from 3,193 in 1977-78 to 3,588 in 1981-82, an increase of 8.9%. Only 13 jurisdictions in our sample (7.5%) reported reducing their number of park sites.

The number of recreation facilities (pools, recreation center buildings, etc.) showed a similar pattern of increase. The total number of such facilities rose from 1,915 to 2,118 (+10.6%) in our sample between 1977-78 and 1981-82. Once again, only 7.5% of all agencies in our sample reported reducing the number of park facilities between 1977-78 and 1981-82.

This growth in the amount of park land and the number of facilities is noteworthy in view of the squeeze noted earlier in park operating expenditures and the sharp drop in park maintenance staff. It appears that park managers continued many park development projects that were planned prior to Proposition 13 even after operating budget problems developed. Unfortunately, we were not able to measure the *quality* of park maintenance before and after June 1978. It has been suggested that park maintenance standards have been dropped to accommodate more acreage with reduced funding and staffing. It is unclear how the public has reacted to any such reduction in maintenance stand-

General Responses to Fiscal Constraints Since 1977-78

Number of jurisdictions: 173

Population served in 1981-82:
Cities (90) **9.2** million
Counties (28) **16.6** million
Special districts **4.9** million

Action Taken	Percent respondents answering yes	
	Overall Sample	Jurisdictions Over 100,000
1. Reduced future employee pension benefits	14.5%	21.0%
2. Instituted new fees or charges	74.2%	78.6%
3. Increased existing fees or changes	89.4%	95.0%
4. Permanently closed a facility that was not being replaced	14.0%	20.0%
5. Reduced the ratio of administrative or support staff to staff providing direct service	46.3%	51.3%
6. Began or increased contracting with the private sector	52.0%	52.5%
7. Reduced the number of days per week any of its services are available	26.8%	35.0%
8. Reduced the number of hours per day when staff handles public inquiries	12.8%	22.5%
9. Reduced janitorial services	55.4%	65.0%
10. Deferred major maintenance project	50.6%	64.1%
11. Used volunteers to replace paid employees	46.2%	51.3%

ards or what long-range costs (if any) may be imposed by such a change.

G. Special Tax Elections

Of 180 districts responding, only 9 (5%) reported holding "special tax" elections under the provisions of Proposition 13 that allows local tax increases with 2/3 voter approval. Of these 9 elections only 3 resulted in passage of a special tax. The three successful elections took place in the City of Hillsborough, Placer County, and the Truckee-Donner Recreation and Park District. No jurisdiction larger than Placer County even attempted a special tax election for park programs.

H. General Responses to Fiscal Constraints

The table on the previous page presents data on the responses of our sample park agencies to a list of 11 general types of actions commonly thought to have been taken in response to fiscal constraints since Proposition 13. One hundred seventy-three different park agencies replied to this question.

As the table points out, there was not a great deal of difference between the replies of the largest jurisdictions and the smaller ones. The most commonly adopted action was to increase existing fees or charges. The least accepted action ws reduction in the number of hours per day that staff were available to respond to inquiries from the public.

Once again, the two largest agencies in our sample, the City of Los Angeles and Los Angeles County, implemented the greatest number of these 11 responses with 8 and 11, respectively. The average number of these measures instituted by the jurisdictions in our sample was 5.

Library of Congress Cataloging in Publication Data

California and the American tax revolt

Bibliography: p.
1. Real property tax—California. 2. Tax and expenditure
limitations—California. 3. Tax and expenditure
limitations—Untied States. I. Schwadron, Terry.
II. Richter, Paul.
HJ4191.C36 1984   336.2'00973   84-8554
ISBN 0-520-05159-9
ISBN 0-520-05215-3 (pbk.)